DATE DUE

DE 2'05			
6			

DEMCO 38-296

WRONG FOR ALL THE RIGHT REASONS

WRONG FOR ALL THE RIGHT REASONS

HOW WHITE LIBERALS HAVE BEEN UNDONE BY RACE

GORDON MACINNES

A TWENTIETH CENTURY FUND BOOK

NEW YORK UNIVERSITY PRESS
NEW YORK AND LONDON

and supervises timely analyses of
domestic political issues. Not-for-
profit and nonpartisan, was founded in 1919 and endowed by
Edward A. Filene.

Library of Congress Cataloging-in-Publication Data

MacInnes, Gordon, 1941–
  Wrong for all the right reasons : how white liberals have been undone by
race-- / Gordon MacInnes.
    p. cm.
  "A Twentieth Century Fund book."
  Includes index.
  ISBN 0-8147-5543-7 (acid-free paper)
  1. United States--Race relations.   2. Liberalism--United States
3. Conservatism--United States.   4. United States--Politics and government--
1993–   I. Title.
E185.615.M22   1995
305.8'00973--dc20   95–32529
                                                              CIP

DEDICATION

In memory of my Dad, who shared his name with me and much more than he ever knew.

FOREWORD

The interaction of race, poverty, and public policy has been tangled in disgraceful partisan jockeying and muddled by competing versions of reality for much of American history. Indeed, in the broadest sense, that history itself is incomprehensible without an appreciation of the deep and abiding influence of the politics of race on issues, debates, and elections. For all the talk of third parties in recent years, a look back provides us, for example, with only one real case of a permanent success: the Republican party, founded largely as a vehicle for opposition to slavery. And significantly, there can be little doubt that the more recent history of the two major parties has been greatly affected by shifts in their perceived positions on race-related issues.

When Franklin Roosevelt reached out to the nation's least fortunate, his party succeeded the GOP as the traditional home of black voters. A generation later, when Northern Democrats broke their unholy and usually unspoken alliance with segregationist Southerners, they starting a process that, in effect, shrunk their own party. And today, the formerly solidly Democratic South is well on its way to becoming almost equally dependable for the Republicans. This shift is a result, in no small measure, of the willingness of some to exploit racial tensions for political purposes. From a historical perspective, in other words, neither of the ascendent parties has an unblemished claim to the high ground on this central issue of American society.

To be sure, the nation has moved beyond the racial ratios which stain our Constitution, the violence of the Civil War, the hypocrisy of Jim Crow, the sit-ins at lunch counters, and the struggle for basic voting rights; but we haven't reached the day when discussions of central domestic problems such as teen-age pregnancy, drug abuse, housing, education, and so forth have no racial or ethnic component. Perhaps there will come a time when political debate and policy outcomes in the United States are not warped by the diversity of our population.

Meanwhile serious discussions of action on domestic issues must move beyond arguments about the facts to include discussions of politics. That premise is the starting point for Gordon MacInnes's work.

MacInnes, formerly a foundation executive and consultant, began this book as an effort to catalogue what works and what doesn't among the approaches to urban poverty. In the course of writing, he found time to be elected to the New Jersey State Senate and reason to shift the focus of his research. He became convinced that the problems of race and poverty cannot be confronted successfully until there is a considerable shift in the approach of liberals and progressives, still the most ardent political advocates of the most ambitious policy solutions.

MacInnes examines the high water mark of national ambitions in this area: Lyndon Johnson's Great Society programs, many of which received bipartisan support. Indeed, considering Republican Senatorial leader Everett Dirksen's pivotal role in the enactment of the 1965 civil and voting rights laws and Richard Nixon's substantial expansion of social and urban programs, the nation, for a time, was united as never before—or since—in its determination to conquer the evils of poverty and racism. He argues, in the pages that follow, that these successes were a false dawn, quickly replaced by a new sort of divisiveness. Central to his argument is the contention that the stifling of honest debate about the effectiveness and success rate of these new programs was a critical factor in reversing the political viability of nearly all the programs initiated during the period.

MacInnes's bill of particulars is lengthy. His ideas for breaking the current pattern of politics on these matters is specific. His call for more open and critical debate among supporters of social programs and for approaches based on need, not race, are spelled out in considerable detail. He notes that there are glimmerings of this sort of thing in the reexamination under way among progressives in both parties, itself a reaction to the recent success of conservative forces. There may be, as well, he notes, new possibilities outside the traditional party structures. Overall, MacInnes offers many provocative points that can help to animate and focus these fresh looks at future national responses to racism and poverty.

One thing is certain: the end of the road toward social justice and reasonable economic equity is not yet in sight. The necessity to confront the peculiar American dilemma is as clear as ever. The importance of candor on these difficult subjects is undeniable. Gordon MacInnes has chosen a topic and an approach, therefore, that compels our attention. On behalf of the Trustees of the Twentieth Century Fund, I thank him for his efforts.

RICHARD C. LEONE, *President*
The Twentieth Century Fund
September 1995

CONTENTS

FOREWORD BY RICHARD C. LEONE   vii

PREFACE   xiii

ACKNOWLEDGMENTS   xvii

INTRODUCTION   1

1   THE POLITICS OF RACE: CONSERVATIVE INDIFFERENCE MEETS
     LIBERAL TIMIDITY   13

2   RACE AND POLITICS IN THE JOHNSON YEARS: FROM MORAL
     MONOPOLY TO POLITICAL SIDESHOW   23

3   THE SOURCES OF LIBERAL DECLINE: FAILURES OF MIND   49

4   THE LIBERAL ABANDONMENT OF POLITICS   73

5   THE COSTS OF BLACK UNITY: POLITICAL ISOLATION   97

6   THE HIGH COSTS OF CONSERVATIVE RULE   117

7   REBUILDING A PROGRESSIVE VISION   145

8   SOLVING PROBLEMS IN POOR CITY NEIGHBORHOODS   167

9   PROGRESSIVE RESTORATION: WITH OR WITHOUT CLINTON   185

NOTES   205

INDEX   223

PREFACE

The ideas in this book first began to take shape as a result of my work with the Mondale-for-President campaign in 1984. I went to Washington to help run the advertising, polling, speech-writing, research, and debate preparation section of the campaign (and, also, to be able to tell my grandchildren that I did everything possible to prevent a second Reagan administration). I came away from that campaign feeling that Mondale's lopsided defeat was not just the result of Ronald Reagan's telegenic smile, but was, in fact, brought on in large measure by the Democratic party's timidity and hypocrisy in dealing with racially charged issues.

The approach to these issues that had come to characterize the Democratic party in the 1980s stood in marked contrast to what I had encountered in Newark's North Ward in 1971, when I first met Steven Adubato, then a Newark school teacher; Adrianne Davis, a teacher's union organizer; and Donald Eshlemann, a Mennonite-Presbyterian minister. Operating out of a small office, they were starting a community organization to help stabilize their polyglot neighborhood and provide new services to its residents. The North Ward Center, still led by Adubato, has always applied a single standard to everyone and is a place where open conversations about race and ethnicity are frank, frequent, and valued.

When the organization was first launched, I was running a foundation interested in urban problems. I recommended giving the group a two-year grant to get it started, and I was pleased to watch it become one of the most thoroughly integrated as well as highly effective service organizations I have ever seen. For me, this Newark organization has kept alive the vision of Martin Luther King, Jr., a vision of an America that judges people by the content of their character, not the color of their skin.

I have watched with growing concern as that vision has been eclipsed by policies that have often been well-meaning but thoroughly wrong-headed. This book represents an effort to explain how progressive forces have taken a wrong turn on racial issues and how they can rectify mistakes that threaten to turn progressive Democrats into a permanent minority in the nation's political debate.

I grew up in California, the son of a Presbyterian minister. I was a "youth leader" who pushed the "adult" church to join Martin Luther King's crusade by fighting racial discrimination in the late 1950s. In college I tutored poor kids in Los Angeles and, later, as a graduate student, in Trenton. With the Episcopal chaplain of Princeton University, I traveled to Mississippi in 1964 to lend support to embattled and isolated workers in the civil rights struggles.

I have spent most of my adult years engaged in public life in New Jersey, a much-maligned state that, in fact, mirrors the nation's demographics of race and ethnicity in many ways. After earning a master's degree from Princeton University in 1965, I moved to Trenton and worked for the city's antipoverty program, believing that the next step in the civil rights struggle was to bring new opportunity to poor blacks in northern cities. I moved on to become a special assistant to the state education commissioner, whose suggestions about school integration between cities and suburbs drew rapid fire. Later, I joined the staff of Governor Richard J. Hughes in the aftermath of the 1967 Newark riots and helped write his special urban message.

For eight years after that, I ran the Fund for New Jersey, a grant-making foundation that emphasized public policy initiatives and urban problems. I also served as chief executive of New Jersey's four-station public broadcasting network.

In addition to my temporary duty in the Mondale campaign, I spent six months in Washington during the Johnson administration working on the staff of a White House task force on cities. Otherwise, I have lived and worked in New Jersey.

Since 1970 I have been deeply involved in the civic life of Morris County. Located in the northern part of the state, within commuting distance of Manhattan, it is one of America's wealthiest and most Republican counties. For six years I served as the president of the Planned Parenthood affiliate that serves seven North Jersey counties; I've also served as treasurer of the battered women's shelter for Morris County and as a member of the boards of a school for students with learning disabilities and a land conservation organization.

Not only have I been living in one of the most Republican places on earth, but also I have spent a good deal of time in what is still a Republican-dominated world of business as the chairman of a $300 million manufacturing company. This experience came about when my father-in-law became incapacitated by a brain tumor in 1988, and I stepped in to represent the family's interests.

Politically, I have spent my life as an underdog. I was the chairman of the Morris County Democratic party for an inglorious three years, and for two years during the Watergate backlash, I represented the county as a Democrat in the New Jersey General Assembly.

In 1993, just sixty days after finishing the first draft of this book, I was elected to the New Jersey State Senate by a margin of 342 votes out of almost 70,000 cast. The same day, Christine Todd Whitman was elected governor, carrying my new legislative district by a 62–38 percent margin. My victory represented the largest crossover vote in any New Jersey legislative election in at least fifty years.

My years as a legislator have further shaped my thinking on the issues that are at the core of this book. In a typical week as a state senator, I attend three or four receptions honoring volunteers or recognizing events at nonprofit organizations. I speak at school principals' retirement dinners, Rotary luncheons, and senior citizens groups. I present resolutions honoring Eagle Scouts, testify at public hearings about sewer lines, and help dedicate new parks and bridges. I talk to police officers, corporate executives, owners of diners, lawyers, lobbyists, preachers, insurance agencies, florists, grieving widows, students, nurses, and teachers. I run in races, walk in parades, and sit on the floors of day care centers. I smile for cameras, shake hands, stand and wave, sit and talk, walk and talk, and drive and talk. And I listen.

As a legislator, I want to solve the problems that are important to the people I represent. So, on the fifty or sixty days a year that the Senate convenes in Trenton, I propose, argue, cajole, plead, wheedle, and joke about laws. I try to find the common ground that will permit a majority of my colleagues to support something I seek or to oppose something I hope to defeat. I am in constant contact with state agencies, pushing for assistance to the towns and organizations in my district, sometimes looking for money, sometimes just seeking a decision, one way or another.

This is the routine, but critical stuff of American politics and government. Through a process of reading and talking, debating and listening, politicians seek to balance competing interests in a search for enough common ground to advance toward consensus. The process is sometimes raucous and always untidy, but it is rooted in some unwritten but strongly held rules about the place of civility and respect for the role of legislatures as institutions.

I am a Democrat, albeit a frustrated one. I have campaigned for Robert Kennedy, Edward Muskie, Morris Udall, Walter Mondale, Michael Dukakis, and Bill Clinton for president. But I do not consider myself a "national" Democrat or an ideologue. I am a fiscal conservative, by which I mean that I believe that we should not borrow money from our children to give ourselves tax cuts and that we should tax ourselves for the services we demand. I do believe in government, however, a belief strengthened every time I drive on a highway, read about the graduates of public universities, fly out of an airport, or pass a cop or a park.

Most important, I believe that a proper role of government is support for the principle of integration, the simple idea that all of the people in this diverse nation should be judged individually, not as members of any group. This means that government must enforce swiftly and certainly laws against racial and gender discrimination. But government must also extend a helping hand to all Americans by providing decent public schools, affordable higher education, free libraries and parks, and accessible transportation.

This book is not a memoir. Nor is it a policy memorandum issued from Washington or from a Cambridge think tank. Rather, it is an assessment of how progressive forces retreated from the battle of ideas, scared off by issues tinged by race. The book will suggest the kind of politics and policies that are needed to restore good sense to this important debate.

My perspective is shaped by years of participation in America's civic culture in one county within one state. That culture reflects the enduring tension between our vigorous individualism and our equally strong tradition of community obligation, a tradition that I believe is now threatened by ideological warfare, Republican irresponsibility, and Democratic timidity.

ACKNOWLEDGMENTS

Writing a book competes with marriage, fatherhood, and running as a Democrat in Morris County, New Jersey as the most difficult and rewarding experience of my life.

Blair MacInnes, my wife, read every word of this book many times over, as well as thousands more that disappeared into some cyber cemetery. She did so with good humor and dispatch, putting aside her own work to question, argue, and exclaim about mine. She put up with the absences and obliterated weekends that go with book-writing. Blair made it possible for me to start and finish this labor, and she deserves first and most fervent thanks.

Richard C. Leone encouraged me as a friend and as president of the Twentieth Century Fund, taking a chance on a heretofore unpublished writer with an unconventional resume. His perspectives and insights are unmatched in my experience for their acuity and freshness. I also appreciate the help of his colleagues at the Fund: John Samples, Jason Renker, Jon Shure, Beverly Goldberg, Kathleen Quinn, Bill Grinker, and Carol Starmack.

This book grows out of thousands of conversations and encounters. Those with Tom Vallely, Charles Kenney, Bill Bradley, Charles Morris, Kathleen Daley, Jim Sleeper, Clement Price, John McLaughlin, Mark Fury, and Wayne Bryant were particularly helpful. Carter Willkie prodded and supported me with jewels and tidbits; Mel Mister argued patiently and effectively.

Steve Adubato inspired this book by his practice of politics and integration. My friends at Newark's North Ward Center work and live as a part of the most thoroughly integrated institution I have ever seen—and as one of the most effective community service organizations.

Miss Juanita Tarr taught me how to type pretty darned fast when I was in 9th grade at the Woodrow Wilson High School in Pasadena. Thanks Miss Tarr.

INTRODUCTION

Bill Clinton's presidency began at a confusing, transitional period in American history. With the collapse of the Soviet Union, he could not do what Ronald Reagan did: borrow enough money in the name of national security to purchase temporary prosperity. President Clinton took office with the opportunity to build a new progressive coalition of working- and middle-class whites, minorities, and liberals—traditional Democratic constituents—to restore credibility to the idea that government plays a constructive role in society and the economy, and to call the bluff of the Republican Right in its refusal to inflict the pain implicit in its antigovernment jihad.

The 1994 elections demonstrated that Clinton had failed to make his case. To be sure, he was exposed throughout his first two years to a relentless, scurrilous, even libelous campaign of defamation and ridicule by the Right. And congressional Republicans appeared more interested in destroying Clinton's personal credibility than in debating policy differences (Senate Republicans used the filibuster more frequently in 1993–94 than at any earlier time in the twentieth century). Questions about Clinton's womanizing lingered from the 1992 campaign. All of this mixed with a personal image of a slick southern politician who restyled his policies at the first sign of opposition.

President Clinton contributed to the creation of that image, demonstrating a lack of steadfastness to the ideas emphasized by candidate Clinton. He was drawn into a fight on gays in the military in the first weeks of the presidency, retreating from his campaign pledge to the gay community and opening himself to the charge of waffling. His cabinet looked like an affirmative action plan. It included four blacks (one a woman), two Latinos, and two white women, but no Republican and no

1

one associated with Ross Perot. He nominated (for a time) Lani Guinier, a black-Jewish, ivy-league law professor, to the highest civil rights job in the Department of Justice, even though she advocated a vision of racial separatism at variance with his own experience as a son of the civil rights struggles. He was slow to translate his central campaign promise to "end welfare as we know it" into a concrete legislative proposal, choosing instead to organize a highly bureaucratic, secretive, and confusing effort to achieve a sweeping reform of the health care system, which failed spectacularly.

During the 1994 congressional elections, President Clinton's achievements were degraded and minimized. The facts that the economy was growing steadily and unemployment was down sharply failed to redound to the Democrats' favor. Clinton had kept his promise to reduce deficits. He ended the antichoice abortion policies of the Reagan-Bush years. Millions of working Americans were aided through expansion of the earned income tax credit he pushed for and by passage of a family leave act that protected workers' jobs during maternity leaves and family medical crises. Even though only 2 percent of American households paid higher taxes under Clinton's budget plan, Republicans accused him (successfully) of raising middle-class taxes.

Clinton's political plight was in no small part a result of wrong turns taken by leaders of the Democratic party during the past three decades. Before the mid-1960s certain values and precepts of American life were so widely supported that they were never the subject of partisan contention. For leaders of what was then the majority party to abandon rather suddenly these shared principles represented a seismic shift in the center of American politics. Nonetheless, consider the following:

▲   Democrats moved from clearly opposing crime and civil disorder to the appearance of excusing black crime and rioting as an understandable reaction to a history of oppression and discrimination;

▲   Democrats shifted from unquestioning acceptance of the role of stable, two-parent families in transmitting society's values from one generation to the next to the suggestion that unwed motherhood and single-parent households were not closely associated with how well-prepared children would be to participate in American society as citizens, parents, and employees;

▲   Democrats were identified in the postwar era with seeking good jobs, full employment, and expanding opportunities for willing workers. By the late 1960s, they emphasized instead the need to protect welfare recipients from the workplace;

▲ Democrats abandoned racial integration in favor of separatism, defining opportunity in terms of membership in a growing list of "protected" groups, from black Americans and Pacific Islanders to women and the disabled.

Thus did the Democratic party cede to the Republicans the role of protector of basic American principles. Until such fundamental values as personal and family responsibility, civility, and work are reestablished as "American" and not "conservative" values, Democrats are unlikely to regain their standing with the voters. Moreover, without an open and full debate on race-framed issues, the words *crime, welfare, family dissolution,* and *idleness* will continue to be political code for blacks.

Progressives need not be defensive. Their goals are widely shared by American voters. I believe that government should stay out of people's way—that a woman, for example, should have the right to decide whether to have a child or not. I believe that taxes that reflect one's capacity to pay them are better than taxes that do not. I admire the entrepreneurial spirit, but I know that sustained economic growth requires government investments in all sorts of activities and facilities that businesses cannot make a go of—activities such as basic research, public transportation, infrastructure, and educational institutions that provide opportunities for everyone. I believe that the parents of profoundly retarded children should be able to look to government for help and that people who work all their lives should have the security of a government-protected pension. I favor the vigorous enforcement of laws prohibiting discrimination based on skin color, accent, religion, gender, or ethnicity, although I oppose granting preferences to persons based on these same attributes. I think government helps determine our quality of life by preserving open spaces and historic sites, building parks, cleaning up rivers and bays, and ensuring our safety from both speeding drivers and violent criminals.

The Clinton presidency could be the harbinger of the restoration of a progressive coalition, one that reunites the black and white working class with traditional Democratic supporters such as Jews, environmentalists, working women, and public employees. Or the Clinton presidency could be just a brief interruption in the conservative Republicans' long-term hold on the White House. In addition to the normal tests of a sitting president—that is, whether jobs are plentiful and the economy is growing, and whether the United States is at peace and our world stable Clinton must contend with a political culture and a media environment that have changed in important ways in recent years.

Politics has seemingly come to be dominated by talk radio populism, "tabloid television," the reduction of complex issues to nine-second sound bites, and a growing cynicism and sourness in the character of public debate. Government, which is supposed to be the source of consensus and agreement on shared public goals, is widely mistrusted, if not despised. A sullen polity looks out on a shrunken economic future, while neither political party offers a concrete vision for restoring prosperity. Triumphant conservatives prattle on about traditional values, yet support policies that diminish savings and investment and that permit government intrusion into the most private and delicate personal decisions. Liberals, terrified to be labeled as such, mask their policies in conservative vocabulary. In the course of the past thirty years, the bipartisan progressive coalition that dominated American politics has been shattered and scattered. This book is about how that happened, and what needs to be done to restore a progressive majority.

A word about nomenclature. I do not attempt in this thin volume to restore liberalism's good name. Liberalism grew out of the New Deal, the economic theories of Keynes, and an acceptance that activist government was essential to referee free enterprise by protecting workers and consumers; to construct a safety net of social insurance for the jobless, elderly, and disabled; and to enforce civil rights. In the 1960s liberalism shifted its emphasis to expanding the legally enforceable rights of all sorts of groups, downplaying conflicts in economic policy. I use the term *liberal* to refer to those who embraced the rights-driven agenda best personified by Senator George McGovern's 1972 presidential campaign. *Liberal* is, here, a political pejorative.

Progressivism had very different roots in the early twentieth century and was much more associated with Republicans like Theodore Roosevelt, Robert LaFollette, Hiram Johnson, and George Norris. It fed on the sweeping populist aversion to the era of railroad, steel, oil, and financial trusts, and emphasized government to improve worker safety, child welfare, consumer protection, and conservation. I use the term *progressive* to refer to those who accept the need for regulation of the environmental, consumer, and labor practices of the private sector; believe in public investment in higher education, research, transportation, and infrastructure as essential to economic growth; advocate programs to protect the helpless and elderly and to offer a helping hand to the economically disadvantaged; push for racial integration and stricter punishment for those who discriminate; and oppose racial preferences and quotas except to offset persistent discrimination.

Progressive is a term of approbation; *liberal* is not.

The 1964 presidential election marked the last hurrah of the fabled Roosevelt coalition. Lyndon Johnson was the last Democratic nominee in the twentieth century to attract a majority of votes from white Americans and to win a convincing margin among Catholic Americans. He was, also, as Thomas and Mary Edsall observed, the last Democrat to be on the right side of the issue of race. The two facts are related.

For the thirty-five months between John F. Kennedy's assassination on November 22, 1963, and the 1966 congressional elections, a progressive policy majority prevailed in Washington. An enduring record was enacted with the crucial participation of Republican "moderates," a species that in the mid-1990s seemed nearly extinct. Most important, this progressive policy majority abolished American apartheid with the passage of the Civil Rights Act of 1964 and the Voting Rights Act of 1965. The automatic pauperization of the elderly was ended by the enactment of Medicare. Federal investment in public transit was inaugurated along with general assistance to public schools. And for the first time, opportunities for higher education were guaranteed to all qualified students through federal grants and loans. Not even the Reagan tide of the 1980s could sweep away public support for these landmarks of the Great Society.

Kennedy's succesor, Lyndon Baines Johnson, and his bipartisan allies were committed to integration, the simple American principle that persons should not be judged or categorized by skin color in defining their access to opportunity and public benefits. Americans responded to the moral force of the civil rights movement, personified by the Reverend Martin Luther King, Jr., with the most effective movement of ordinary citizens in the nation's history. President Johnson's advocacy of equal opportunity for all Americans and an end to legalized segregation prevailed as a moral and political argument. To be sure, support for equal opportunity did not prevent massive white resistance to the dismantling of the dual school systems in the South nor a contemptuous hostility to northern blacks who moved into white neighborhoods. Most whites accepted integration in theory but made no special effort to make it a reality in their daily lives.

By 1968 the progressive coalition was broken. Richard Nixon was elected president in a campaign dominated by two issues: the war in Vietnam and rising crime rates in American cities. Democrats were blamed for both, and they had no good answer for either (neither, as it turned out, did Nixon).

Something quite extraordinary had happened between 1964 and 1968. The liberal Democrats, who would come to dominate their national party, lost their will to argue about these racially charged issues (but not about, say, Vietnam or weapon systems). Plenty of issues were devilishly complex and deserving of the fullest ventilation, issues that revolved around the expectation and hope that black Americans would participate fully in American society after centuries of oppression. But instead of turning to a full exploration of what had to be done to improve the educational performance or employment opportunities of poor black Americans and to strengthen black families, liberals retreated from the challenge and remained silent in the face of ideas that were morally insupportable, practically ineffective, and politically fatal. They were mute in the face of demands and proposals from the Left and "professional blacks" that demanded rejoinder and debate. By their servility and ineptness, liberal Democrats handed over to conservative Republicans a series of racially framed issues of such potency that they would help determine the outcome in the 1968, 1972, 1980, 1984, and 1988 presidential elections.

Moreover, in their ineptness white liberals manifested enormous disrespect for black Americans collectively, for the American political process, and for the working- and middle-class Americans who were formerly at the heart of the Democratic coalition. By the mid-1990s liberals still did not respect the ideas of black Americans enough to argue with them. Yet because they avoided such arguments, Democrats found themselves tagged with ideas that were anathema to most voters. Democrats did not endorse muggings, but they sought to defer a crackdown against violent criminals until the "underlying conditions of poverty" had been corrected. In taking this view they showed greater sympathy for the rights of criminals than they did for the rights of victims, who are disproportionately black Americans.

In the end, liberals implicitly accepted the arguments of professional blacks that the nation's sad history of slavery and legalized segregation required that black Americans be granted extraordinary preferences. Preferences mean that different, inevitably lower standards are set for some individuals solely on the basis of their skin color, a notion that collides with broadly accepted notions of a colorblind society. Even such an ardent integrationist as Martin Luther King, Jr., argued for temporary preferences for black Americans modeled on the incentives, subsidies, and preferences granted veterans under the popular GI Bill. Liberals appeared to agree with assertions that any differences between black and white Americans in everything from illegitimacy and homicide rates to scores on standardized tests could best be explained by the legacy and continuation of racial oppression.

If there were a moral case to be made for temporary race preferences because of the systematic and persistent oppression of black Americans, the argument was much weaker when it came to Asian-Americans, Pacific Islanders, and Latinos. Although they surely had faced prejudice and occasional discriminatory laws, they had never been enslaved nor legally segregated. Despite the clash with bedrock American values, liberals uncritically extended preferences to other ethnic groups, as well as to women. And they adopted these radical policies without an open debate that would illuminate their rationale or allow for dissenting views. The long-term result of this thinking has been devastating for Democrats at the polls and of questionable consequence for the intended beneficiaries.

Nowhere have the cumulative effects of liberal thoughtlessness been more apparent than in the quest for a sensible approach to the problems of the urban poor. Because liberals would not acknowledge the role that individual behavior, responsibility, and effort must play in any policy that deals with poverty, they have been left to advocate unconvincing alternatives that require unrealistic levels of spending. Defensive about the consequences of concentrations of lower-class families in city neighborhoods, Democrats have understated the difficulties of proposals, such as job training or school reform, and underestimated the capacities of the poor themselves. They have been reduced to slogans for "more Head Start," "urban Marshall Plans," and "good jobs at good wages." In the meantime, the quality of life in poor neighborhoods has declined precipitously, with violent crime, idleness, and family dissolution rates soaring so high they define a culture alien to the rest of America.

In sum, liberals were arrogant—and not just about urban poverty or what was best for ethnic neighborhoods. The same attitudes prevailed in the evolving policies about Vietnam in the Kennedy and Johnson administrations. It was the hubris of the "best and brightest" that allowed defense planners to assume that superior logistics and bomb tonnage would subdue Vietnam and that Washington bureaucrats could best design solutions for the residents of Watts and the South Bronx.

Democrats are reputed to be good, scrappy politicians, which helps explain how they continued to do so well in state and local elections for so long despite the wanderings of the national party. This makes it all the more ironic that in trying to solve racially framed issues, national

Democrats abandoned the political process. The liberal reformers who took over the party in the 1970s intentionally excluded elected Democrats from the national convention, as if their success in politics had contaminated them.

Democrats retreated from trying to advance the civil rights agenda through legislation, a demanding process of argument and compromise that narrows differences to build consensus among widely divergent interests and philosophies. Instead, liberals turned to the federal judiciary and civil rights bureaucrats to advance ideas that they could not carry legislatively. Support for busing to integrate schools lost its congressional majority (even among most Democrats) by the late 1960s, so civil rights organizations used the courts and federal agencies to desegregate northern schools. The use of quotas to evaluate compliance with job discrimination laws was put to a congressional vote only once (by President Nixon), yet it evolved as national policy through successive federal court decisions and bureaucratic rule-making. Democrats said they opposed quotas, supporting instead "goals and timetables" (which in practice turned out to be indistinguishable from quotas). They never put such revolutionary ideas to the test of legislative argument, however, and scurried away from them in campaigns.

Finally, Democrats showed no respect for working- and middle-class Americans. They would not acknowledge the efforts of millions of black Americans who finished school, got jobs, started families, and joined the mainstream. To praise such progress was seen as defusing efforts to assist those who remained mired in poverty; it blunted the argument made by professional blacks that systematic discrimination persisted. Liberals blamed the white working and middle classes for opposing even dubious schemes such as locating large-scale public housing projects in the midst of residential neighborhoods. The white liberals who righteously condemned such opposition tended to live in neighborhoods not faced with such housing. By 1972 the national Democratic party—led by highly educated white males—was suggesting that the greatest enemies of progress and justice were white males, a message that has not gone unnoticed by the white males who have come to be the group that most consistently supports Republican presidential candidates.

So maladroit were the Democrats that the Republicans were able to draw off huge segments of traditionally Democratic voters, even though these voters' economic interests are better served by the Democrats' support of organized labor, protectionist trade policies, and Keynesian pump priming. The Republican appeal to "traditional values," such as law and order and patriotism, and opposition to "social engineering" and welfare overcame the historic antipathy of white Southerners and northern working-class voters to Republican economic policy.

The 1970s marked the end of America's postwar global economic hegemony and with it, the low unemployment, stable prices, and rapid growth in real income that had characterized much of the postwar period. For almost three decades, white male high school graduates had found jobs that allowed them to provide for their families and enjoy a rising middle-class standard of living. Taxes rose through this period, but incomes rose faster. With the onset of a voracious inflation in 1973, however, American families found themselves on an economic treadmill that went faster and faster. To stay even, married women went to work (in 1960 only one-third of married white women were in the labor force; by 1990 two-thirds were). As real incomes stalled and inflation eroded purchasing power, taxes continued to rise, bringing on the conditions for a tax revolt. In combination with Democratic silliness on cultural and social issues, this economic scenario laid the groundwork for Ronald Reagan and the right wing of the Republican party to take over the national government.

Reagan was not conservative in the same sense that Barry Goldwater, Robert Taft, or William F. Buckley were. Traditional conservatives hold a long-term perspective, and they believe in balancing current spending and revenues and in stimulating savings and investment. Theirs was a dour economic vision that emphasized cutting programs such as Social Security. In contrast Reagan's offer was irresistible—a 30 percent cut in income taxes—and not to worry: because of previously unforeseen multipliers observable only to supply-side economists and the editorial writers at the *Wall Street Journal*, this generous giveback would be accomplished without unbalancing federal budgets. Of course, as George Bush observed only a few months before accepting Reagan's vice presidential offer, all this was "voodoo economics." But Reagan presented it with such ebullience and optimism, and financially strapped Americans so wanted to believe it, that the nation crossed its fingers and spent the tax cut.

Reaganism was built on the proposition that government was the cause of economic stagnation and moral decline. Where traditional conservatives understood the need for public investment in transportation, housing, and education, Reagan attempted to sharply reduce federal spending in these areas. He argued that welfare explained unwed motherhood. When even the Republican-controlled Senate opposed his proposed cut in Social Security benefits, Reagan blamed the failure of his supply-side promise on Congress's "tax-and-spend Democrats." Federal programs remained in place because the American people did not want Reagan to dismantle public services.

Reagan accelerated spending for a new war on crime and drugs, federalized drug offenses, and promised to close the borders to illicit drugs. During his presidency, prisons filled beyond capacity, yet drug-related crimes helped turn city neighborhoods into some of the most dangerous places on earth. Since Vietnam, there had not been a more spectacular failure of policy or program.

In fact, Reagan lost the argument about government. When given the choice, voters opted for continued indexing of Social Security benefits, expanding Medicare coverage, maintaining loans and grants for higher education, subsidizing mass transit, and expanding open spaces (the Republican Right rationalized its defeat on domestic programs as the victory of "special interests"). But Americans also wanted to believe that they could maintain public services, enjoy a massive tax cut, and still balance federal budgets. In accepting Reagan's deal, they became the first generation of American citizens in peacetime to demand more of their government than they were willing to pay for.

Part of Ronald Reagan's legacy is that he defined the terms of debate for the next two presidents. For George Bush, it meant a single term. His disavowal of one of the most memorable campaign pledges ever made—"Read my lips, no new taxes"—set off an attack from the Right that ruined the 1992 Republican convention and encouraged Ross Perot to run, drawing off traditional Republican votes. When Bill Clinton assumed office on a promise to "end welfare as we know it" and to reform health care, he found himself caught like a fly in the amber of Reagan's deficit trap. "What public service will you reduce or eliminate to cut the deficit?" was the question that ensnared him. So, Clinton's modest plans for economic stimulus disappeared, while his welfare and health visions shrank to modest proportions.

In 1988 Michael Dukakis, the Democratic presidential nominee, tried to sell the American public on the idea that he was the only true conservative in the race for president and that George Bush was something else. Dukakis studiously avoided admitting himself a liberal until ten days before the election. In 1992, when Clinton was accused of being a liberal, he responded: "That's a bunch of bull. . . ." "Do anything," say liberal politicians, "but don't call me 'liberal.'"

Liberal has become a political pejorative, and I, too, use it as such in this book because liberals should have learned by now that they will always lose the argument with American voters by walking away from it. Their credibility was destroyed when they wandered off in the company of a small band of leftists and professional blacks and abandoned the field to conservative Republicans. Now, the traditions of self government and republicanism are endangered by a new brand of right-wing populism that declares all public activity a misguided, corrupt, ineffective waste of time. It seeks to shortcut the complexity and frustrations of representative government through referenda, term limits, and recall.

Progressives need to respond with an affirmation that there is much that the nation must do with a sense of common purpose and public investments and a respectful regard for the rights and opportunities of everyone. And they must demonstrate by their actions and words that they have absorbed the lessons of the Liberal Misadventure with divisive interests and caucuses and are ready to resume the hard fight for true racial and economic progress.

1 »

THE POLITICS OF RACE: CONSERVATIVE INDIFFERENCE MEETS LIBERAL TIMIDITY

CLINTON RECLAIMS THE CENTER

In June 1992, Bill Clinton's presidential candidacy was in deep trouble. True, he had just scored big primary victories in New Jersey and California on June 2. The nomination was beginning to look more like a sentence than a prize, however. The mid-June Gallup presidential preference poll showed Clinton a distant third, with only 24 percent support against 32 percent for Republican President George Bush, and 34 percent for independent candidate Ross Perot, the Texas billionaire. Surveys suggested that voters neither trusted Bill Clinton nor showed much interest in his campaign. Clinton was better known as a draft-dodger and womanizer than for any public accomplishment or serious proposals about America's future. Some Democrats whispered that there was still time for the party to come up with a stronger candidate.

That was the situation on Saturday, June 13, when Clinton appeared before the Rainbow Coalition meeting in Washington for what looked to be a routine effort to generate some enthusiasm in the party's left wing. The coalition had always belonged to the Reverend Jesse L. Jackson: he convened it, chaired it, and set its agenda. Jackson described the June meeting as an "emergency" gathering "between [riots in] Los Angeles and the [Democratic convention in] New York." The agenda included a gathering of black ministers to talk about crime, a breakfast with labor leaders, a symposium on Jackson's proposal to invest $500 billion in infrastructure projects, and a panel of rap and hip-hop artists.

Jackson's political agenda was clear: to move Clinton leftward, closer to the Democratic party's base among unions, urbanites, and minorities. Although Perot was likely to split the anti-Bush vote, Jackson argued that the Democrats' only chance was to mobilize the liberal-left side of the party: "Those who cannot touch the rim when it's 51 inches high, can slam dunk when its lowered to 34 inches," was Jackson's basketball analogy for the 1992 political math.[1]

One of the rap artists featured at Jackson's "youth summit" on June 12 was Sister Souljah, a self-described "rapactivist." The rapper, whose real name was Lisa Williamson, had previously appeared as a warm-up act for Public Enemy, one of the better-known rap groups, and had issued her debut album just six months earlier. After the Los Angeles riots, she had gained some prominence as a spokesperson for young black Americans, an interpreter of their "rage and frustration." Bill Clinton's candidacy was about to turn a corner on Sister Souljah's words.

Some advisers pressed Clinton to use the Rainbow speech to solidify his base of support, to rally the Democratic party's left flank and Jackson himself to Clinton's candidacy, and to repair the earlier damage in their relations.[2] Indeed, that is how Clinton started his remarks. He praised the coalition and Jackson for honoring blacks and whites who had reached across racial lines at personal risk before and during the riots in Los Angeles. He outlined his proposals to invest in infrastructure improvements, a subject dear to Jackson. It was, in short, a routine campaign speech—until he turned to the remarks of Sister Souljah. Jackson had singled her out for prideful attention, but Bill Clinton said:

> You had a rap singer here last night named Sister Souljah. . . .
> Her comments before and after Los Angeles were filled with a
> kind of hatred that you do not honor today and tonight. Just lis-
> ten to this, what she said. She told *The Washington Post* about
> a month ago, and I quote, "If black people kill black people
> every day, why not have a week and kill white people? . . . So
> if you're a gang member and you would normally be killing
> somebody, why not kill a white person?". . . . Last year she said,
> "If there are any good white people, I haven't met them. Where

are they?" Right here in this room. That's where they are. . . .
If you took the words black and white and reversed them, you
might think that David Duke was giving that speech.[3]

Clinton had not only criticized Sister Souljah, he had criticized Jesse
Jackson's judgment in front of Jackson's most loyal supporters. Jackson,
usually confident and aggressive, was taken aback. After the speech, he
said: "I don't know what [Clinton's] intention was, I was totally surprised." Two hours later he called a press conference to say that Clinton
had used "very bad judgment." About Sister Souljah, Jackson opined:
"She represents the feelings and hopes of a whole generation of people.
She should receive an apology."[4]

Clinton's political prospects were significantly altered by these brief
words about an obscure rapper. Most voters never heard about the confrontation at the Rainbow Coalition, but the fallout with Jackson opened
the way for Clinton to appeal to white working- and middle-class voters.
Many of these voters had come to equate Jackson with the Democratic
party's policies that offended their work ethic and with crime policies
that seemed to favor the criminal over the victim. To be sure, economic
stagnation and George Bush's miscalculations were influencing voters,
but Clinton resuscitated his campaign with the Rainbow confrontation.
By early July Clinton led Bush in the two-way polls by a few points, and
in the week after the mid-July national Democratic convention, his lead
grew from nineteen to twenty-seven points. Perot announced his (temporary) withdrawal from the race during the Democratic convention citing the "revitalization" of the party.[5]

It is a measure of how far liberal Democrats had fallen in their standards of intellectual integrity and common sense that a candidate's criticism of someone for advocating racial violence would seem noteworthy.
Typically, white liberals had taken to standing in quiet acquiescence in the
presence of statements by black Americans, however outrageous they
might be. And when these liberals were criticized by a black American,
their response was to retreat, explain, apologize, or overreact. This pattern was so well established by 1992—particularly after the presidential
candidacies of Hubert Humphrey, George McGovern, Walter Mondale,
and Michael Dukakis—that Clinton's criticism stunned Jackson, the
Rainbow Coalition audience, and the press.[6]

The confrontation over Sister Souljah was the result of increasing
political friction between Clinton and Jackson. When Clinton had chaired

the Democratic Leadership Council (the group he helped establish to push the party back to the political center), he had excluded Jackson from a speaking role at the council's 1991 conference in Cleveland, and he had fought successfully for a resolution opposing racial "discrimination of any kind—including quotas." Jackson had accused Clinton of practicing "exclusion," appealing to "white suburbanites," and using "ugly, suggestive, and race-based" statements on equal opportunity.[7] When Jackson told the *New York Daily News* in April 1992 that he thought he should be the vice presidential nominee and that he might not support the Democratic ticket if he were not given serious consideration, Clinton had expressed "surprise" that Jackson had not talked to him about his interest. He said it was premature to even talk about the number two spot before the nomination was won (Jackson backed off, claiming "misunderstanding").

After the Sister Souljah speech, Jackson led the counterattack (presumably just as Clinton hoped he would).[8] Jackson said Clinton's words were part of "a consistent attempt to provoke me" and that Clinton "was invited as a guest and he used the platform . . . to embarrass us."[9] In an interview on June 18 with the chief political correspondent of the *New York Times,* the surest route to national coverage, Jackson accused Clinton of staging "a very well-planned sneak attack without the courage to confront but with the calculation to embarrass" him. Clinton had "exposed a character flaw" with his criticism of Souljah "purely to appeal to conservative whites by . . . isolating Jackson." Jackson went on to praise Ross Perot, implying that his defection to the Perot camp would take away millions of votes that Clinton had taken for granted.[10]

For speaking out against violence, Clinton was attacked by a chorus of professional blacks, the white Left, and white liberals. Jackson received immediate support from black journalists and scholars. His chief academic advisor, Ronald Walters of Howard University, weighed in:

> I would be the first to condemn anyone who said and meant that "blacks should kill whites," but I believe that was beside the point of Bill Clinton's attack. The point was that by attacking Sister Souljah, Bill Clinton's strategists intended to accomplish the objective of having him appear strong and independent by standing up to a "special interest" of the party, putting blacks "in their place" and in the process, appealing to the white middle class. . . . Bill Clinton's foray into the cultural politics of the black community was as offensive as it was crassly opportunistic, making his calls for racial harmony ring hollow.[11]

Walters's criticism was classic. First, he said the content of Souljah's remarks was unimportant, but if it were important, he claimed he would be even stronger than Clinton in his criticism. Second, what counted was Clinton's intent, which, according to Walters, was to appeal to a group that would cast most of the votes in the November election. Third, Walters asserted that Clinton had no right (presumably because he was white) to comment on something that Walters considered the exclusive domain of the black community.

Other prominent blacks were quick to jump in. Roger Wilkins, professor and columnist, said of Clinton's criticism, "it was a message to white people that Bill Clinton is a big, strong man who can protect them and is strong enough . . . to stand up for them to black people."[12] Derrick Jackson, a columnist for the *Boston Globe*, wrote:

> For white Democrats, Clinton hands out free Bubbagum. Like all nominees before him, he will go to church and expect the African-American vote to go to him in November, because he is the lesser of two evils. . . . It may seem like political suicide, but there is a feeling, far from the unity of convention halls, that not voting the top of the ticket is preferable to bootlicking a boot that has kicked you.[13]

The *Boston Globe*, a good place to find contemporary examples of classic liberalism as practiced in the 1970s, also ran an editorial that called Clinton's criticism of Sister Souljah "a cheap shot." "For a candidate desperately seeking to come from behind in the polls," opined the *Globe*, "the Rainbow meeting, and Souljah's participation, provided a perfect opportunity—not for courting members of the party's core constituency, but for kicking them to the curb."[14] Anna Quindlen of the *New York Times* added:

> Bill Clinton generated considerable heat, but no light, when he . . . decried [Souljah's] anti-white comments . . . sounding the white-guy clarion call, that hatred is as bad when it goes black to white as when it goes white to black. All things being equal this is true. Only all things are not equal. . . . Mr. Clinton got to shout across from the white side of the racial divide that black folks can be racist.[15]

Left-liberal journalists Alexander Cockburn and Andrew Kopkind concluded from Clinton's Souljah criticism, "if racism is not in Clinton's heart, as he blandly insists, it is evident in his behavior, which is after all what counts." They went on to surmise that the "Clinton culture" is "suffused with a gestural sentimentality about racial harmony, but its commitment is to white power and privilege."[16] Cockburn and Kopkind hoped to weaken Clinton sufficiently to induce Jesse Jackson to initiate a fourth-party candidacy.

SILENCE MATTERS

In the past, an attack of this seriousness instigated by Jackson against the Democratic nominee would have produced immediate signs of surrender: Michael Dukakis and Walter Mondale had each responded to Jackson with alacrity, and reassurances of "respect." Each piously said Jackson would be considered a serious candidate for the ticket (when both men knew that such a choice would be disastrous). In each case, after entreaties from the designated Jackson intermediary—Bob Beckel in Mondale's campaign, Paul Brountas in Dukakis's—a well-publicized peace meeting was organized at which the Democratic nominee gave way on the nomination rules, a prime-time speech slot, and a symbolic platform issue or two. Jackson invariably wound up looking stronger than the candidates who had beaten him in primary after primary.

Reversing the trend of liberal timidity, however, Clinton held firm against Jackson's onslaught. Perhaps some of this confidence came from the fact that Clinton had already shown himself to be very effective at attracting the support of black politicians. Even when Virginia Governor Douglas Wilder was still a presidential candidate and had some presumptive hold on politicians of color, Clinton received substantial support from blacks, particularly from black southerners like Representatives Mike Espy (later named secretary of agriculture) and John Lewis. At no time did Clinton act on the view common to liberal candidates that the only road to the hearts and votes of black America was through Jesse Jackson.

Not all black politicians and commentators were put off by Clinton's statement. Clarence Page, a respected Chicago columnist, wrote:

> We [black Americans] are notsaposta hang our dirty laundry in public, we are told, because it might weaken the movement's ability to resist attacks by political enemies. But what actually happens is almost the opposite. We end up making the enemy

look better. Bill Clinton has courageously admonished whites in the blue-collar North and the deep South to reach out to blacks. Now he's gambling that we African-Americans, after centuries of abuse, will embrace graciously a similar appeal for harmony with whites. I know I'm notsaposta think he's right. But I hope he is.[17]

Carl Rowan, the *Washington Post* columnist, exclaimed:

Underdog Democrat Bill Clinton moved a badly needed step toward the presidency last Saturday by angering Jesse Jackson. . . . Jackson acted as though he thought Clinton was on his turf, and had no right to say anything about Sister Souljah or anyone or anything else that he thought Jackson would object to. Sycophants are telling Jackson, "Clinton insulted you; don't give him your blessing!" Jackson must realize that his "blessing" becomes a curse if it requires Clinton to endorse even by silence an outrageous advocacy of murder.[18]

Clinton did not back down in the face of the counterattack by Jackson and his chorus. Criticized for his "rudeness" and his failure to warn Jackson of his remarks, Clinton said: "[I didn't] say anything that I hadn't been saying since I first started running. . . . I called for an end to division."[19] Pressed to retract his criticisms, Clinton responded, "I grew up in a segregated society, and I have devoted my public life to trying to overcome feelings of prejudice. That is what I have worked for."[20]

Clinton did something no Democratic nominee had done for twenty-five years: he demonstrated enough public respect for a black leader's ideas to argue with him in public. Bill Clinton ended the silence in the presence of alien ideas, and this simple, otherwise unremarkable action was essential to his election.

It is difficult not to personify the white liberal dilemma in recent elections and argue that Jesse Jackson was the source and symbol of the politically damaging ideas. He not only portrayed himself as the representative of the black race, he advocated leftist domestic and foreign policy agendas. As a result, he required as the price of his support that Democratic candidates offend the one-half of the national electorate that is white suburban. The efforts made by Democratic candidates to appease Jackson were costly because white suburban voters cast six or seven times the number of votes that black Americans do—votes cast overwhelmingly for the Republican candidates.

Because Dukakis and Mondale had been afraid to argue with Jackson, the only route to restore common sense to a Democratic presidential campaign ran through Jackson's front yard—he had to be confronted as the proponent of unpopular positions and the apologist for Fidel Castro, Yassir Arafat, and Louis Farrakhan. Jackson had survived because his white opponents and the press were unwilling to treat him or his ideas seriously.

Unfortunately, the source of the problem was not Jackson, but the liberals themselves. As one critic put it:

> The problem is not with the black leaders—they are merely taking advantage of the timidity and intellectual vacuity of the liberals who run the national Democratic Party. The problem is with the liberals who fail to respect the ideas of black Americans enough to argue with them . . . and who view 30,000,000 black Americans as a racial monolith.[21]

Black activists have taken advantage of white liberals since the symptoms of white guilt were first identified. *White liberal* is a pejorative term that connotes a well-educated, well-intentioned person who does not respect black Americans enough to treat them as individuals, but who is willing to support their leadership in plans that do not affect the liberals or their families in any direct way.

Ironically, Clinton, who was so disciplined as a candidate in distancing himself from the unpopular ideas associated with his predecessors, would demonstrate considerably less agility as president. He nominated Lani Guinier to the Justice Department despite her view of America's white majority as relentlessly racist. The administration also argued a New Jersey lawsuit on the side of using race as the decisive criterion in layoffs.

Clinton's stand regarding Sister Souljah was more than artifice; it would not have worked had it only been served up as clever politics. It worked because Clinton's criticism was consistent with his public record, philosophy, and personality as governor and presidential candidate. He was a product of the segregated South, but he had always pressed for an end to all forms of racial classification and discrimination. Moreover, the process of integration applied to himself and his family as it applied to others; for example, his daughter, Chelsea, attended the Little Rock public schools (although not the Washington, D.C., public schools), which meant that she was bused as a part of a court-ordered integration plan. In addition, Clinton relied on a biracial coalition to win the governorship in Arkansas.

His appeal to black voters went beyond his ability to cut deals with black political leaders; he was a Baptist, as were most blacks, and he spoke easily and naturally with them. One of the early and prominent themes of his presidential campaign was a promise to "bring us together," to unify Americans for their shared interests and problems, and not to divide them for their differences, racial and otherwise.

Some may balk at the idea that Clinton was somehow a very different Democratic candidate simply for opposing racial violence and supporting a simple view of race and equal opportunity. But that is precisely the point: white liberals had failed politically because they supported—actively or by their silence—ideas about race and racial issues that violated America's civic culture.

One has to go back to 1964 find a Democratic presidential candidate whose views on racial issues were compatible with those of most Americans. Lyndon Baines Johnson devoted much of his presidential power to dismantling southern segregation and ameliorating the problems facing northern blacks. In 1964 and 1965 Johnson enjoyed enough popular support to lead the nation to a new understanding about the problems that were percolating in northern ghettos. Understanding the Democratic experience with racial issues requires taking a look at LBJ's most visionary effort to untangle those problems for the American public—and examining Johnson's retreat when his ideas were attacked by his "friends" in the civil rights community and in the leftist salons.

2»

RACE AND POLITICS IN THE JOHNSON YEARS: FROM MORAL MONOPOLY TO POLITICAL SIDESHOW

President Lyndon Baines Johnson made the nation whole, at least for a short period of time. He stood on the shoulders of ten generations of black Americans to liberate their descendants in the eleventh generation from enslavement and segregation. At the time, Johnson was as powerful as an American president could get. The 1964 elections installed the 89th Congress, the first since 1936 to have the votes needed to keep the coalition of conservative Republicans and southern Democrats from blocking progressive legislation. Johnson moved with energy, relentlessness, and passion to legislate his vision for a Great Society: Medicare for older Americans, Medicaid for poor Americans, federal aid for public schools, federal assistance for mass transit, a war to end poverty, and programs to beautify and preserve the environment. Most of these programs had been long opposed by major interests such as the medical profession and the highway lobby; according to the conventional wisdom of the time they had no chance of passage. Yet he shepherded them through Congress.

More than anything else, however, Johnson wanted to do right by America's blacks. He funneled the nation's emotional response to President John F. Kennedy's death into passage of the Civil Rights Act of 1964, which outlawed discrimination in government programs, employment, and public accommodations. Johnson reached across the aisle to recruit conservative Republicans to join with liberal Republicans and Democrats in fashioning a bipartisan consensus to undo the tragedy of a segregated South and an indifferent North. The enactment of the civil rights laws in 1964 and 1965 did what the Old Confederacy could not do for itself. By eliminating state laws that classified persons by race, it moved the South into the mainstream of economic and social life in the United States. Building on the moral force unleashed by the civil rights movement, Johnson helped erase (or at least, lighten the darkest smear on America's history, the failure to treat black Americans as human beings).

As the 1960s began, the South still practiced apartheid: public facilities were strictly segregated; black southerners were routinely intimidated and humiliated, brutalized and exploited. For blacks, practicing one's citizenship by registering to vote could mean the loss of a job, a warning shot through a window, or worse. Particularly in the Deep South, political candidates competed to be the most extreme advocates of the continued subordination of black residents (George Wallace promised, after losing the 1958 Alabama gubernatorial primary to a harder-line segregationist, "boys . . . I ain't ever going to be out-niggahed again"[1]). After the Supreme Court's decision in *Brown* v. *Board of Education* outlawing segregation, candidates were judged on the creativity and efficacy of their schemes to circumvent orders to abolish dual school systems. The South maintained its ways through massive resistance to federal intervention, frequent use of the filibuster in the U. S. Senate, and a devil's compact with the Democratic party that exchanged electoral votes for a promise of nonintervention in its subordination of black southerners.

THE MORAL HIGH GROUND

Ultimately, black southerners did what liberals and federal judges' decisions could not do—they focused and mobilized the nation's moral outrage against the immorality of segregation. They did so with a discipline, persistence, courage, and effectiveness unmatched by any mass movement in American history. The appeal was direct and simple—give black southerners only what all Americans believe is theirs as an inalienable right—the right to equal treatment under law. The suffering of black southerners at the hands of southern officials was the instrument mobilizing public opinion.

The coalition that pushed the civil rights laws through Congress was bipartisan and biracial and stretched across the political spectrum from conservative Republican to Democratic Socialist. It encompassed Protestant, Catholic and Jewish clergy; corporate leaders and organized labor. Its moral force came from the philosophy of nonviolence advanced by Dr. Martin Luther King, Jr., and practiced by thousands of southern blacks and white allies. "We will soon wear you down by our capacity to suffer," Dr. King told white Americans.[2] The political force followed. King's message of what black Americans sought fit squarely within the American political theology: what blacks wanted was an opportunity to be educated, to be considered for good jobs, and to secure the blessings of personal liberty and the benefits of prosperity.

Segregationist politicians and sheriffs responded with a level of official violence that only the most rabid racist could support. Fire hoses, water cannon, tear gas, police dogs, and cattle prods were used on hymn-singing columns of blacks and whites, young and old—events frequently captured for television audiences across the country. Black churches were bombed, civil rights workers and marchers were murdered. Mobs of screaming, cursing whites menaced earnest black students who dared to integrate public universities.

Dramatized in this way, the cause of black southerners became the cause of students on northern campuses, preachers and rabbis, the editors of magazines and great newspapers, and individuals moved by the simple goal of equality before the law. The result was that the civil rights movement had a monopoly on morality in the early 1960s, and its adversaries were seen not only as crude, violent, and ignorant, but wrong.

GHETTO DREAMS AND BITTERSWEET REALITY

Black Americans in 1965 expected that their recent victories would set the stage for their full integration into American society. That meant integration into the booming economy, integration that would give black men and women good jobs that would support a family and give hope to their children. Integration also meant access to quality education that would prepare black children to compete successfully for places in good colleges and for good jobs after college. Integration meant being treated justly by police, merchants, and realtors. It meant the chance to live in safe, clean neighborhoods.

The civil rights laws of 1964 and 1965 clearly helped black southerners. But by then, 45 percent of the black Americans no longer lived in the Old Confederacy. They had moved North in pursuit of jobs, liberal governments, programs such as public housing and unemployment compensation, and the freedom to vote and participate in the system.

The North, however, was hardly the promised land. Black newcomers were concentrated in the poorest, most crowded neighborhoods. Many of those who could afford to move were blocked by antiblack real estate covenants and discriminatory practices. (At the time, no one thought the enforced mixing of poor and middle-class blacks was an advantage—it was one more negative consequence of racial discrimination. Only after the black teachers, police, social workers, doctors, lawyers, and business people moved out to leave concentrations of poor, struggling families was it clear that a new, more intractable, class-based problem had to be faced.)

The northern ghettos could not be blamed on Jim Crow laws and segregationist evil. Yet there was plenty of prejudice, and the discrimination practiced by some personnel offices and craft unions was as hardened and damaging as anything found in the South. In 1960 the average earnings of black college graduates were less than those of whites who had only one to three years of high school. Whites made it painfully clear that they wanted no black neighbors, and real estate agents went along. Black neighborhoods were redlined by mortgage lenders.[3] The federal government collaborated with the residential segregationists: the Federal Housing Administration and Veterans Administration essentially classified mortgages to black families as "bad" mortgages.

White northerners had developed a strong notion of the right "place" for blacks. Blacks could sit in the front of the bus—they could even drive it, but white bus drivers would not work for a black owner; northern whites would work alongside blacks—but not for them. The occupational pigeonholes were strongly walled: black workers could carry hod but not run wire; they could stock shelves, but not wait on customers; bus dishes, but not take orders. Even public jobs were stratified. Black college graduates might work as postal clerks, social workers, or school teachers, but few black high school graduates could hope to get a firefighter's job. Hurtful stereotypes abounded. Even as liberals hailed the civil rights movement's successes in the South and in Congress, their white neighbors worried about blacks moving too fast and upsetting customs and traditions that served to keep "them" in their place.

After the apartheid of Alabama or Mississippi, the North was a very confusing place for blacks. The prevailing public attitude in the North was that racial discrimination was immoral and irrational. Most states and cities had strong antidiscrimination laws. Business leaders were frequently represented in groups such as the Urban League and showed up on the boards of interfaith, interracial assemblies. Editorials in northern newspapers called for understanding and cooperation among the races. The clergy in many northern churches and synagogues had participated in southern civil rights marches and now sought ways to bring "the cause" into their own congregations and communities.

But evidence of the North's racial hypocrisy quickly surfaced. Alabama Governor George Wallace, an avowed white supremacist, received 34 percent of the vote in the 1964 Wisconsin presidential primary against Governor John Reynolds, Lyndon Johnson's stand-in. In a state with a black population of only 3 percent, Wallace's message against black crime and disorder and federal "meddling" found a receptive audience. In Maryland, Wallace took 43 percent of the Democratic primary vote, winning by landslide proportions in Catholic areas.

When pressed about the implications of such votes, President Johnson maintained an Olympian detachment, deciding not to enter any presidential primaries, but to "do the very best job I could as President for all the people up until convention time, and then let the delegates. . . make their choice freely."[4]

Johnson faced a devilish, perhaps irreconcilable, political problem in 1965. The boundaries of black neighborhoods were stretching and breaking under the weight of growing populations. The neighborhoods encroached upon by this growth were populated most frequently by white ethnic Catholics, who opposed the black "invasion." One of the few things the new neighbors shared was a loyalty to the Democratic party. In 1964 about 96 percent of black votes and 79 percent of ethnic Catholic votes went to Johnson. The two largest and most loyal Democratic constituencies were competing for living space and public benefits in the great and gray cities of the North and Midwest. The tensions between these groups created a serious political problem for the newly elected president and for the big city Democratic mayors who were among his most effective supporters.

For the first time law and order was becoming a national political issue. William Brink and Louis Harris found in a 1966 survey that while 44 percent of the nation was "personally uneasy about the threat of racial violence," the numbers for Italian-Americans and Polish-Americans, who were more likely to live in central cities, were 69 and 67 percent respectively.[5] Democrats wavered on crime, first denying that it was getting worse (blaming the increases instead on improvements in statistical methods), then settling on eliminating its "underlying causes." They advocated "soft" solutions that were vague and untested. Republicans were "tough," calling for a national "war" they could not lead. The reason crime was up, conservatives asserted without a whit of evidence, was because the Supreme Court was protecting criminals.

Crime was not the only pressure. Black men wanted jobs in craft unions that provided middle-class wages to the sons, nephews, and cousins of Irish, Italian, and Polish families. They wanted a fair shot at the best public sector blue-collar jobs, but firefighting and police slots were viewed as tribal inheritances by Irish, Italian, and other ethnic families. Black families wanted better housing in safe neighborhoods; the closest and most affordable of these neighborhoods were home to white ethnics. Black parents wanted their kids to go to better public schools; they had been told by judges and experts that black schools could not be good schools.

President Johnson knew that the federal government would have to help defuse the growing tension in northern cities. Because of the 1964 election, the problems of black Americans were now the inheritance of the Democratic party. "Black equals Democrat" was the equation in the public mind. Ghetto residents needed more concrete opportunities to be educated, to get good jobs, and to be protected from crime. The nation needed to show some patience and understanding for the heavy disadvantages borne by black Americans. Johnson needed to move quickly before the ghettos blew up. It was so fragile—a bunch of sixteen-year-old kids in any one of a hundred cities could undo the balance. The Democratic coalition was at stake.

JOHNSON'S UNCONDITIONAL WAR

Forty-seven days after becoming president, Lyndon Johnson stood before Congress to deliver the State of the Union address. In stentorian tones he said, "This administration today, here and now, declares unconditional war on poverty in America." Many Americans, he declared, "live on the outskirts of hope—some because of their poverty, and some because of their color, and all too many because of both." He did not wait for a strategy, or an analysis of the enemy, or an estimate of the costs, or evidence of whether the war could even be won. He pledged that the war would be fought without increasing taxes or the federal budget.

Johnson's War on Poverty was not built on systematic thinking, careful analysis, or even an energetic pursuit of truth, but on hunches, guesses, and, in the end, arrogance. White liberals approached northern ghettos like American tourists overrunning a small, foreign village: they knew little about its history or culture but were certain that its residents welcomed their presence and would benefit from their attention. And then they were off to see the next cathedral.

In the 1960 presidential campaign, the drive for civil rights for black southerners was an issue. In fact, in the closest election in the nation's history, it may have been decisive. Candidate Kennedy responded to Martin Luther King's October imprisonment for civil disobedience with a sympathetic call to Mrs. King; Nixon was silent. King's father switched his support to Kennedy, the word traveled the grapevine of black America, and Kennedy received the northern black vote by margins wide enough to carry Illinois, Michigan, and New Jersey. The party of Lincoln was shedding its ties to black voters.

But nowhere were the growing black ghettos themselves an issue. Nicholas Lemann traces the embryonic and superficial efforts that underlay the Kennedy and Johnson administrations' programs to transform northern ghettos in *The Promised Land,* his important book about the northward migration of black sharecroppers. He concluded that among "public policy experts, the idea that an important national problem was brewing in the black slums of the Northern and Western cities was not at all a part of the conventional wisdom."[6]

Only a few scholars and visionary foundation executives were studying or acting on the problems of blacks in northern cities. In fact, it is difficult to find a single work on the subject before Kenneth Clark's *Dark Ghetto,* published in 1965. Paul Ylvisaker had convinced the Ford Foundation to start the "Gray Areas" project in 1959 to encourage mayors, charitable organizations, unions, and public schools to pay attention to ghetto problems in a few cities. The foundation-supported projects in New Haven, Oakland, Washington, and Pittsburgh were to be particularly valuable in planning the community action program in the War on Poverty.

Elsewhere, few influential purveyors of ideas and issues paid any attention to the intersection of discrimination, crime, and poverty found in black neighborhoods. In the early 1960s, a loyal reader of *Atlantic, Harper's,* the *Saturday Review,* the *Reporter,* or the *New York Times Magazine*—never mind *Time* or *Newsweek*—would have remained largely ignorant of the race-poverty problem. One exception was Theodore H. White, who offered a prescient analysis in his 1961 best-selling book on the 1960 presidential campaign. White analyzed the results of the 1960 census, reporting on the suburbanization of the nation and the displacement of white city residents with black southerners, and he noted:

For what has happened over the past twenty years, as Negro progress has come so swiftly, is that the gap between its own advanced leadership and the troops of its rear echelon has widened almost as fast as progress. If Negro education, Negro culture, Negro responsibilities have soared, so, sickeningly, has the heritage of a past now sampling life with an abandon once choked by Southern white cruelties.

Perhaps the most dramatic and alarming of the figures attendant on the release of the Negro from his previous Southern punishments has been the rise in the proportion of illegitimate Negro births as the Negro has moved North. . . . But attendant on those figures [of illegitimacy and broken families] are all the figures and delinquency and street violence; and the political implications thereof.[7]

One segment of the Kennedy administration that paid attention to the black ghettos was the President's Committee on Juvenile Delinquency, a tiny group located in the Justice Department and run by Attorney General Robert Kennedy's prep school friend, David Hackett. The committee, set up at the suggestion of Kennedy's sister, Eunice Shriver, gave grants to experiments such as Mobilization for Youth in New York, most of which had been started by Ylvisaker's Ford Foundation dollars.

The Kennedy presidency is celebrated for the energy and glamour it brought to the practice of politics and government. It was as if the nation had traded in its gray Buick Dynaflow for a bright red Mustang. The "best and the brightest" took over Washington, introducing new operating assumptions, one of which appeared to be: *There is no consequential public problem that smart, energetic, white men cannot solve.* National wars of liberation? *No problem, we'll invent the Green Berets and air mobile tactics.* Soviet superiority in aerospace? *We'll focus American industry and government on beating the Russians to the moon.* Dangerous combinations of frustration and poverty in ghetto neighborhoods? *We'll mount the War on Poverty.*

On the second day of his presidency, Lyndon Johnson directed Walter Heller, the chair of the Council of Economic Advisors, to get to work organizing a War on Poverty. Heller sketched out a plan before Christmas, and spent the holidays working out the details at the Johnson ranch. What is amazing, in hindsight, is the great weight put on the results of such a hurried effort for an initiative central to a new presidency.

Johnson put a Kennedy brother-in-law and the founding director of the Peace Corps, Sargent Shriver, in charge of his war. Shriver inherited an interagency task force that was split between those who advocated services, such as job training and early childhood education that would be managed by existing federal agencies and their state or local counterparts, and those who emphasized process, specifically "community action." Community action was based on the premise that existing service agencies had failed to serve the special needs of poor blacks in cities and that the only way to motivate the "system" was to empower those left out to bring pressure to bear on traditional agencies. Community action programs would not report to city hall, and would include representatives of the poor themselves. This requirement was pushed, in part, to ensure that southern blacks—the poorest group in the poorest region—would not be cut out by white-run local governments.

Shriver avoided a decision by endorsing both approaches. He proposed creation of a new federal agency to run the war—the Office of Economic Opportunity (OEO). It would also operate some programs directly, such as the Job Corps, and it would fund and monitor community action programs (CAPs) at the local level. The Labor Department would operate the Neighborhood Youth Corps; the Department of Health, Education, and Welfare (HEW) would be responsible for programs battling adult illiteracy. From the outset, the war was hampered by the untidiness of funding and organizational relationships and by the vagueness of the charge to the CAPs. Charles Morris, an early poverty warrior, captured the spirit of the early days of the War on Poverty:

> To the technocrats, overcoming poverty was just another systems problem like managing the economy or winning the race to the moon. . . . Complicated flowcharts showed how the poor would be processed smoothly through various stages of life-skills education, literacy training, and job preparation into permanent employment. . . . Community organization was discussed as a subtle form of input-output analysis, a somewhat complicated question of Skinnerian stimulus and response—adroit dollops of social pressure here would produce just the desired outcomes over there. McNamara-style program budgeting would bring entire arrays of social services to bear on each poor family—health care, treatment for drug addiction and alcoholism, marriage counseling, mental health services, whatever—to support the communal march forward to social respectability and economic independence.[8]

The War on Poverty was put together by smart, confident, elite white men. Few of them had any experience working in poor neighborhoods or with poor blacks. They worked for an impatient president who was uninterested in the practical and conceptual problems the task force faced. He wanted action and big numbers. Johnson had run the National Youth Administration in Texas during the Depression—it had helped people; it worked. With thirty years of experience and new approaches, why shouldn't his war do just as well? Nicholas Lemann put it this way:

> The idea that the federal government might have trouble solving a large problem was completely foreign to Shriver and his associates, whose formative experiences were watching Roosevelt defeat the Depression and then the Nazis. Because all the key participants . . . were white and from the North, they didn't have that ingrained awareness of the tragic potential of the national enterprise that virtually all African-Americans, and many white Southerners, possessed; to them, America almost by definition couldn't fail at anything.[9]

Concurrently with the planning for the War on Poverty, other groups of self-confident white men were huddled in the White House and Pentagon making plans to control events and change behavior in a far-away land about which they were as ignorant as were the poverty warriors. No matter to them. The Vietnam and Poverty wars proceeded in parallel except that, as a consequence of the former, the latter received steadily diminishing attention from President Johnson, political support from Capitol Hill, and fiscal resources. Both wars ended in failure and in a loss of public confidence in the Democratic party and the policy entrepreneurs who launched them.

The logic of the poverty planners was straightforward: for every characteristic of poverty that was thought to be important, an off-setting federal program would be created with a name that suggested corrective action. Poor families did not give their kids the same preparation for school that middle-class families gave theirs; ergo, Head Start. Many poor adults had only a few years of inferior education and were, thus, unequipped to compete for a good job; the answer: a program in adult literacy. Poor kids had higher jobless rates than suburban kids; the result: the Neighborhood Youth Corps. And if poor people felt unconnected and lacking in influence to change their neighborhoods and lives, then the War on Poverty would provide a community action program to give them authority and pride.

One of my jobs in the Trenton CAP was to put together a "coordinated, comprehensive attack" on poverty in an area slated to be cleared for urban renewal. The funding proposal to OEO reported agreements with thirty-three public and nonprofit agencies for everything from visiting homemaker and nursing services, legal representation, and separate counseling for families, alcoholics, and disturbed youth, to Girl Scout troops and summer field trips. By the time OEO approval was received, a director recruited, and contracts signed, most of the carefully identified 230 families had moved away.

One observer in 1969 offered a scathing critique of the centerpiece of the War on Poverty, community action programs:

> This is the essential fact: *The government did not know what it was doing*. It had a theory. Or, rather, a set of theories. Nothing more. The U.S. Government at this time was no more in possession of confident knowledge as to how to prevent delinquency, cure anomie, or overcome that midmorning sense of powerlessness, than was it the possessor of a dependable formula for motivating Vietnamese villagers to fight Communism. . . . The divergence of the various theories was such that what would serve to cure in the one case would exacerbate in the other. A *big* bet was being made. No responsible persons had any business acting as if it were a sure thing.[10]

The words are particularly damning because they are not those of an outside observer, but rather are from someone who had supplied President Johnson with many ideas regarding race and poverty: Daniel Patrick Moynihan.

MOYNIHAN'S SEARCH FOR ORDER AND HIS DESPAIRING PROPHECY

No clear focus guided the War on Poverty, no grand strategy or concept unified the scattered programs. The crucial questions—What is the main problem? How do we attack it? Why do we think it will work?—went unasked and unanswered. The leadership was too busy—reviewing proposals, fending off unfriendly congressional inquiries, awarding funds, and trying to secure IBM Selectrics for their secretaries—to answer these first, simple, big questions. This was the setting for Moynihan's introduction—in a bit part—onto the national stage.

In 1965 Moynihan had become, at the age of thirty-eight, the assistant secretary of labor for policy planning and research. Moynihan had grown up for a time in Manhattan's predominantly Irish slum, Hell's Kitchen. After working briefly as a longshoreman, he enrolled at the City College of New York, finished his bachelor's degree at Tufts, and earned a doctorate at Tufts's Fletcher School of Law and Diplomacy in 1961. He went on to teach at Syracuse University, study in London, and serve on the staff of New York Governor Averell Harriman.

Moynihan would prove himself to be a street-smart scholar with a reporter's instinct for a story and a speechwriter's flair for the memorable phrase. He was neither shy about expressing himself directly and clearly nor about departing from the prevailing wisdom with big, bold ideas. On top of all this, he would demonstrate enough political dexterity to be elected U. S. Senator from New York and to be twice reelected.

THE MOYNIHAN REPORT

In March 1965, Moynihan circulated a 48-page report entitled "The Negro Family: The Case for National Action."[11] The report argued that the federal government had good reason to organize its scattered antipoverty efforts around the objective of strengthening the black family. Known as the "Moynihan Report," this little-read, oft-cited document would generate bitter attacks on its author.

The report, produced some nine months after the Economic Opportunity Act setting up the OEO was signed, was Moynihan's attempt to bring the normally drab statistics of government tables and reports alive with social commentary and policy implications. Moynihan avoided specific program or policy recommendations, saving those for shorter, follow- up memoranda directed at the president and the small audience of men in the White House and around official Washington who could influence the president to shift dollars and programs to the Labor Department.

Moynihan began his report with an uncontroversial assertion: the family is the basic unit in American society for transmitting values about work, education, and savings; and families that have both parents present are much better off. He offered much evidence concerning illegitimacy, divorce, and desertion that indicated that the black family was not doing as well as the white family. The report argued that:

▲   The black family had been exposed to uniquely destructive forces from slavery through Jim Crow and was particularly susceptible to instability in times of high unemployment.

▲   Black men had been robbed of their manhood, with increasingly disastrous consequences not only for them but also for black women and children. When the economy dipped, black men were much more likely to be laid off; with no job, their self-respect was decreased and they deserted their families. Unemployment and desertion explained most of the rise and fall in welfare caseloads until—ominously—1963, when cases continued upward even as black male unemployment declined.

▲   Too many black children grew up in poor homes without fathers. Social values, especially those concerning education and family, were not effectively transmitted in such an environment. Too many girls repeated the experience of their mothers by having children when they were very young and before they were married.

The report suggested that legalized discrimination was not the main problem facing most black families in city ghettos. It declared that, if one were able to eliminate in one stroke all the discrimination practiced against blacks, they would still be at a competitive disadvantage against the rest of American society. The report made clear, however, that dealing with the crumbling black family and its dismal prospects was the responsibility of the larger society:

> In this new period [following enactment of the 1964 civil rights law] the expectations of Negro Americans will go beyond civil rights. Being Americans, they will not expect that in the near future equal opportunities for them as a group will produce roughly equal results, as compared with other groups. This is not going to happen. Nor will it happen for generations to come unless a new and special effort is made.
>
> There are two reasons. First, the racist virus in the American blood stream still afflicts us; Negroes will encounter serious personal prejudice for at least another generation. Second, three centuries of sometimes unimaginable mistreatment have taken their toll on the Negro people. The harsh fact is that as a group,

at the present time, in terms of ability to win out in the competitions of American life, they are not equal to most of those groups with which they will be competing.

Individually, Negro Americans reach the highest peaks of achievement. But collectively, in the spectrum of American ethnic and religious and regional groups, where some get plenty and some get none, where some send eighty percent of their children to college and others pull them out of school at the 8th grade, Negroes are among the weakest.[12]

Moynihan wanted to sound the alarm and to offer a coherent and practical rationale for government policy. He argued that the problem was critical enough that the government should adopt racial preferences to guarantee that blacks got their fair share of jobs, education, and income. In fact, the Moynihan Report is one of the few "official" examples of an open argument in favor of racially preferential treatment. Moynihan's policy recommendation was offered in two sentences:

The policy of the United States is to bring the Negro American to full and equal sharing in the responsibilities and rewards of citizenship. To this end, the programs of the Federal government bearing on this objective shall be designed to have the effect, directly or indirectly, of enhancing the stability and resources of the Negro American family."[13]

One would be hard-pressed to imagine a policy that could be more openly racial than the one advanced by Moynihan. Moynihan was alarmed by numbers and trends that demonstrated sharp differences in the fortunes of black families compared with whites. He sought to convert a national program that had been conceived to deal with millions of poor whites living in rural America, as well as the poor minorities in cities, to a program for poor blacks.

To the reader a generation later, Moynihan's description and analysis would appear reasonable and supportable, if debatable. But, in the report, Moynihan provided the intellectual foundation for three radical departures that would wreak havoc with liberal politics:

▲   He "racialized" poverty, concentrating attention on black poverty.

▲   He justified a racially conscious poverty program on the basis of slavery and segregation, even though the family deterioration he documented had not accelerated until the 1950s, when the black American culture became increasingly an urban, ghetto culture.

▲ He played on the guilt of contemporary white America for the sins of the past.

Moynihan's observations—sympathetically posed and depressingly accurate in the rereading—set off fierce attacks. These attacks came from a chorus of the Left, black activists and scholars, and a few white liberals; mainstream conservatives were quiet, despite the radical conclusions Moynihan reached.

None of this would have happened if Moynihan's report had disappeared into a White House file cabinet. But by May 1965, barely two months after he had completed the report, Moynihan was working with Johnson's speechwriter, Richard Goodwin, on a major presidential address that would take public the findings and implications of the report. Moynihan emphasized two troubling trends that were emerging in the statistics about black families. The first was the accelerating increase in the proportion of births to unwed mothers, growing from 16.8 percent in 1940 to 23.6 percent by 1963. This trend, plus higher separation and divorce rates, was producing what Moynihan characterized as a startling increase in the welfare dependency. Secondly, for the first time ever, welfare rolls had grown while the unemployment rate for black men was falling. Moynihan was eager to highlight the crisis caused by the crumbling black family structure through a speech by the president.

THE ADDRESS AT HOWARD UNIVERSITY

In his address at Howard University on June 4, 1965, Lyndon Johnson went further to identify with black Americans than any white American politician before or since. He reached up to draw a high-water line that is still visible today, a line marking the apex of black America's moral purchase on those who govern the nation. Johnson understood that there were profound differences between the situation and expectations of black Americans living in the South and those packed into northern ghettos. And he knew that the American public would not accept the argument that the two situations were born of the same sins of the white majority.

The president laid out plans for "the next and most profound stage in the battle for civil rights."[14] The speech signified that the president was shifting his considerable energies from the problem of segregation in the South to the problems in northern ghettos and that he was prepared to share ownership of his new poverty war with the civil rights movement. Johnson's argument followed the analysis and policy implications of the Moynihan Report, declaring that the roots of black poverty were different from the poverty faced by waves of European immigrants. Although the Negro, like the immigrant, "will have to rely mostly on his own efforts . . . he just cannot do it alone," the president said. For the Negro American "equal opportunity is essential, but not enough." In his Howard University speech, Johnson advanced four startling, even radical, ideas.

First, the American ideal of equal opportunity was insufficient when contending with the problems facing black Americans:

> You do not wipe away the scars of centuries by saying: Now you are free to go where you want and do as you desire and choose the leaders you please. You do not take a person who . . . has been hobbled by chains and liberate him, bring him to the starting line of a race, and then say you are free to compete with all the others, and still just believe that you have been completely fair. . . . This is the next and most profound stage of the battle for civil rights. We seek not just freedom but opportunity. . . not just equality as a right . . . but equality as a fact and equality as a result.[15]

Second, Johnson argued that black poverty was different in kind from the poverty of other Americans: "Negro poverty is not white poverty. . . . There are differences—deep, corrosive, obstinate differences—radiating painful roots into the community, the family, and the nature of the individual."[16]

Third, Johnson claimed that white America was responsible for the deterioration of the black family: "For [the breakdown] white America must accept responsibility. It flows from centuries of oppression and persecution of the Negro man. It flows from long years of degradation, and discrimination, which have attacked his dignity and assaulted his ability to provide for his family."[17]

Fourth, Johnson said that the process of figuring out how to accomplish the goal of "equal results" required a partnership between government and the black leadership. Thus, Johnson explicitly equated the War on Poverty with the civil rights movement. Johnson pushed at the edges of white America's patience and tolerance. In the land of liberty, equality, and justice for all, he called for a special deal for black Americans based on what white Americans had done to their ancestors. The time was ripe if it were ever to be so: Americans of both colors were benefiting from a sustained growth in jobs and the economy and were ready to support a more active role for government in guaranteeing the rights of minorities. But practically no Americans in 1965 supported explicit racial preferences. (Brink and Harris found white respondents opposed to job preferences for Negroes by a 90-to-4 margin in their 1966 survey for *Newsweek*—the ratio had been 93-to-3 in 1963.)[18]

Johnson, true to Moynihan's report, made it plain that the unusually severe problems of instability, desertion, and illegitimacy facing the black family were best explained as consequences of white discrimination. He said that many of the federal programs under way or proposed in housing, health, education, and job training would help poor Americans, white or black. These efforts would not be enough for poor blacks, however, not because they were black, but because they were the victims "solely and simply . . . of ancient brutality, past injustice, and present prejudice." The focus of federal efforts to bring hope to the ghetto, in Johnson's view, would be the black family:

> When the family collapses it is the children that usually are damaged. When it happens on a massive scale the community itself is crippled. So, unless we work to strengthen the family, to create conditions under which most parents will stay together—all the rest: schools and playgrounds, public assistance and private concern, will never be enough to cut completely the circle of despair and deprivation.[19]

What did this talk of family mean for concrete programs or for the organization and conduct of the War on Poverty, then ten months old? The president was confident that "scholars and experts," the leaders of civil rights groups, some government officials, men of both races could unlock the mystery. He called for a national gathering to come up with the answers, a White House Conference "To Fulfill These Rights."

The Howard speech had far-reaching effects; Johnson, for lack of a more precise term, had *racialized* poverty. The president had said black poverty was different from white poverty, suggesting that something as yet unknown would have to be discovered to deal with poor blacks. One might charitably argue that presidential rhetoric was finally catching up with presidential policy. After all, the early administration of the antipoverty program, particularly the Community Action Program, emphasized the preference to be given to black community activists in the governance and patronage of the program. The popular connection between "black" and "poverty," and, particularly, with "poverty program," would further weaken already tenuous congressional support for the "unconditional war."

In his speech, Johnson invited the civil rights movement to assume ownership of the national effort to abolish poverty. The movement was a reasonably united front directed at dismantling southern segregation, and Johnson had earned the respect of its leadership by frequent consultations concerning the civil rights bills—but the civil rights leadership was ill-equipped to manage a role in the antipoverty war. Like the planners of the War on Poverty, they had no operating insights on how to deal with what Moynihan called the "tangle of pathology" in northern ghettos.

In these departures from conventional American politics, Lyndon Johnson was following the script laid down by Daniel Patrick Moynihan. The Howard speech, which received prominent attention in the daily press and news magazines, would reinforce the growing notion that Democrats were cutting a special deal for blacks.

As it turned out, Johnson's infatuation with Moynihan's ideas was short-lived. The president mentioned the special problems of black families in public only once after Howard—in the immediate wake of the Watts riots. If President Johnson had intended to rewrite the American creed with the Howard address, as conservatives had suggested, his intention flagged badly in the months immediately following the speech. His growing preoccupation with Vietnam became clear. (Between June 1965 and June 1966, the ceiling on American troops in Vietnam jumped from 75,000 to 400,000.) But there was something more: the Moynihan analysis did not "take" with Johnson: he never returned to the language and approach he outlined at Howard University. Johnson needed programs that would deliver numbers and buy peace, not ambiguous, open-ended proposals that would subject him to vitriol.

Writing in 1967, Moynihan called the period around the Howard speech "the moment lost." In Moynihan's view:

> [T]he plain and ascertainable fact was that the nation was going through a moment that had never occurred before—and could not persist indefinitely—in which a willingness to accept a

considerable degree of social innovation was combined with genuine feeling for the problems of Negroes. The world was at peace. The President had enormous majorities in Congress. The success of the New Economics was by then manifest: the Bureau of the Budget was already forecasting a $45 billion increase in the level of federal revenues by 1970. . . . It was, in addition, a moment of racial calm.[20]

SUPPRESSION AND CENSURE: THE NEW ORTHODOXY IS ESTABLISHED

The response to Moynihan's report shaped much of the future debate of national antipoverty policies. In combination with rapid and dramatic changes within the civil rights movement itself, the treatment of Moynihan and his ideas chilled the atmosphere for scholars, journalists, and politicians to the point that, a full generation later, only a few academics and fewer politicians were prepared to deal with the questions Moynihan raised and analyzed.

The suppression of the Moynihan Report—and suppression is the right word—sent a cold, clear message to scholars, activists, journalists, and politicians: You can talk about the cruel effects of white racism, the underfunding of government programs, or America's history of shameful treatment of black Americans. But you run the danger of personal attack if you mention individual or family responsibility or point to negative statistical correlations about black Americans.

The approach and language of the Moynihan Report's initial critics should sound familiar to the contemporary reader. Consider a recent description of the report by a respected black scholar, Adolph Reed, Jr., and the erstwhile *wunderkind* Julian Bond: they called it "Moynihan's racist, scurrilously misogynous 1965 report."[21] Jewell Handy Gresham, writing in 1989, summarized the uses of the report in these words:

> Those who found the Moynihan report useful were presumably unaware that the archetypal sexism on which it rests is *inextricable from its racism*. At any rate, the report signaled, at the very height of the civil rights movement, that Northern whites would pick up where the South was forced to leave off in blocking the long black struggle for parity with whites in American life.[22]

Moynihan's early critics succeeded in defining a new orthodoxy, an orthodoxy that prescribed the boundaries for public debate for all, except for conservatives who found the orthodoxy silly, and a few progressive black scholars such as William Julius Wilson who had the gumption to speak up.

The Moynihan Report was never in the headlines. (The 1965 and 1966 indices for the *New York Times* carry no mention of it by name.) The report was clumsily released by the White House in August 1965—some say to demonstrate concern and expertise as the Watts riot played out. By that time, Moynihan had resigned to seek office in New York City; his views were without strong sponsorship among his former colleagues either in the Labor Department or the White House.

Meanwhile, Moynihan's critics formed a chorus to shout down anyone so bold as to question their version of the race and poverty story. The Left welcomed any ally or evidence that aided its argument that the American economic system had failed and was pervasively unfair, corrupt, exploiting, and racist; professional blacks, preying on white liberal fear and blaming white racism for the difficulties facing black Americans, preached a message of cultural, political, and intellectual separatism; liberals, black and white, tended to be the weaker voices, holding the coats for the Left and black combatants as they attacked Moynihan.

Moynihan's most effective assailant was William Ryan, then a psychologist at the Harvard Medical School. In a single article provocatively entitled "Savage Discovery," in the November 22, 1965 issue of the *Nation,* Ryan, a vivid, engaging writer, wrote the textbook for black activists and their radical white camp followers for confining the debate about the issues of race and poverty to the narrow ground they favored. Following a review of what Ryan characterized as "methodological weaknesses" and "misstatements" in the report, he launched his attack.

Ryan's first tactic was to accuse anyone who sought to discuss problems that disproportionately afflict black Americans of "blaming the victim." Here is a sample of Ryan's artistry.

> The explanations almost always focus on supposed defects of the Negro victim as if those—and not the racist structure of American society—were the cause of all woes that Negroes suffer. The Moynihan Report . . . singles out the "unstable Negro family" as the cause of Negro inequality. But the statistics. . . reflect current effects of contemporaneous discrimination. They are results, not causes.[23]

Later, in his 1971 book, *Blaming the Victim,* Ryan explained the motivation and practice of the "Victim Blamer":

> Victim-blaming is cloaked in kindness and concern, and bears all the trappings and statistical furbelows of scientism. . . . In observing the process of Blaming the Victim, one tends to be confused and disoriented because those who practice this art display a deep concern for the victims that is quite genuine. . . . Its adherents include sympathetic social scientists with social consciences in good working order, and liberal politicians with a genuine commitment to reform. They . . . indignantly condemn any notions of innate wickedness or genetic defect. "The Negro is *not born* inferior," they shout apoplectically. "Force of circumstance," they explain in reasonable tones, "has *made* him inferior." And they dismiss with self-righteous contempt any claims that the poor man in America is plainly unworthy or shiftless or enamored of idleness. . . . No, they say, he is "caught in the cycle of poverty." He is trained to be poor by his culture and his family life, endowed by his environment (perhaps by his ignorant mother's outdated style of toilet training) with those unfortunately unpleasant characteristics that make him ineligible for a passport into the affluent society.[24]

Ryan radically dismissed any assignment of individual responsibility or family obligation in the case of blacks; in doing so, he suggested the most unkind motives for Moynihan's report. Ryan's tone further trivialized Moynihan's effort:

> To sustain this ideology, it is necessary to engage in the popular new sport of Savage Discovery, and to fit the theory, savages are being discovered in great profusion in the Northern ghetto. The all-time favorite "savage" is the promiscuous mother who produces a litter of illegitimate brats in order to profit from AFDC.[25]

There was no pattern of black behavior—from illegitimacy to crime to educational performance—that Ryan would concede could be attributed to anything other than systematic white discrimination and oppression.

More than a quarter of century after Ryan's lesson in rhetorical warfare, one did not have to look too far to find devotees of his tactics.

The nation's most influential newspaper, the *New York Times,* regularly alloted its valuable op-ed pages to Ryan's ideological descendants. The Reverend Mr. Cecil Williams, a prominent black pastor in San Francisco, for example, wrote that the epidemic of crack cocaine usage in black neighborhoods was best understood as "genocide": "I am talking about the spiritual and physical death of a race."[26] This astounding allegation begged for the identification of who or what is behind genocide. Williams's answer: "The very raising of the question minimizes the seriousness of the issue. The answer is not nearly as important as the steps we take to reverse the genocide." Others may use crack, but Williams argued that "its full destructive fury was unleashed in the black community."[27] Like Ryan, Williams argued that any bad behavior of poor blacks is not their fault.

Ryan's second tactic followed closely on the first: deflect attention to white shortcomings. For example, according to Ryan, the disparity in the ratio of illegitimacy rates for blacks and whites distorted the real truth, which is that blacks and whites engaged in premarital sexual intercourse in about equal proportions. (Whites make more use of contraception, illegal abortions, and "shotgun" marriages.) If what Ryan suggested was true in 1965, it still would not change the facts that Moynihan reported about illegitimate black births and the consequences. (The Moynihan Report, incidentally, did not impute higher illegitimacy rates to greater promiscuity among blacks.)

Ryan used the same kind of "analysis" to explain higher black crime rates and poorer educational performance. A frequent argument using the deflection technique is that white crime is just as pervasive as black crime, except that it is practiced with computers and advertising, not burglary tools and street weapons. Of course, it is true that much white-collar crime goes undetected or unreported, but people do not move out of neighborhoods because of a neighbor's check-kiting scheme, and they can walk past the house of convicted embezzlers without fear.

Ryan's third tactic was to cite white racism as the single explanation for any example of black behavior that seemed aberrant, pathological, or undesirable:

> If we are to believe the new ideologues, we must conclude that segregation and discrimination are not the terrible villains we thought they were. Rather, we are told the Negro's condition is due to this "pathology," his values, the way he lives, the kind of family life he leads. The major qualification—the bow

to egalitarianism—is that these conditions are said to grow out of the Negro's history of being enslaved and oppressed—*generations ago*. It is all an ingenious way of "copping a plea." As the murderer pleads guilty to manslaughter to avoid a conviction that [might] lead to his being electrocuted, the liberal America today is pleading guilty to the savagery and oppression against the Negro that happened 100 years ago, in order to escape trial for the crimes of today.[28]

Although written a quarter century ago, nothing in Ryan's approach or language is dated: the same arguments are still offered reflexively by the Left and professional blacks in response to any effort to untangle the mess in our cities that does not explicitly blame the problem on white racism. Ryan persisted in arguing that Moynihan was either out of step with a fundamental assumption of American society—equality—or was untruthful in asserting that the concept of equality applies to blacks:

The theme is "The Negro was not initially born inferior, he has been made inferior by generations of harsh treatment." Thus we continue to assert that the Negro is inferior, while chastely maintaining that all men are equal. It is all rather painful, as well as fallacious. For the fact is that the Negro child learns less not because his mother doesn't subscribe to *The Reader's Digest* . . . but because he is miseducated in segregated slum schools.[29]

This type of clinching, shut-your-mouth argument was made by others. James Farmer, best known as the erstwhile director of the Congress of Racial Equality, criticized Moynihan in a December 1965 syndicated column. Like Ryan, Farmer attacked Moynihan for blaming blacks for individual and family decisions that Farmer said were better explained by past and present white racism. Moreover, employing Ryan's second tactic, Farmer claimed that Moynihan was guilty of ignoring the pathology in "'an orderly and normal' white family structure that is weaned on racial hatred." Much of what Farmer attributed to Moynihan was in the report, including the view that blacks must earn their freedom and stop buying Cadillacs and that "mental health should be the first order of business in a civil rights revolution."[30]

Then, notwithstanding Farmer's liberties in representing Moynihan's report, he proceeds to provide an excellent example of the fourth, and most destructive, rhetorical tactic of professional blacks and white radicals—the charge of racism:

> [Moynihan's] well-enough intentioned analysis *provides the fuel for a new racism* . . . it succeeds in taking the real tragedy of black poverty and serving it up as an essentially salacious "discovery." . . . It has been the fatal error of American society for 300 years to ultimately blame the roots of poverty and violence in the Negro community upon Negroes themselves. I honestly felt that the Civil Rights and Voting laws indicated that we were rid of this kind of straw-man logic, but here it is again, in its most vicious form, *handing the racists a respectable new weapon* and insulting the intelligence of black men and women everywhere. . . . I am convinced that the author . . . did not consciously intend to write a racist tract . . . but the fact that it may be used as such makes [his] innocence inexcusable.[31]

Unhappily, one need not limit a search for contemporary instances of the "racism" charge to the irresponsible charges of street leaders such as New York's Al Sharpton. In the scholarly journal *American Prospect*, Professor Kenneth Tollett excoriated the author of an article about the conservative Supreme Court with these words:

> [Cass R. Sunstein's] deemphasis on race condones or rationalizes the crypto-racism of this kind of so-called liberalism and progressivism which cares more about protecting the right to kill fetuses, to bird-watch spotted owls, and to practice sodomy than saving black children, employing black males, and reviving the nuclear family, thus stemming the tide of female-headed households, a veritable plague in the black community, especially when it means children having children.[32]

There may have been other episodes of intellectual intimidation, but none were as effective as the suppression of the ideas in the Moynihan report: the subject of race was now to be governed by new rules of intellectual engagement. For the better part of two decades, liberal scholars, politicians, journalists, and other opinion leaders either styled their public discussion of the issues Moynihan had raised to conform to the approved orthodoxy or they simply walked away from research, debate, and the search for solutions altogether. Liberals left the discussion of family and individual responsibility to conservatives, who were quick to seize the opportunity.

The chill lasted a very long time. Ironically, the orthodoxy was most powerful on university campuses, but the new constrictions on the free exchange of ideas were visible in church assemblies, legislatures, and newsrooms. In the vigorous search for solutions, one was no longer able to frame problems honestly, and hence, effective solutions became that much more difficult to identify, debate, and test.

One thing should be made clear about the chill: critics such as William Ryan and James Farmer are not to blame. The failure rests with the liberals who obligingly shut up about ghetto problems, who patronized the ideas of vocal blacks solely because of their color, and who accepted as truth the view that less should be expected of a black child because of the legacy of white racism. Liberal politicians stopped arguing about race, about affirmative action, and quotas. Instead of treating black colleagues with respect for the arguments they advanced, liberals nodded in agreement, afraid their black friends could not withstand criticism or inquiry. The resulting damage has been enormous to all involved.

THE LEFT AND THE RIGHT OWN THE DEBATE

The withdrawal of liberals from the debate about race and poverty in America in the mid-1960s did not end the debate. The discussion moved to the fringes of American politics, to the Left and the Right. The conservatives, who had supposedly been buried in the Johnson landslide of 1964, were very much alive and increasingly in control of the Republican party machinery, particularly in the New South. Intellectuals who were not prepared to accept the new strictures laid down by the response to the Moynihan Report were speaking out as neoconservatives. (Irving Kristol defined a neoconservative as "a liberal who's been mugged.") In the quarterly journal *The Public Interest*, neoconservatives analyzed and criticized the liberal orthodoxy on public policy issues such as housing, education, and, most effectively, crime. Their arguments went largely unopposed by white liberals, who were too timid and clumsy to fight for the idea of integration or for a true black-white partnership within the Democratic party.

3 »

THE SOURCES OF LIBERAL DECLINE:
FAILURES OF MIND

Having been too sanguine and too self-righteous about their part in the civil rights movement, [liberals] are too easily prey to despair when their contribution is rejected by those they presumed to help. Torn between a nagging guilt and a secret desire to turn on their black tormentors, white liberals have become spectators watching with frozen horror as their integrationist ideals and favorite public programs disintegrate amidst violent black rebellion. . . .

Aaron Wildavsky, 1968[1]

THE FADING OF THE GREAT SOCIETY

Lyndon Johnson anticipated that his dream of a great society could become a reality if his administration were able to transform the black ghettos that had been created in inner city areas across the United States. In overseeing the transformation, Johnson wanted to see numbers: how many laws were passed, programs started, dollars delivered, and people enrolled. He assumed that if the numbers got high enough, the problems could be tamed. While he was trying to move the numbers up in the ghetto neighborhoods of northern cities, however, these neighborhoods blew up on him and on his Democratic party.

49

The rise and fall of the Great Society occurred during the brief period of Lyndon Johnson's presidency, between the passage of the civil rights
laws and Richard Nixon's election in 1968. What happened to the search
for solutions in these few years?

President Johnson was surrounded by self-confident men who were
dead certain that there was not a problem they could not resolve, even
problems that they did not know much about or that were not very well
defined. Northern ghettos were such a problem. So was Vietnam. Daniel
Patrick Moynihan tried to spell out the precise nature of the problem
with his report on the black family, and for a few months in the spring of
1965 he enjoyed the support of Johnson's senior advisers. After his ideas
were put forth by the president at Howard University, however, they disappeared from official view.

Despite the lack of a clear definition of the problem, there seemed to
be no lack of "solutions." The proposals that were floated largely origi-
nated from three "schools." The Left offered a theory of empowerment
and confrontation that emphasized organizing poor neighborhoods, welfare clients, parents of schoolchildren, and workers to press for greater
benefits, jobs, public facilities, and a formal part in making decisions.
Empowerment was mixed with redistribution programs modeled on the
health and welfare programs of Western European socialists. The Left in
the United States was permanently marginalized, however, for its rejection
of democratic capitalism—the "mixed" economy—and for its denial of
the idea that individual, family, and community responsibility must play
key roles in grappling with ghetto pathologies.

A second school was led by social work theorists and professionals who advocated "enriching" the ghetto by greatly increasing expenditures for a wide range of social and medical services that would,
presumably, make lower-class people more like middle-class people.
The welfarists assumed that traditional professional social services
would be efficacious for the poor if only sufficient tax dollars were
appropriated and the services themselves were efficiently coordinated.
No one was very precise as to the amounts required, and school bureaucrats, United Way executives, settlement houses, community action programs, mayors, and others competed vigorously for the designation of
"coordinator."

A third view borrowed a bit from the Left and social welfarists but
placed the greatest emphasis on integration. It was this approach that
would receive the most attention.

LIBERALS AND INTEGRATION

Integration was a terribly powerful idea in the United States of the early 1960s—it was the goal of the civil rights movement and of its personification, Martin Luther King, Jr. White liberals viewed integration not only as the moral objective of the civil rights struggle, but also as the answer to the increasingly visible practical problems of the black lower class in northern cities. They had faith that deserving blacks would gradually be absorbed into the majoritarian society one by one; they gave little thought to what would happen to those not included or to neighborhoods dominated by those who could not be absorbed.

At the time, many white Americans generally supported the idea of integration. Since the end of World War II, white opinion had shifted from a general belief in white superiority to at least lip service in support of equal opportunity. There was overwhelming support among white Americans in 1965 for equality in voting rights (91 percent) and access to public accommodations (87 percent) as well as for integrated schools (72 percent).[2] White receptivity to integration declined steeply, however, as the idea moved from the general to the specific; for example, about half of all whites were "upset" by the prospect of black families moving into their neighborhoods,[3] and less than half supported government intervention to achieve school integration.[4]

Liberals viewed integration as the nearly inevitable result of enacting antidiscrimination laws, a view strengthened by their experience during the civil rights movement. They had been gratefully and warmly received in black churches, in which inspiring messages about equal opportunity and nonviolence were preached. What quickly became most noticeable about integration plans for the North, however, was that they tended not to affect white liberal enclaves in any direct way. The plans for northern school integration almost always mixed children from poor and working-class black families with children from working-class white families. (In a few metropolitan areas such as Boston, liberals organized voluntary one-way busing schemes to suburban schools for city students, and some smaller cities and towns voluntarily integrated their schools.) Housing integration meant building low-income housing projects in white working-class neighborhoods, not in the neighborhoods in which white liberals tended to live. Job integration meant opening up good blue-collar jobs to blacks in the construction industry and in police and fire departments—jobs not avidly sought by white liberals or their children.

Kenneth Clark's *Dark Ghetto,* published in 1965, was one of a very few serious analyses of the problems to be overcome in integrating the black lower class. His findings about family instability, welfare, and black male unemployment were very compatible with Moynihan's, but Clark placed more emphasis on the differences between the middle and lower classes. He offered neither hope nor despair, but he was certain about the minimal conditions required to face the challenge:

> If the civil rights struggle is going to be successful, it will require white participation and commitment, even though a number of Negroes believe the white is no longer relevant. The simple fact of arithmetic decrees otherwise. Negroes are one-tenth of the American population. Without white support and without the white power structure the civil rights struggle is doomed to failure.[5]

Clark called liberalism the "Negro's affliction," and chided liberals for a "persistent verbal liberalism that is never capable of overcoming an equally persistent illiberalism of action."[6] Clark's understanding of the need for genuine integration of fact resulted in a rare effort among white liberals to discuss integration and the ghetto with any specificity.

Popular support for integration grew, even as it was discredited by many black leaders. In 1966 the Student Nonviolent Coordinating Committee (SNCC), which was founded in 1960 to organize black college students to conduct nonviolent protests against Jim Crow, ousted its integrationist leaders (including John Lewis, who was later elected to the U.S. House from Atlanta) and replaced them with leaders who favored a diminished role for whites and tolerated an ideology of racial separatism.[7] By 1967 the idea that came to be known as Black Power was highly visible among black Americans—and Black Power derided integration. Stokely Carmichael, the militant head of SNCC, and Charles Hamilton, a political scientist, wrote at the time:

> The goals of integrationists are middle class goals, articulated primarily by a small group of Negroes with middle class aspiration or status. Their kind of integration has meant that a few blacks "make it," leaving the black community, sapping it of leadership potential and know-how . . . those token Negroes—absorbed in a white mass—are of no value to the remaining black masses. They become meaningless show-pieces

for a conscience-soothed white society. . . . "Integration". . .
speaks to the problem of blackness not only in an unrealistic
way but also in a *despicable* way."[8]

What was despicable to the adherents of Black Power was the equation of
quality with "white," whether in describing schools, neighborhoods, or jobs.

Every effort to force integration on working-class neighborhoods in
the North met with fervent opposition. As early as 1964, the term *white
backlash* entered the political vocabulary to explain George Wallace's
spectacularly successful forays in the presidential primaries in Wisconsin,
Indiana, and Maryland against stand-ins for Lyndon Johnson. He
opposed "forced integration," a message that appealed to the primarily
Catholic, blue-collar neighborhoods that were most directly affected by
the continuing expansion of ghetto boundaries.[9] While "national
Democrats" such as Robert Kennedy and Senator Eugene McCarthy
opposed all antibusing legislation, the numbers of northern Democrats
who supported restrictions on federal courts and bureaucrats grew steadily in the late 1960s. Among the newly converted were several white
Democratic House members from ethnic districts.[10] Integration was a
middle-class idea, the product of black and white middle-class activists
who mixed easily when Jim Crow was the enemy. But once these activists
expanded beyond the South, integration faced mounting opposition in
the geographically segregated reaches of the North.

The 1964 election accelerated the transfer of partisan loyalties among
two significant blocs of voters: one was composed of Southern segregationists, who gave Republican Senator Barry Goldwater his only victories
outside Arizona, thus building a new "white party" in the Old
Confederacy; the other was black Americans, who gave Johnson 96 percent of their votes, ending black allegiance to the "Party of Lincoln."
After 1964 black problems became Democratic problems.[11]

And the clock was ticking. In 1964 the Great Society liberals had
received a powerful mandate from voters to solve the nation's racial
woes. They hoped that expressions of goodwill and concrete program
proposals would buy time and peace. No one was clear about what was
to happen in the meantime, the time between promise and delivery,
between Head Start and Job Corps, between rumble and explosion. The
conference that Johnson promised in his Howard University speech—to
bring the best minds together to figure out how to "fulfill these rights"
to equal opportunity and equal results—was held in November 1965.
Instead of focusing the attention of the civil rights coalition on the

complexities of fighting poverty and the need for black "self-help," the conference emphasized increased federal spending. Conference director Berl Bernhard opened the meeting by quipping: "I want you to know that I have been reliably informed that no such person as Daniel Patrick Moynihan exists."[12] Moynihan was, in fact, present and eager to defend his report. The tide, however, was running with his critics. The question of fragile families and a national family policy was stricken from the agenda.

Lyndon Johnson believed in the efficacy of government. An ardent New Dealer and veteran of twenty-two years on Capitol Hill, he measured effective government by laws enacted—"let's nail those coonskins [laws] to the wall, boys," he would urge his staff—and federal programs created. Johnson's partner was the 89th Congress, elected in the 1964 Democratic sweep. Together they altered the balances in the federalist system, giving the federal government a commanding role in areas in which it had previously been a bit player. The 89th Congress enacted the first programs of general federal assistance for elementary and secondary education, mass transit, and land-use planning. Over the opposition of America's doctors, it enacted Medicare for the elderly and Medicaid for the poor. It broadened higher education opportunities beyond veterans and science majors. The Voting Rights Act constituted a radical intrusion in the electoral mechanics of southern states, but it was stunningly effective in extending the vote to black southerners.

President Johnson's penchant for programs meshed with the liberal faith in social services as an important way to transform the black lower class. He was convinced that the comprehensive and coordinated attack on city slums embodied in the Model Cities Act of 1966 would inevitably succeed. Johnson wrote in his memoirs:

> I believe this law will be regarded as one of the major break-throughs of the 1960s. It posed two basic challenges to our ability to handle urban problems. First, it forced cities. . . to plan their own reconstruction with financial assistance from the federal government. . . . Second, this legislation provides a graphic test of the federal government's ability to work in harmony with other levels of government.[13]

Joseph Califano, Johnson's principal domestic policy advisor, confirmed the president's sweeping hopes:

Johnson was ready to . . . rebuild ethnic slum neighborhoods in American cities and in the process provide jobs for the unemployed in the ghetto. Instead of urban renewal programs that moved poor people out of their neighborhoods . . . he envisioned a program that would allow them to stay there, in remodeled or new dwellings, with jobs, police protection, recreation, and community health centers.[14]

THE LIBERALS SKIP CLASS

Kenneth Clark, Daniel Moynihan, and others had warned about the problems brewing in the black lower class. Among the few progressives who had thought about the ghettos, there was strong agreement about the crucial differences between the prevailing middle-class ethos and the growing lower-class subculture. Harrington observed in his influential 1962 book, *The Other America,* "to be a Negro is to participate in a culture of poverty and fear that goes far deeper than any blow for or against discrimination."[15] Similarly Clark noted a critical difference between white and black America:

> White America is basically a middle-class society; the middle class sets the mores and the manners to which the upper class must . . . seek to conform . . . and which the lower class struggles to attain or defensively rejects. But dark America . . . has been assigned to be a lower-class society; the lower class sets the mores and manners . . . from which the Negro middle class struggles to escape.[16]

The relative scarcity of liberal discussions of class differences during this period is surprising because liberals believed—privately—that the unsatisfactory behavior and life consequences of poor black Americans was much more a function of class than of race. The crucial policy question was this: What can government do to replace or supplement the family role among lower-class individuals to produce middle-class Americans?

If this has been the objective of liberal programs, why is it so rarely mentioned publicly, even now? There are three parts to the answer. First, Americans do not like to acknowledge the existence of class, preferring to believe that everyone is middle class, and if they are not, they are taking steps to ascend. "Upper-class" is hardly mentioned. A patrician like George Bush pretended that his favorite food was pork rinds, country and western tunes his favorite music, and horseshoe pitching his preferred sport. Benjamin DeMott wrote that the first assumption of America is its classlessness:

> The mind of the middle isn't absorbed with the subject of class, doesn't engage ceaselessly in placing itself and others, and lives without detailed maps of social difference. . . . The people in question know . . . that although they may sometimes speak of themselves as men and women of the "middle class," only with an effort of will—only by contrivance—can they imagine themselves to *be* members of a class. Normally they feel themselves to be solid individual achievers in an essentially classless society composed of human beings engaged in bettering themselves.[17]

Second, black nationalists and the white Left have routinely condemned the middle class for its mores and goals. The primary reason the civil rights movement succeeded in the early 1960s was that its goals were clearly in line with the American middle-class culture. But as the black leadership split over style and substance, the militants not only abandoned the goal of middle-class aspiration, but condemned middle-class culture as racist.

Black nationalists have viewed the middle-class ethos as a white ethos, oppressive and alien to the values of the black community. Moreover, the Left requires the existence of a permanent lower class to prove its assertion that any capitalist system inevitably produces an exploited class, a situation that must be rectified by social and economic restructuring. Laura Carper, in her attack on the Moynihan Report in *Dissent,* wrote, "What is destructive to the Negro man and woman is social impotence . . . and what rehabilitates them is social power and the struggle for it."[18] The Left's insistent, romantic notions of revolution cannot work in a society that accepts the middle class as both the norm and the objective.

The Left and professional blacks reserved their most potent venom for those who ventured into a discussion of class and race. Edward Banfield published a book in 1968 that made a simple and well-documented case that the problems played out in ghetto neighborhoods were a consequence of concentrated *lower-class* populations.[19] Race was not the critical issue, he said. The black poor, Banfield suggested, were no different from other (white) lower-class Americans: they had no fondness for work, no strong family ties, an easy acceptance of criminal behavior, no brief for schooling, and no future perspective. All these characteristics violate the middle-class ethos that defines America's political culture, and Banfield argued that even well-run government programs could not undo the harm caused by class differences. His was a particularly dangerous formulation for the liberal-Left orthodoxy because, if accepted, it would undermine the rationale for government redistributive programs and blunt the racism-explains-all-ills theory. For this sin, Banfield was effectively banished from one campus after another, his books vandalized, his lectures shouted down, and his sponsors threatened.[20]

The third reason why liberals avoid mentioning class as a factor is that no one knows how to orchestrate the conversion from lower to middle class. Kids who grow up in poor families that inculcate the values of education, work, and other middle-class values can easily be put on the right track through educational opportunity. For the lower-class poor, however, no approach or program has been proved to work; nonetheless liberals have continually accepted the self-serving assertions of social service and educational professionals that they have the solution. Social workers and educators hedge their guarantee with all sorts of qualifiers, but in truth, many of the conditions required for "success" are beyond the realm of social services.

LIBERALS AND THE SOCIAL SERVICES INDUSTRY

In the mid-1960s liberals hoped the push for social services would cool the ghetto until integration rendered its problems manageable. Thus, in 1967 and 1968, liberals spoke about the simultaneous strategics of "enriching" the ghetto, while "dispersing" its residents.

President Kennedy had relied on a social services approach in his welfare reforms of 1962, which authorized psycho-social counseling and other services as a means to assist recipients move off the rolls. The alliance between liberals and social services was not fully cemented until the Great Society, however. The War on Poverty, for example, increased the number of direct services financed by the federal government: Head Start, Job Corps, the Neighborhood Youth Corps, adult literacy training, legal services, neighborhood health clinics, and foster grandparents. It also established community action programs (CAPs) in each city to plan and coordinate "comprehensive" services for poor residents. These residents were "empowered" to help run the CAPs themselves, bringing pressure on city hall for more and better public services.

As the number and variety of programs proliferated, the social service sector ranged from disorder to chaos, and seemingly all of it received funding. Catalogues as thick as the Manhattan telephone directory described the array of federal programs; a cottage industry of consultants evolved to help local and state governments, charitable organizations, and universities gain access to pots of cash that seemed to be available in the corners of federal offices. The Model Cities Act was passed to rationalize the impact of federal and state programs, to reduce confusion and duplication, to concentrate limited resources to maximum effect, and to coordinate the actions of distant bureaucracies. Planning funds were supposed to overcome the protective and insular instincts of federal bureaucrats, their loyal constituencies in cities and states, mayors, newly established CAPs, school districts, public housing authorities, and voluntary agencies. At the same time, Congress was enacting legislation to coordinate other federal funds—for transit and water, for example—on a metropolitan basis. Meanwhile, mental health funds were "coordinated" by "catchments." Somehow, all this was to be coordinated and rationalized by interagency task forces and Bureau of the Budget circulars. It never happened.

Instead the emphasis was on "more." Liberals and their professional allies argued that the programs were well designed, but there was a need for an "urban Marshall Plan" and "expenditures at scale." In 1966 Roy Wilkins, head of the NAACP, and a coalition of progressive organizations pushed for the adoption of a "freedom budget" to spend $185 billion over ten years. After the Newark and Detroit riots, the Kerner Commission would recommend a $30 billion (about $120 billion in 1994 dollars) increase in annual federal spending for city programs—at a time when Johnson could not convince Congress to approve a $14 billion tax increase for fighting the Vietnam War. Black leaders warned that failure to increase funding would lead to more violence.

The Great Society sought to improve the lives of poor blacks by providing social services. As it turned out, it achieved success in a different way: by providing jobs to the aspiring black middle class. Between 1960 and 1976, the black middle class tripled in size, primarily because of increased government and nonprofit agency employment. A study by Michael Brown and Steven Erie in 1981 estimated that the Great Society created two million jobs in public schools, nonprofit agencies, and welfare and health agencies. The number of black Americans in such jobs rose from 400,000 in 1960 to 1.25 million in 1976; the increase in other public jobs was twofold, from 412,000 to 835,000 (there was, for example, a twelvefold increase in the number of black law enforcement officials between 1960 and 1990). On the down side, Brown and Erie also found that the primary impact of the Great Society on *poor* black Americans was an increased reliance on welfare, and a decreased reliance on earnings.[21] Nobody expected that the primary beneficiaries of legislation and appropriations to assist the poor would be professionals, teachers, and social workers, yet that is what happened.

With the growth in social and educational service jobs, professional associations and unions saw enormous gains in membership. Again, black professionals were the prime beneficiaries. Between 1960 and 1980, the number of employed Americans increased from 68 million to 97.6 million—a 43.6 percent rise. In the same period, however, the census reported that the number of social workers and welfare workers went from 96,000 in 1960 to 476,000 by 1980—a 394.1 percent increase—and the number of black social workers jumped from 10,616 in 1960 to 88,021 in 1980—up 729 percent! Public school teachers more than doubled from 1.3 to 2.75 million (110.8 percent). Again, black Americans greatly benefited: there were 116,423 black teachers in 1960, and 290,389 by 1980—an increase of 149 percent. Although the increase in the number of public administrators grew less dramatically than welfare and education categories (from 198,351 in 1960 to 536,549 in 1980), the number of black administrators grew almost tenfold, from 3,075 to 30,109.[22] But expanding public and nonprofit jobs for black strivers did not meet the needs of the poorest black Americans.

THE YLVISAKER GROUP

To 1960s liberals, it seemed that every problem could be solved through specific legislation accompanied by the creation of a new federal bureau or agency. Johnson's chief domestic policy adviser, Joseph Califano, described how many new programs were born:

> The President offered little guidance. He would occasionally say that he wanted "a program for the cities," or an "Asian Development Bank," or "something to help the Negro male and his family." At other times he spoke of a "fair-housing bill," or a "consumer program to help housewives buying groceries and

veterans buying cars and homes." But he expected me to put flesh on the bones "with the finest minds in the country." He wanted the best ideas "without regard to politics. You let these intellectuals get me the ideas. I'll worry about the politics." He would often add, when irritated, that "The trouble with the Democratic party is that all the intellectuals want to be politicians and all the politicians want to be intellectuals."[23]

In 1966, Califano put together a task force on the cities that was chaired by Paul Ylvisaker, the former Ford Foundation executive who had prodded the nation's largest foundation into investing in new approaches to ghetto problems and consulted with Shriver's planning group for the War on Poverty. Ylvisaker had as much experience as anyone in breaking through political, bureaucratic, and racial barriers to fashion concrete opportunities for poor people in cities. His task force included some of the finest minds on city problems: Theodore Sizer from Harvard's School of Education; John Dunlop, the respected labor mediator; Ivan Allen, the "New South" mayor of Atlanta; Anthony Downs, a Chicago housing expert; and Edwin "Bill" Berry, the director of the Chicago Urban League. They were joined by experts on systems analysis and the quantification approach to problem-solving then popular in the Pentagon, as well as experts on urban renewal, urban planning, and labor. I was the group's deputy staff director.

The Ylvisaker group was an important opportunity for experienced, thoughtful, concerned, liberal white men (Berry was the only black member, and no one seemed to notice that there were no women) to identify the pieces to the nation's biggest puzzle, to address the questions Moynihan had posed but left unanswered. The search was quiet; there were no press leaks or inquiries, no attacks from black militants or leftists to worry about. Califano and his deputy, Larry Levenson, showed interest without interference, and the task force delivered its report to the president in July 1967—five days before the Newark riots.

The group was charged with laying the groundwork for the Great Society's next big step, presumably in Johnson's second term. Convened at the height of the Vietnam escalation, the group assumed that the war would be over before long—throwing off a large fiscal dividend in federal revenues—and that the economy would continue its uninterrupted expansion (in its fifty-seventh month and counting in January 1967).

The task force report, never made public, was an urgent and heartfelt appeal for integration as the main answer to the problems of the ghetto, and its principal conclusions (which would be echoed in the celebrated report of the Kerner Commission nine months later) were unambiguous:

> *The overriding problem of our cities is segregation by race and income. No solutions of the nation's urban problems are valid unless they deal directly with the questions posed by segregation.*
>
> A dangerous confrontation is building in most of our metropolitan areas between white and Negro, rich and poor, growing suburb and declining central city. . . .
>
> We see no prospect that these disturbing trends will be arrested by "natural" forces or by current programs at present scale.
>
> The nation is at a turning point. . . . A century ago, President Lincoln risked the Union in order to preserve it against the threat of internal division. Today, a comparable venture in national leadership is called for to heal the rift between the ghetto and growth sectors of American society.[24]

The Ylvisaker task force called on Johnson to strengthen his already historic commitment to black Americans by making the case for integration with white America and by fighting entrenched interests to reorganize federal urban programs. The first recommendation to the president was that "integration . . . be explicitly stated as national policy; that it become the first criterion by which . . . programs are tested, that . . . powerful incentives be devised to accelerate integration; and that employment and educational opportunities for the urban poor be sharply increased."[25]

The task force made some prescient warnings: cities were losing the competition for good jobs; the proliferation of categorical programs was atomizing and confusing antipoverty efforts; suburbs were discriminating against all low-income families regardless of race; mayors were being bypassed by semi-autonomous authorities working in league with federal bureaucrats; and school integration was valueless if middle- and lower-class kids did not attend the same schools.

To counter these forces, the group recommended that federal policy should not try to reverse the large economic forces that were speeding the development of suburban economies; that federal grant programs be pooled and allocated on the basis of clear performance criteria (advancing integration) to governors and mayors; that antidiscrimination orders and laws be vigorously enforced; that integration be made the primary determinant of housing funds and mortgage guarantee programs; and that "bonuses" of $1,500 (or about $6,400 in 1994 dollars) be offered to suburban schools for every black student and poor white student residing in cities that they enroll. The task force advocated placing a high priority on the enrichment of ghetto families through higher, federalized welfare payments, job training stipends, and education and housing bonuses. It also recommended a dispersal strategy that shut off federal funds to discriminatory towns and tied grants to housing, job, and educational integration.

There were many practical and political problems with the group's proposal. The task force called for spending for federal urban programs to triple, to $27 billion. At the time, Johnson was fighting the new 90th Congress, which had been elected with a mandate to put a stop to his furious expansion of federal spending and experimentation. Moreover, distrust of state and local governments was endemic to the Washington culture; every federal dollar was subject to the approval and audit of presumably honest federal bureaucrats.

The task force's emphasis on integration came just when the word and idea were beginning to disappear from the vocabularies of black and white liberals. The group recognized that only vigorous presidential leadership (in combination with a tripling of federal funds for urban programs), would work: "The growing apartheid of our urban populations, segregating by race and income, presents this nation with an ugly fact and an ominous future—and a possible threat to our security which may too soon overshadow that of Vietnam."[26] But it was too late. Vietnam already preoccupied Johnson, and the new Congress was intent on cutting urban programs, not on tripling their appropriations.

In some ways, the Ylvisaker group fell victim to the orthodoxy of permissible inquiry established after the attack on the Moynihan Report. It paid no attention, for example, to achieving integration between people from different classes, even though integration by class was applauded. The questions Moynihan had raised about the ability of black Americans to compete effectively under new circumstances were similarly ignored. But to today's reader, the most obvious bow to post-Moynihan orthodoxy was the group's failure to use the word *crime*. At the time of the report, crime was a growing problem, and liberals would pay dearly for sidestepping it.

LIBERALS STUMBLE ON CRIME

Liberal self-censorship allowed the public debate about race and poverty to remain focused on those areas "approved" by the Left and professional blacks. Liberals adopted positions and language that would prevent personal attacks from the Left, but the eventual price was defeat at the ballot box. Crime and riots were the killer issues.

Beginning in 1963, crime rates had begun to rise very rapidly across the nation. Between 1963 and 1968, for example, the rate for robberies—the most random, threatening crime—doubled across the nation. There was a ready explanation: the number of young men and boys—the usual perpetrators of such crime—was increasing rapidly.

Few persons would accept the idea that random violence can be excused. Yet, in the post-Moynihan era, that is precisely what liberals tried to argue. At first, they suggested that the police were just getting better at collecting statistics and that the victims were reporting crime more often. Some liberals, noting the wide disproportions in the number of blacks convicted of crimes, argued that the criminal justice system was racist and that it preyed on black men. Liberals felt that street criminals should not be criticized—that would be "blaming the victim"— but that crime should be "understood" as an appropriate expression of "rage and frustration." These ideas were nonsense to most Americans who believed that the courts were too lenient, that parents were too irresponsible to discipline their children, and that there were too few cops on the street.[27]

Among prominent liberal Democrats, only Robert Kennedy plainly condemned crime and disorder and those who excused it. Kennedy may have enjoyed special license—his martyred brother was revered, particularly among blacks and Catholic Americans (the core of the white backlash, which he also condemned). In a speech at the University of California at Berkeley, he attacked rioters and their defenders:

> Yet, however much the condition of most Negroes must call forth compassion, the violence of the few demands condemnation and action. . . . Still far more disturbing is that the chaotic self-destructive violence of Watts or Oakland are the statements of a very few Negro spokesmen—those who have called for hatred to fight prejudice, racism to meet racism, violence to destroy oppression.[28]

Kennedy was also a solitary liberal critic of Black Power.[29] Liberals took their lead much more from Ramsey Clark, Johnson's attorney general during the era of civil disorders and rising crime rates. Clark typified the liberal philosophy of crime control. He became notorious enough that Richard Nixon routinely promised during his 1968 campaign to fire him, an unremarkable, but apparently effective pledge. Clark suggested viewing ghetto crime as the direct product of racism:

> The most tragic and dangerous risk of racism in America today is that it may cause us to misconstrue the meaning of crime among poor blacks. That crime flows clearly and directly from the brutalization and dehumanization of racism, poverty and injustice. Black America has shown itself to be far gentler and more humane than white America. There is nothing inherent in black character that causes black crime. On the contrary, the slow destruction of human dignity caused by white racism is responsible. This is the most pitiable result of this huge wrong of the American people.[30]

Clark firmly believed that only society—white society—could be held responsible for the surge in crimes that began in the 1960s.

Liberals were painting themselves into a corner with their own timidity and thoughtlessness. They made excuses for violent crime, blaming government's failure to spend more money on more programs. Liberals blindly urged action against the "root causes" of crime, skipping over the inconvenient question of what was to be done in the meantime. In 1967 the President's Commission on Law Enforcement and Administration of Justice argued the classic liberal line:

> The Commission finds, first, that America must translate its well-founded alarm about crime into social action that will prevent crime. It has no doubt whatever that the most significant action that can be taken against crime is action designed to eliminate slums and ghettos, to improve education, to provide jobs, to make sure that every American is given the opportunities and the freedom that will enable him to assume his responsibilities. We will not have dealt effectively with crime until we have alleviated the conditions that stimulate it . . . widespread crime implies a widespread failure by society as a whole.[31]

The commission announced its findings in the midst of the nation's longest economic expansion, when unemployment was 3.7 percent overall (4.9 percent for black males twenty years of age and older), family incomes were increasing, prices were stable, and the sense of economic improvement and well-being was strong among all Americans.

A corollary to the issue of root causes was the liberal assertion that crime is a universal, that there is larceny in every heart. The difference between solid citizens and young criminals, liberals argued, was not the violent nature, but rather the flamboyance of the latter's crimes and the greater willingness of biased cops to arrest them. William Ryan, in his book, *Blaming the Victim,* put it this way:

> Crime is . . . endemic. We are surrounded and immersed in crime . . . most of our friends and neighbors are law violators. Large numbers of them are repeated offenders. A very large group have committed serious major felonies, such as theft, assault, tax evasion, and fraud. Few of them are ever arrested, still fewer tried, and only a tiny number are ever imprisoned. This "hidden crime". . . is not petty or negligible. . . .[32]

Ryan went on to make the case that so-called law enforcement has little to do with arresting criminals—because all of us as a matter of routine break laws—and everything to do with arresting black people and poor people to maintain not just the public order, but the social order.[33]

The argument that black rage was an explanation for black crime also found support among liberals. In 1968 two black psychiatrists wrote a book entitled *Black Rage* that received wide attention. The authors, William Grier and Price Cobbs, explained that crime and riots were akin to a contemporary slave rebellion:

> At bottom, America remains a slave country which happens to have removed the slave laws from the books. The question we must ask is: What held the slave rebellion in check for so long? The racist tradition is pervasive and envelops every American. For black men it constitutes a heavy psychological burden. From the unemployed, illiterate ghetto dweller to the urbanized man living in an integrated setting, careful examination shows psychological scars. Black men fight one another, do violence to property, do hurtful things to themselves while nursing growing

hatred for the system which oppresses and humiliates them. Their manhood is tested daily.[34]

Rage—and its twin, frustration—would become more than an explanation for black violence; for liberals, it would become an excuse. In time, the argument regarding black rage would spawn conspiracy theories holding that white society had initiated a genocidal campaign—featuring police assassination and government-sponsored drug and AIDS epidemics—to combat the threat of black violence.

The liberal search for solutions to the root causes of crime was half-hearted and confused, and it ignored the problem of lower-class behavior in city ghettos. Moreover, the rapidly rising number of crime victims were disinclined to view the promised payoff from Head Start and other social programs as solace for their trauma.

In early 1968 the Gallup Poll reported that "crime and lawlessness are viewed by the public as the top domestic problem facing the nation for the first time since the beginning of scientific polling in the mid-thirties."[35] But those, such as Johnson's former speechwriter Ben Wattenberg, who warned Democrats that appearing to favor muggers over their victims was a fatal political strategy were dismissed as neoconservatives or racists.

CIVIL DISORDERS AND THE KERNER COMMISSION

Between March and September 1967, civil disorders broke out in 163 towns and cities in every part of the nation. Eighty-three persons died, almost nineteen hundred were injured, and thousands of businesses and homes looted and burned. The worst rioting took place in Newark and Detroit; the Detroit riot was put down only after Army paratroopers were sent in and forty-three people killed.

Republicans condemned the violence, anarchy, and the rioters and called for swift and stern law enforcement measures. Televised footage of widespread looting led the scholar Edward C. Banfield to call it "rioting mainly for fun and profit."[36] But the Democrats seemed ambiguous, a sense captured by Vice President Hubert Humphrey's earlier observation:

I'd hate to be stuck [in] . . . a tenement with rats nibbling on the kids' toes . . . with garbage uncollected . . . with the streets filthy, with no swimming pools or no recreation. . . . I think you'd have more trouble than you have had already, because

I've got enough spark left . . . to lead a pretty good revolt under those conditions.[37]

On July 27, with Detroit still smoldering, Lyndon Johnson addressed the nation, promising to appoint a commission to find out what happened. Known since then as the Kerner Commission after its chairman Otto Kerner, then Illinois governor, the National Advisory Commission on Civil Disorders would take its place as the archetypal expression of 1960s liberalism.

The commission issued its report on March 1, 1968, in the midst of one of the most turbulent periods in American history. North Vietnam had just launched the Tet offensive throughout South Vietnam; a small unit had even fought its way onto the American embassy grounds. Brutal fighting continued throughout February. On March 12, Senator Eugene McCarthy almost beat Lyndon Johnson in New Hampshire's presidential primary (McCarthy had been given no chance by politicians or journalists). Four days later, Robert F. Kennedy announced his candidacy for the nomination. Johnson then stunned the nation with his March 31 announcement that he would not seek reelection. And just four days later, Martin Luther King, Jr. was assassinated in Memphis, setting off a week of riots in more than one hundred cities that required the call-up of over 50,000 federal and National Guard troops and resulted in thirty-nine deaths.

In such turbulent times, the Kerner Commission report might have suffered the usual dusty-shelf fate of government reports—except for the inclusion of a hastily added two-page introduction, in which these sentences appeared:

This is our basic conclusion: Our nation is moving toward two societies, one black, one white—separate and unequal.

What white Americans have never fully understood—but what the Negro can never forget—is that white society is deeply implicated in the ghetto. White institutions created it, white institutions maintain it, and white society condones it.[38]

Two other equally memorable sentences followed:

Race prejudice has shaped our history decisively in the past; it now threatens to do so again. White racism is essentially responsible for the explosive mixture which has been accumulating in our cities since the end of World War II.[39]

The Kerner Commission report remained, twenty-five years after its publication, a symbol of liberal excess: indiscriminate invocations of white guilt, blanket amnesty for the criminal acts of rioters, and an unchallenged faith in the efficacy of federal programs.

The report was really two reports. The first was the introduction that raised the warning about racial and class segregation and white complicity. This was the "Kerner Commission report" most frequently cited. The second report was an analysis of central city problems that assumed the government was fully capable of solving those problems if it had the will to tax, spend, and organize still more programs. The report represented the culmination of the Great Society approach: an undifferentiated batch of categorical programs offered with the unstated hope that they would turn lower-class individuals into middle-class citizens. As was customary in the post-Moynihan period, the Kerner Commission rested its recommendations on four assumptions:

▲   The gap in black achievement could best be explained as the consequence of past and continuing racial discrimination and the lack of adequate government funds and programs to reduce this gap.

▲   The rapid growth in the black middle-class offered no lessons or hope.

▲   The responsibility for responding to black-white differentials rested entirely on the government and majority society.

▲   The failure to act with speed and urgency at the scale recommended was likely to lead to more riots, which was not only predictable, but understandable.

The Kerner Commission, like the Ylvisaker group, predicted an accelerating concentration of black residents in central cities and a continuing out-migration of white residents. Discriminatory real estate practices would continue to bottle up middle-class black families in center cities. The commission identified three broad policy choices: the continuation of present policies, inviting more trouble; the enrichment of the ghetto through higher welfare payments, a million public sector jobs, educational vouchers, and expanded housing subsidies; and integration through federal subsidies for schools serving broad geographic areas, tough new open housing laws, and a massive increase in low-income housing outside ghettos.[40]

The commission acted quickly. At the request of the president, it investigated and succinctly dismissed the theory that the riots were planned.[41] Like the planners of the War on Poverty, the commission had no solid evaluations of public programs, and it ignored the difficulties associated with raising the lower class. The commission fell back on an approach that pleased activists, professional blacks, the Left, and the liberal academics: the nation should do everything it thought possible, at whatever cost, or expect more violence. The commission made hundreds of policy recommendations, covering everything from police training to property insurance to a new national income guarantee. It made no effort to rank its suggestions according to urgency or cost-effectiveness. Nor did the commission acknowledge the confusion, rigidity, and thoughtlessness endemic in the management of those public programs most relevant to the poor. As Wildavsky observed, the report was a continuation of a liberal policy that "angered whites and did not help blacks."[42]

Government commissions are not appointed to find the whole truth. Few elected officials feel a need to increase the amount of public criticism to which they are subjected; nor do they need to be reminded that "resources are limited" or that "problems are complex." Commissions serve important, albeit limited, purposes—they buy time and they help build consensus. A commission is assembled to represent divergent interests and to make recommendations that are compatible with the policies and politics of its appointor. The Kerner Commission was typical: its chairman was a loyal Democratic son of the Illinois Daley organization (and, later, the first convicted federal judge in history); its vice-chair, John V. Lindsay, was the Republican mayor of New York. The commission included two U.S. senators and two U.S. representatives—a Democrat and a Republican from each chamber; one corporate CEO; the president of the steelworker's union; one woman (a former Kentucky commerce secretary); Roy Wilkins, the director of the NAACP; and the Atlanta police chief.

John Lindsay was a white, Protestant Republican in his first term as mayor of a Democratic, ethnic, Catholic, and Jewish city. Lindsay gave concrete expression to the liberal model: he believed that black New Yorkers would do much better if white New Yorkers—particularly those living in Brooklyn and Queens—would just give them a chance. He believed that civic peace was possible only if the city's leadership tilted to the needs of black and Latino neighborhoods. He opened "little city halls" to provide information and to coordinate city services. He increased garbage pick-ups in black neighborhoods (up to nine times a week in some neighborhoods in summer). At a time when street crime was rising dramatically, Lindsay pushed to establish a civilian review board to hear complaints of police brutality (he lost badly). He proposed low-income housing projects for middle-class neighborhoods and redistricted school attendance boundaries to integrate a dwindling number of white students with growing numbers of minority students. He supported an experiment in community control of schools in Ocean Hill–Brownsville that produced anti-Semitic intimations and a citywide teacher's strike. He supported liberalization in the administration of welfare—and then expressed betrayal when the welfare rolls skyrocketed to almost one million.

Lindsay hijacked the commission, with the help of David Ginsberg, its staff director. Peter Goldmark and Jay Kriegel, members of Lindsay's staff, working with Ginsberg's deputy, Victor Palmieri, drafted the famous introduction at the time the commission was wrapping up its business. Lindsay and Ginsberg insisted that the introduction be included, even though it had not been seen (only heard) by the other members.[43]

Lyndon Johnson refused to accept the Kerner report, refusing even to exchange the usual letters of acknowledgement and thanks.[44] The commission staff, however, had arranged for immediate commercial publication of the report: in the first eleven days, it sold 750,000 copies, exceeding the sales of the Warren Commission report on the assassination of President John F. Kennedy.[45] The editorial response was dramatic. The *New York Times* praised the report and counseled that "the younger more restless Negroes are increasingly prone to violence because they feel trapped. Their sense of entrapment is not imagined."[46] The *New Republic* supported the commission's most notorious conclusion: "The Commission is saying in effect: Don't blame conspirators, outside agitators . . . Stokely Carmichaels . . . drugs, neglect in childhood, hangover of slavery, sloth, dirt, rats. Blame Whitey. It's a harsh judgment, and true."[47]

White racism, as an explanation for black behavior, gave government no purchase with which to move against the problems in black ghettos. When everyone is responsible, no one is responsible. This is not to say that white racism is not a problem or even that it is not the most important explanation for black-white divisions. As a policy recommendation, it leads to nothing, except a paralyzing guilt that freezes debate and halts the search for helpful answers. Most critically, it produces an imbalance in which black apologists dismiss all suggestions of individual responsibility for rioting, drug abuse, and the abandonment of children.

THE LIBERAL LEGACY

Liberals, rather than stand up to their sometime allies, sometime tormenters on the Left, went soft instead. They meekly withdrew from direct conversation with black militants who insisted that white Americans had no role in maintaining the progressive coalition that helped enact the civil rights laws of 1964 and 1965. Liberals seemed willing to accept the blame and guilt for the entire nation. They excused black violence, allowing cities to be held hostage.

Maybe there was no consensus to be found in the United States of 1968 because the divisions were so wide and violent. But liberals stopped trying. They shrank from the hard political work of advancing ideas and arguments, negotiating, shaving differences of opinion, and fashioning alternatives. Instead, liberals fell back on the Senate filibuster to block the adoption of antibusing directives; their allies in civil rights organizations turned increasingly to sympathetic federal judges and bureaucrats to advance more radical notions of equal opportunity. All the while, the national consensus was building toward a conservative policy majority on social and racial issues. So total was the intellectual surrender of white liberals that the Democratic party began to lose credibility on basic issues that had previously never divided American politics. By the 1968 presidential campaign, Republicans could make a credible charge that the Democratic party opposed efforts to maintain law and order in America's cities.

4 »

The Liberal Abandonment of Politics

As Lyndon Johnson's presidency drew to a close, the Democrats' moral leverage on the nation was slipping. The violent clashes at the Democratic National Convention in Chicago in 1968 symbolized growing divisions over Vietnam, the emerging cultural wars between traditional and new values, and the liberals' efforts to reform the Democratic party. After Richard Nixon defeated Hubert Humphrey in the November elections, liberals focused on taking over the Democratic party. Their short-lived triumph culminated in the nomination of George McGovern as their presidential candidate in 1972 and accelerated the Democrats' loss of credibility with American voters.

The Roots of Reform at the State Level

In spring 1968, I became the deputy manager of Senator Robert Kennedy's "noncampaign" in New Jersey's presidential primary. (This grand title meant that I did grunt work for Kennedy's only New Jersey visit, a boisterous rally in Camden.) Kennedy had bypassed the New Jersey primary and had instead put all his efforts into California—a winner-take-all event involving 174 convention delegates held the same day as the New Jersey primary, which selected 82 delegates.

Kennedy decided that New Jersey was not essential, and the feeling was mutual. New Jersey's Democratic party was run by "regulars" who cared much more about winning county elections than opposing a Democratic president on anything as remote as Vietnam. Control of county government meant jobs, contributions, contracts, and the right to decide who ran on the organization line for state and federal office. (At his farewell dinner in 1968, Essex County's longtime chairman delivered a plain message: "And don't worry about me in retirement. Y'll not be havin' to throw any bingo games for Denny Carey."[1]) In return for the support of party loyalists, the county chair would award members jobs, services, or small favors. The selection of national convention delegates was yet another opportunity for the leader to conduct business, rewarding the faithful for year-in, year-out service with the chance to take a nice trip, attend a few parties, and do a little political business of their own; there was no place for newcomers or ideologues.

Kennedy stayed out of New Jersey, knowing that a good showing in other primaries was his only hope of unlocking the organizational support that had nominated his brother in 1960. As LBJ's presumptive heir, Vice President Hubert Humphrey focused his campaign on appealing to southern and organization Democrats who remained loyal to Johnson; he had announced his candidacy too late to participate in primaries. (Johnson did not announce his retirement until March 31, by which time the filing deadline for primaries in most states had passed.) As a result, New Jersey's primary produced sixty-three uncommitted delegates (sixty-two of whom would eventually vote for Humphrey in Chicago) and nineteen for Eugene McCarthy.

The McCarthy delegates were elected from suburban, Republican areas where the Democratic party structure was weak. The exclusion of antiwar Democrats from consideration as delegates in strong Democratic counties led to the unprovable assertion by McCarthy loyalists that, in a fair and open fight, they would have won more than their eighteen committed delegates. When they returned from the tumult of the Chicago convention, they were ready to do battle with the regular organization Democrats, even if it meant allying with the followers of the martyred RFK to form the New Democratic Coalition (NDC).

The New Jersey NDC attracted white liberals, most of whom were well-educated, well-compensated professionals motivated by opposition to the war in Vietnam. A 1970 survey of seven hundred NDC members and more than eight hundred county committee members ("regulars") found an astonishing 87 percent of NDC respondents employed as professionals or managers.[2] Jews were overrepresented and Catholics underrepresented among reformers, while 40 percent of the reformers claimed no religion at all. By contrast, 58 percent of the regulars were Roman Catholic and only 7 percent listed no religion.[3] The NDC also included representatives of progressive unions such as the United Auto Workers, some renegade black politicians, and even some organization Democrats—nimble antiwar incumbents who represented suburbs. The New Jersey NDC was typical of the upper-middle class reformers who would create a new national Democratic party at the 1972 convention.

What was the tone of an NDC gathering? Two characteristics stand out: zealotry and a numbing emphasis on procedural purity. The extreme McCarthy supporters distrusted Robert Kennedy, whom they saw as the gutless exploiter of McCarthy's New Hampshire success. To prevent Kennedy loyalists and suspect McCarthyites from "stealing" the NDC, the McCarthy extremists insisted on elaborate safeguards regarding notice and conduct of meetings, strict adherence to rules of order, and cumbersome reviews of any public statements. Many of those attracted to the NDC were "professional meeting attenders" who had honed their parliamentary skills at League of Women Voters conferences, Episcopal synods, bar associations, or social worker councils. No point was too small to evade challenge, review, resubmission, reconsideration, amendment, or amendment to the amendment. Meetings were a nightmare of resolution-drafting, caucus sessions, and procedural pedantry.

For the McCarthy zealots, there was no room for accommodation with anyone morally tainted by support of the Johnson-Humphrey wing, which limited the potential appeal of the NDC to traditional Democrats. The sons of white working-class families were fighting the war (much more so than the sons of NDC members), but the NDC made little effort to include working-class people. The sons of black families also were overrepresented in Vietnam, and Martin Luther King had stood strongly against the war, but the NDC was a very pale group. Much of the language and ideology of the New Jersey reformers stressed the plight of the poor and minorities, and advocated more taxes and spending to help them. But the plea was bloodless, abstract, and, for most NDC members, devoid of any personal connection to the problems being decried.

The NDC did not last long—it announced its establishment in November 1968 and dissolved in June 1969—but its effects in New Jersey were substantial and largely positive. The NDC's leadership, enduring parliamentary torture and personal abuse, labored to moderate the extremes and to freshen the Democratic party. Recognizing the energy of the NDC and the need for rejuvenation in the party, the leader of New Jersey's regular Democrats, Governor Richard J. Hughes, gave the NDC his stamp of approval. A man of uncommon graciousness, shrewdness, and resilience, Hughes had been praised by all combatants for the dignity and fairness with which he chaired the credentials committee at the Democratic National Convention in Chicago. That experience convinced him that the Democrats had to accommodate the newly energized reformers. On the NDC's establishment, Hughes opined: "Change is being forced upon us. We have no choice. Rejecting [the Coalition] ideas would mean the early destruction of the party."[4]

In January 1969 the New Jersey NDC held its first and only convention. More than 2,000 Democrats registered for a day of workshops on party reform, riots, racism, and tax policy; to elect officers (a slate of "moderates" was elected overwhelmingly against a ticket of McCarthy purists); and to hear Senator George McGovern and the antiwar organizer Allard K. Lowenstein. It was the largest such gathering of New Jersey Democrats, making the NDC an immediate force in the upcoming gubernatorial primary. For a time, it appeared that the NDC might entice seasoned, antiwar Representative Frank Thompson to run against the conservative former governor, Robert B. Meyner. "Thompy" eventually declined, leaving the NDC to endorse an ideologically satisfactory, but electorally unexciting, candidate, Representative Henry Helstoski. Meyner won the primary. Amidst warnings from Hughes and others that he needed to show deference to the coalition, Meaner named an NDC activist as vice-chair of the Democratic state committee (a meaningless position) and chose NDC chairman Dan Caby to be the head of the newly established Democratic Policy Council.

When Meyner sought the NDC endorsement for the general election, he was rejected by its executive committee as too conservative and insufficiently energetic in his opposition to the war. In response, Caby resigned from the NDC. His vice-chair declared the New Jersey New Democratic Coalition dissolved and strode out.

Despite its short lifespan, the NDC succeeded in propelling its reformist goals to the top of the Democratic party agenda in New Jersey. After Meyner lost the election, the Democratic Policy Council went to work as a shadow government, attracting a broad cross-section of Democrats to work on major issues. When reform Democrat Brendan Byrne was elected governor four years later in the wake of the Watergate scandal, much of his program for fiscal, governmental, and campaign finance reform reflected the council's recommendations, and many of his important appointments had been NDC activists.[5]

The NDC experience in New Jersey contains an object lesson for reformers. The New Jersey NDC was a vehicle for attracting and channeling the energies of hundreds of motivated Democrats who wanted to end the Vietnam War and open up the party. For all the sanctimoniousness of its rhetoric and its sometimes paralyzing procedural rigor, the NDC leadership understood the character of its mission—to change the Democratic party and win general elections. From its first day in public, the NDC appealed to organization Democrats, seeking to broaden the party's base and strengthen its coalition.

Moral outrage against the Vietnam War was a powerful force in 1968, and its aftereffects brought a new generation of activists into the Democratic party. If many later drifted away, enough stayed to give the party a reservoir of talented, progressive politicians, who became the dominant force in Congress and in many northern statehouses. But, when it came to demonstrating good sense and inspiring leadership in national campaigns, the legacy of liberal reform is decidedly different.

1968: THE LAST GATHERING OF THE REGULAR DEMOCRATS

The purpose of a national party is to organize the process of nominating and electing presidential candidates. Until 1972 Democratic national conventions were gatherings of politicians whose main purpose was to make judgments about who could win the White House. State delegations were led by governors, mayors, legislators, and labor leaders. The Democratic party was, by reason of its breadth and depth of support, either a coalition party or a losing party. Leaders negotiated with candidates to guard their prerogatives, to ensure that they would be consulted about federal appointments in their jurisdictions. Platforms were drafted to ensure that all major interests and regions in the party could stand comfortably on them. It is easy to romanticize the pre-1972 conventions, to understate the villainy and corruption of some of the leaders, and to overlook the exclusion of black Americans (conventions were virtually all white until 1936). But what cannot be too strongly emphasized is that the convention was a place for politicians to practice coalition politics.

All this was very frustrating to the Republicans. Much more cohesive ideologically, racially, and economically, Republicans marveled at how a mixture of white southerners, city Catholics, Jews, and blacks could come to together with western ranchers and midwestern farmers and agree on a platform and candidate—a process that had regularly defeated the Republicans since 1932. Democrats knew how to select attractive candidates and build electoral coalitions.

There was no *national* Democratic party. The national committee arranged the quadrennial convention and did little else. It was the state parties that decided who would go to conventions. For a century, southern states sent white Democrats whose primary objective was to trade electoral votes for guarantees that the federal government would not disturb segregation. Not until 1964 did a national convention even question the right of a state party to exclude blacks. At Atlantic City that year, Democrats agreed to seat two at-large delegates from the integrationist Mississippi Freedom Democratic party, and to set up a Special Equal Opportunity Committee to consider changes at the 1968 convention.

Even without the ferment brought on by the Vietnam war, the 1968 convention in Chicago would have pursued the integration of the southern delegations. Since the Voting Rights Act, black southerners were registering in huge numbers—as Democrats. The tradition of an inert national party had ended in January 1968, with the adoption of standards against racial discrimination and secret party proceedings. The pace of change in the hands of the regular Democrats was slow, however: black delegates increased from 2 percent in 1964 to just 5 percent in 1968.

At Chicago, the Democrats nominated Vice President Hubert Humphrey, the badly bruised legatee of Lyndon Johnson, who kept Humphrey on a short leash; Johnson vetoed any platform language remotely critical of his Vietnam policies. With no flexibility to compromise with the antiwar Democrats on Vietnam, Humphrey released his delegates to support party reform resolutions, if they chose to.

Two-thirds of the delegates arrived at Chicago formally unpledged to any candidate. The southern delegations were overwhelmingly supportive of LBJ and opposed to radical party reform (meaning rapid integration). Humphrey received 440 of 527 votes from the states of the Confederacy (the only significant defections came from the two delegations—Mississippi and Georgia—that were successfully challenged by integrated slates). Humphrey also captured the large industrial states, with their tradition of organizational politics representing organized labor and working-class Democrats. Liberal on economic and social insurance issues, but conservative on social, racial, and cultural issues, party regulars were put off by McCarthy and his "kids." Humphrey took 112 of 118 delegates in Illinois, 104 of 130 in Pennsylvania, 94 of 115 in Ohio, 72 of 96 in Michigan, 62 of 82 in New Jersey, and 45 of 49 in Maryland.

McCarthy did best in Massachusetts, Wisconsin, Oregon, California, and New York, picking up a total of 601 delegates. George McGovern, a late entry to attract the assassinated Bobby Kennedy's delegates, received 146 votes, most of them from California and South Dakota.

Humphrey was terribly damaged by the convention: he looked like an LBJ puppet while the streets of Chicago were turned into scenes of blood and disorder as Vietnam protesters clashed with the Chicago police. And all of it was on national television. The party left Chicago badly divided on the issue of Vietnam, with many liberals threatening to sit out the general election. Even so, Humphrey only narrowly lost what turned out to be one of the closest elections in American history, an election confused by Governor George Wallace's strong showing (he got 13.5 percent of the vote and electoral votes from Alabama, Arkansas, Georgia, Louisiana, and Mississippi).

THE REACTION TO THE "SIEGE OF CHICAGO"

The ugliness of the Chicago convention produced calls for reform from two different kinds of Democrats. First and loudest were supporters of Senator Eugene McCarthy, who wanted to overthrow regular Democrats and end the Vietnam War. They protested that the true strength of the antiwar movement was not represented at Chicago because of tricks and traditions of regular party organizations. They pointed out that six hundred delegates had been selected before McCarthy even announced his candidacy and that delegates in most states were picked in private with no participation by grass-roots Democrats.

In fact, the picture was a good deal murkier than the one McCarthy enthusiasts painted. Their man had won only six primary elections, and five of them were against no declared candidates (Johnson beat McCarthy by 230 votes in New Hampshire as an undeclared *write-in* candidate). Oregon was the only truly contested primary that he won. Moreover, grass-roots Democrats showed limited support for McCarthy: a mid-May Gallop Poll showed Humphrey leading with 40 percent, followed by 31 percent for Kennedy, and only 19 for McCarthy.[6] McCarthy had no visible support among organized labor, regular Democrats, white southerners, or minorities. Nonetheless, McCarthy's adherents were adamant that the nomination had been won by political shenanigans.

The other Democrats pressing reform were regulars who foresaw the consequences to the party if the frustrations of newly energized antiwar and minority Democrats were not addressed directly. New Jersey's Governor Hughes was the most consistent voice of reform among party regulars. He chaired the Democratic party's Special Equal Rights Committee, which put forth a plan containing six basic elements of standards and procedures for ridding the party of racially discriminatory practices. Their adoption in early 1968 constituted the first step in the reduction of state party autonomy and led directly to the unseating of the regular Mississippi delegation and half of the all-white Georgia delegation at the Chicago convention. The Special Committee also recommended that the 1968 convention establish a commission on party structure to shape new procedures for the 1972 convention.[7]

Hughes accepted the chairmanship of the Credentials Committee for the 1968 convention, where he had to deal with challenges to fifteen state delegations, including Texas, Michigan, and Pennsylvania. Theodore White said of Hughes's performance:

> The Credentials Committee hearings might have degenerated into a succession of brawls. Fortunately, the Party's National Committee had chosen as its chairman Governor Richard Hughes of New Jersey, and they could have made no better choice. Hughes, a man of the old politics, a stern commitment man on the war, was a judge by profession and instinct, a man of absolute fairness whose honor insisted on review of facts. . . .[8]

The Credentials Committee's work would be overlooked during the tumult of the Chicago convention, but it would serve as the point of entry for the reformists. The committee's proposal to establish a commission on party structure and reform was approved as an afterthought by the full convention. Meanwhile, the Rules Committee's parallel recommendation for a commission to implement rules forbidding winner-take-all primaries—the "unit rule"—and favoring "timely" primary elections of delegates pledged to specific candidates was the subject of vigorous debate before adoption by a narrow vote. Humphrey delegates provided the margin of victory.

After Chicago, the reformers had an opportunity to open the party without pushing out the regulars and to integrate the southern delegations without reverting to quotas. Many regulars were progressive and open to debate. Hubert Humphrey, in defeat, became a distant advocate of reform and set a precedent that other party nominees would follow. Like Mondale and Dukakis, Humphrey had traded the nomination for new rules to appease the left wing of the party that would bind future candidates and conventions. If Humphrey had been elected to the White House, the new rules would not have been a consideration because incumbent presidents usually enjoy easy renomination. Humphrey pushed the process along with his selection of an Oklahoma populist, Senator Fred Harris, as party chairman in January 1969. Harris wanted proponents of reform for the Commission on Party Structure and Delegate Selection and found a working majority.[9] George McGovern was appointed chair and served until he resigned in 1971 to seek the presidential nomination, at which time Representative Donald Fraser of Minnesota replaced him.

REVOLUTION BY RESOLUTION AND COMMITTEE REPORT

The liberals were playing in a forum where their comparative advantage was greatest, where issues of procedure could mask the power struggle, and where the argument only had to carry a small group, with little attention from the media to alert somnolent regulars. Hubert Humphrey was concentrating on a 1970 Senate election, not on Senator McGovern's commission. The regulars on the commission were inattentive (I. W. Abel of the steelworkers union, for example, did not attend a single meeting); furthermore, they were unrepresented on the staff, all of whom were handpicked by Senator McGovern. The questions of who would vote at national conventions and, more important, how presidential candidates would be nominated, were answered in a series of close votes among the twenty-four commission members.

Revolution is a word cheapened by overuse, but revolution describes what the McGovern-Fraser commission achieved. The reforms would result in a *national* party structure, animated by presidential elections, and quite distinguishable from the state and local party organizations that otherwise represented Democrats. Between 1968 and 1972, the Democrats who ran states and cities and represented the party in Congress were purged. Their places were taken by delegates who represented presidential candidates, not party organizations. The host of the 1968 convention, the most powerful Democratic leader in the nation, Mayor Richard Daley, was not seated at the 1972 convention even though he had been elected a delegate in the Illinois primary. Only 30 of 255 Democratic members of Congress were delegates. (By the 1976 convention, fewer than half the Democratic governors and only 14 percent of Democratic U.S. senators and 15 percent of Democratic representatives were officially seated.)[10] Thus were Democratic officeholders excluded from the process of selecting their presidential nominee.

Instead of letting governors or party leaders choose delegates, the new Democrats adopted quotas. The McGovern-Fraser guidelines required proportional representation for blacks, Latinos, women, and younger voters. Theodore H. White portrayed the action as a betrayal of liberalism:

> From the founding of the country on, the central instinct and pride of the American liberal has been to keep opportunity for individuals open. For two centuries the wars of American liberals—against King George, against the banks, against the slave holders . . . against the bosses—have reflected a doctrine which is more than politics, a doctrine which is of the essence of the culture of the nation: No man must be locked into or hammered into a category from which he has no opportunity to escape. He must not be locked in by the color of his skin . . . ; he must not be locked in by lack of educational opportunity; he must not be locked in by birth, or parentage, or age, or poverty.
> The quota idea was a wrench from this tradition.[11]

The vote of the McGovern-Fraser commission was ten to nine. By a single vote did the party of equal opportunity "wrench" from its tradition. Between the 1968 and 1972 conventions, women delegates increased from 13 to 38 percent; black delegates from 5 to 15 percent.

In January 1970 the Democratic National Committee approved the McGovern-Fraser Commission's report with little discussion. Nearly every state Democratic party would have to revise its procedures, state laws, and party regulations to comply. Confusion reigned. The simplest way for states to avoid legal challenges was to opt for primaries that elected pledged delegates selected by the presidential candidates.

Primaries, previously nothing more than a sideshow to the nominating process—as with John Kennedy's victory over Hubert Humphrey in West Virginia in 1960 or George Wallace's guerrilla raids on LBJ in 1964—dominated the process by 1972. The number of states holding primaries increased from seventeen to only twenty-three; the percentage of delegates selected in primaries increased from nearly half to two-thirds. But the biggest difference was in the proportion of delegates formally bound to a candidate: in 1968 only 36 percent were committed; by 1972,

58 percent were.[12] The unit rule was out, except that California was allowed to retain its winner-take-all primary. Elected officials and party leaders were no longer granted *ex officio* delegate seats. Suddenly, state party organizations faced bewildering new requirements, and the decision on whether to comply was taken out of their hands. The new Democratic party became a regulatory commission, a nose-counting, rule-invoking, lawyer-driven council run by faceless functionaries who issued edicts to governors, mayors, and state chairs. The blood was running out of Democratic politics.

The nominating rules had been changed by politicians who could not win otherwise. "Fairness" was their public rationale, but control of the nominating process was their real objective. Before 1972 the process favored leaders with broad appeal to the Democratic base, who could bring regional or ethnic strength and who could get along with the major constituent groups in the party. The nomination required careful coalition- building. Coalitions mean compromise, and compromise usually pushes one toward the center of the political spectrum, where American elections are won. Finding common ground is the defining political skill—not only for winning the nomination, but for winning general elections and for governing.

The new incentives favored candidates who could generate enthusiasm among policy activists and organized interests such as teachers, candidates who could appeal to the media, raise funds, mount highly visible campaigns in crucial early state contests—and understand the rules well enough not to get tripped up in the extensive regulation of the process. The public nature of the new process gave additional power to the media, which sought significance in otherwise insignificant facts. In 1972 McGovern spent twenty-four days campaigning for primary votes in tiny, Republican New Hampshire and was rewarded with a mere 35,000 votes. He lost by a landslide margin of almost 10 percent to Maine Senator Edmund Muskie. In the new politics, however, McGovern was the winner. Early surveys had given Muskie 65 percent of the votes, and the media had built up expectations for the New England senator. When Muskie fell short, the media said he was faltering. By 1976 the process was so misguided that Jimmy Carter established his candidacy by drawing 27 percent of the votes from the 10 percent of Iowa Democrats participating in neighborhood caucuses. The obsession of the media transformed the 150,000 or so Democrats who attended the Iowa caucuses and voted in the New Hampshire primary into the new kingmakers.

The end result is that Democratic primaries have become "policy auctions" in which candidates bid up the intensity of their commitment in exchange for the support of Democratic interest groups. The differences between constituent groups are highlighted, not their commonalities. Thus, Jewish groups hear promises for relocating the American embassy to Jerusalem, black groups hear declarations for set asides and affirmative action, teachers unions are assured about opposition to school "choice" plans, and feminists are promised unqualified defense of abortion rights. In return, candidates hope to receive the enthusiastic support from interest groups without much regard for the effect these promises will have in the general election.

THE NATIONAL DEMOCRATS: IDEOLOGUES, PARLIAMENTARIANS, AND NOSE COUNTERS

The clash between traditional and new Democrats reflected the divisions of America's cultural war of the late 1960s and early 1970s. This was in many ways a class war that set those who opposed the Vietnam War against those who fought in it; well-educated feminists derided stay-at-home mothers and emphasized the career opportunities of professional women over secretaries, factory workers, and store clerks. It was a battle between the casually religious or agnostic and the devout. Liberals looked at graffiti on city walls and saw folk art; traditionalists saw defacement. Liberals heard the four-letter words shouted at student sit-ins as the poetry of self-expression; the traditionalists heard the crudity of the ill-mannered. White liberals called for "understanding for the rage and frustration" of rioters; traditionalists said "lock them up." White liberals seemed particularly enthusiastic about school busing and low-income housing proposals and left it to the traditionalists to say "not in my back yard." In every case the new Democrats supported the culturally liberal against the traditional. And, in just about every case, a majority of the electorate took the side of the traditional against what it perceived to be the disruptive, disorderly, and destructive.

The accession of the antiwar reformers coincided with the rise of the women's movement, the increased militancy of racial and ethnic minorities, and the homosexual rights movement. These groups gravitated to the Democratic party, where they found a warm reception from the white liberal reformers who were looking for allies in their war with the regulars. For many of the feminists, gays, and minorities, the party was just another forum. Their loyalties were to their causes and movements, not to the party. They wanted acquiescence to their demands, not compromises and coalitions. By 1972 feminists, blacks, Latinos, gays, and lesbians had organized caucuses within the party (the first three were granted their own seats on the Democratic National Committee's executive committee, which was expanded to an unwieldy 410 members to accommodate the "protected" classes).

At precisely the time that national Democrats were purging the traditional bases of their party, the representatives of new causes infused the Democrats with energy, ideas, and troops. They also made the new Democrats appear disorganized and fractious, embarrassed by patriotism, and—more often than not—on the side of the robbers against the cops and the welfare recipient against the worker. These groups also conveyed another persistent, plain message: We do not much like white, straight males. White, straight males got the message.

Senator McGovern typified the new Democrats in several ways. First, he was defined by his avid opposition to the Vietnam War. Second, he had limited firsthand experience dealing with black Americans. He came from Mitchell, South Dakota, which in the 1970 census reported 22 blacks out of 13,425 residents. The crunching issues of race, crime, disorder, and school busing were remote from the concerns of his constituents. But he was generous with his sympathy about the plight of blacks. Third, he was an inept politician. Although he mastered procedure and reform, he could not exercise sufficient leadership to control his own nominating convention.

The Republicans could not believe their luck—here was their rival party, claimant to the loyalties of fully half the American electorate, adopting procedures and requirements that substantially decreased its capacity to nominate a winning presidential candidate. It would take twenty years, four Republican victories, and a right-wing Republican government for the Democratic party to recover from the damage inflicted by the 1972 convention and campaign.

The platform adopted at the 1972 convention reflected the air of unreality that had seized liberal Democrats. The platform is an important element in presidential campaigns because it paints a simple picture that the party wants voters to see. In 1972 the Democratic platform attracted attention for its support of measures considered radical by most voters. Consider these positions:

▲   On Vietnam: "We will end that war by a simple plan . . . the immediate total withdrawal of all Americans from Southeast Asia."

▲ On American society: "We must restructure the social, political, and economic relationships throughout the entire society in order to ensure the equitable distribution of wealth and power."

▲ On poverty: "an earned income approach to ensure each family an income substantially more than the poverty level, ensuring standards of decency and health."

▲ On school busing: "Transportation of students is another tool to accomplish desegregation."

Although the McGovern platform did not promise socialism, it did pledge to eliminate—through government guarantee and dicta—any manifestation of free enterprise that could potentially produce inequality or failure. It promised to use the tax system and federal law enforcement to redistribute income and wealth. And it said the Democrats would study whether corporations should be chartered as federal institutions.

The McGovern Democrats were just as radical when they considered the divisions brought on by the nation's raging cultural war. As Thomas and Mary Edsall emphasized in their 1991 book on the decline of liberalism, the Democrats "were committed to continuing the rights revolution—a revolution that many working- and lower-middle class voters saw as threatening to traditional, deeply valued, if inequitable social arrangements." And most strikingly, the Edsalls noted, "at a time when crime was rising at an unprecedented rate, the Democratic platform devoted more attention to the restoration of constitutional rights to released convicts than to efforts to combat street violence."[13] The platform endorsed quotas for "historically under-represented groups," including the poor; the right of welfare recipients to be represented by union-like organizations when dealing with welfare agencies; and special employment and educational rights for the mentally retarded and physically disabled. Everybody, it seemed, was handed specially tailored rights by reason of their age, race, gender, handicap, income, or military service—except for the middle- and working-class voters who cast most of the votes every November.

The McGovernites thought their platform was just right. Gary Hart, the McGovern campaign manager, reported on the platform in one sentence in his memoirs: "The platform evolved essentially as we had hoped, angering only the Wallace supporters by the pro-busing plank, militant women's rights advocates with a moderate abortion plank, and some

welfare leaders with a moderate welfare plank."[14] McGovern blamed
Hubert Humphrey and the press for distorting his true positions and
painting him into a "radical" corner. Critics called the Democrats the
party of "acid, abortion, and amnesty."[15]

Because the 1972 Democratic convention was organized by politicians who favored openness, inclusion, and participatory democracy in
party affairs, everyone had a say, and thus 80 million prime-time viewers
of the convention were "treated" to nominating and seconding speeches
for seven hopeless candidates for vice-president. Having satisfied the procedural imperatives of reform, the presidential nominee was offered the
dais at 2:48 A.M. Eastern time to deliver what he considered the best
speech of his life. George McGovern wasted the best opportunity he was
to be given to speak directly to the nation.

The capper was McGovern's selection of Missouri Senator Thomas
Eagleton as his running mate. Eagleton had to withdraw from the ticket
when his history of mental health problems was made public, despite
Senator McGovern's initial insistence that he supported Senator Eagleton
"1000 percent."

McGovern was inept. He claimed, for example, that he wanted
Mayor Daley and his Illinois delegation seated but that he could not control the McGovern delegates on the credentials committee.[16] Both he and
Hart described their strategy as winning over regular Democrats first, even
as they pushed issues, such as school busing, unilateral withdrawal from
Vietnam, and racial and gender preferences, that working-class Democrats
overwhelmingly opposed. Over and over, McGovern blamed others for distorting his positions to make him appear radical. He portrayed himself as
a liberal centrist, who took a strong and principled position against the
Vietnam War but otherwise appealed to the American center.

Self-deception is not rare in politics. The most important rule to
remember in political campaigns is the one most frequently violated:
never confuse the campaign with real life. Campaigns are surreal hot-
houses. The normal divisions of the day and week are without importance. Campaigns punish their participants physically and emotionally.
There is too much information, too many rumors, too many opportunities. In a presidential campaign, the separation between candidate and
voter is even more extreme. A candidate's life is defined in an airplane in
which are seated, day after day, the same crew of trusted aides and con-
fidants with whom one visits a succession of airports, assembly halls,
and hotels, trailed by a pack of fatigued reporters. In this atmosphere,
bad judgments are about the only ones that can be made, which is why

successful candidates are normally those who follow the more detached directions from a central directorate "on the ground." McGovern's campaign was particularly confused because the candidate himself lacked clear and strong convictions to anchor his decisions about key issues, such as the selection of a running-mate.

McGovern's reformist coup drove from the national party its best politicians. They were excluded by McGovern and his supporters as too white, too male, too ambiguous about the Vietnam War. Their places were taken by reformers who believed that the United States had not only embarked on an immoral and disastrous war, but that the nation itself was diseased and could be saved only by radical surgery. This view was rejected in November 1972 by the largest margin in history. One in three Democrats voted for the Republican incumbent.

MEANWHILE, IN THE WHITE HOUSE

While reform Democrats were working to purge their party of the working class, their ancient foe, Richard Nixon, occupied the White House. Nixon continually confounded his friends as well as enemies. He neither ended the Vietnam War as promised nor dismantled the Great Society as threatened. Having spent most of his public career as a fervent anti-Communist, he opened relations with the People's Republic of China. Much has been made of the ironies in Nixon's conduct of foreign affairs; much less of his efforts to formulate and launch the nation's last war on poverty.

To hear Richard Nixon tell it, he was oblivious to the cultural and racial wars that had so much to do with his 1968 election and 1972 reelection. Nixon would have his observers believe, for example, that Strom Thurmond, the South Carolina senator who was the key player in Nixon's southern strategy, cared, first, about a strong national defense and, second, about textile trade quotas. Civil rights? "Thurmond knew my position was very different from his," Nixon wrote in his memoirs. "I was for the Civil Rights Act of 1964; he was against it." [17]

Nixon ran his 1968 campaign like a clinic in the politics of race, a clinic that would guide Republican presidential candidates for twenty years and would drive Democratic candidates into fits of futility, timidity, and stupidity. The Republican party in 1968 was still recognizable as the "party of Lincoln." In the Northeast and through much of the Midwest, the party was dominated by racial liberals such as John Lindsay,

Nelson Rockefeller, and Jacob Javits of New York; Senator Clifford Case
and Representative William Cahill in New Jersey; Senator Edward Brooke
in Massachusetts; Senator Charles Percy in Illinois; Senator Hugh Scott in
Pennsylvania; and Governor George Romney in Michigan. These men
believed that the civil rights of black Americans deserved the unwavering
support of the Republican party. Nixon understood the danger of taking
any positions that would offend liberal Republicans. When Martin Luther
King was assassinated, Nixon went to Atlanta to pay his respects to his
family, returned for his funeral, and suspended his campaign for two
weeks.

Richard Nixon understood that the Democrats, with their close identification with social and civil rights legislation, had handed the
Republicans an opportunity. White southerners, once the most loyal
Democratic voters, felt betrayed by Lyndon Johnson and northern liberals. Working-class Democrats in and around northern cities were fright-
ened and angered by black riots, crime, and school busing plans, yet the
new Democrats showed no concern. What Nixon mastered was the
vocabulary that allowed him to express understanding and sympathy for
white southerners and ethnic northerners without offending racial moderates in his party.

Nixon reflected the ambivalence of white voters on racial issues; he
favored racial justice and an end to state-approved segregation but
opposed an intrusive federal government in implementing civil rights laws
and court decisions. Thus, Nixon supported the *Brown* v. *Board of
Education* decision ending segregation in schools and opposed school
busing; he favored voting rights for black southerners, even as he tried to
limit the Justice Department's power to veto decisions normally reserved for
southern states. He was an early critic of the Kerner Commission's indict-
ment of white racism: "One of the major weaknesses of the [report] . . . is
that it . . . blames everyone for the riots except the perpetrators. . . . Until
we have order we can have no progress."[18]

Nixon's selection of Spiro Agnew as his running mate symbolized his
approach to racial issues. Governor of Maryland for only eighteen
months, Agnew had previously served one term as the executive of
Baltimore County. Agnew's thin public record met one crucial test—he
was acceptable to Strom Thurmond. At the time, he was best known for
his carefully staged scolding of Baltimore's black leaders in the aftermath
of the rioting that followed Martin Luther King's assassination. Liberal
Republicans were thrown off by his lack of public record, but Agnew
appeared liberal because he had supported Nelson Rockefeller's presidential

candidacy at one time. In just ten years, Agnew would rise from his first
elected position—as the vice president of the Loch Raven, Maryland,
Kiwanis Club—to vice president of the United States.

MOYNIHAN'S RETURN

As Nixon turned to governing, he would take a surprising path in his
first two years as president. In fact, Nixon would propose the nation's last
war on poverty, betraying his campaign rhetoric and the expectations of
conservative supporters and liberal critics alike. No one was surprised
when he named Robert Finch, his closest political associate and former
lieutenant governor of California, to be the secretary of health, education,
and welfare. From Finch, Nixon was assured of a steady stream of advice
from the liberal edge of the Republican ideological spectrum. The appointment of George Shultz, a highly regarded labor economist from the
University of Chicago, as labor secretary was equally unsurprising. But his
appointment of Daniel Patrick Moynihan as the director of a newly established Council on Urban Affairs in the White House indicated a radical
departure.

Moynihan was back, not quite four years after his unceremonious
departure from Washington. He had not been totally invisible during his
absence from the nation's capital, but his light had been dimmed.
Moynihan had returned to academia after his stint in the Kennedy-Johnson
administrations, chairing a joint Harvard-MIT program on urban policy
and cochairing a comprehensive review of the Coleman report, the
nation's largest-scale investigation into the performance of schools and
students. Although many of his liberal critics retreated from the search for
solutions to the puzzles of poverty and, specifically, the black lower class,
Moynihan persisted.

The Nixon government did not back away from tangled problems of
the ghetto—at least, not at first. It proceeded on two fronts and in both
cases adopted approaches that had been rejected in the late days of the
Great Society. One front was opened with the most aggressive public
effort ever made by an American president to impose racial quotas. The
Philadelphia Plan was a part of Nixon's advocacy of black capitalism as
the best alternative to the "social engineering" of the Johnson years. The
public rationale for the Philadelphia Plan was to open high-paying unionized construction jobs to black workers, who had been excluded by all
sorts of gimmicks and excuses. Privately, Nixon delighted in driving a

wedge between two powerful Democratic constituencies, organized labor and civil rights organizations.[19] The plan required unions and contractors to meet specific goals for minority workers on any construction involving federal funds. Nixon became the only president to obtain congressional authorization for the use of racial quotas when the Philadelphia Plan was approved in Congress. It was opposed by the most conservative Republicans and southern Democrats and a few northern Democrats from heavily unionized areas.[20] After Nixon's victory in Congress, Secretary Shultz extended the Philadelphia formula to nineteen cities that displayed the same pattern of underrepresentation of minority workers in the construction trades.[21]

Nixon received no credit from civil rights leaders for his surprising and aggressive move. The NAACP's spokesman, Herbert Hill, characterized the Nixon administration's plan in confused and confusing terms: The "abandonment of the Philadelphia Plan" was a "payoff to the building trades unions for their support of the war in Indochina." Hill went on to describe the extension of the Philadelphia Plan to other cities as "a meaningless hodgepodge of quackery and deceptions, of double talk and doublethink."[22] It was ironic that Nixon's most visible appeal to traditionally Democratic blue-collar workers for support of his Vietnam policies would be directed at people in the same construction trades that were singled out for such unfavorable treatment in the Philadelphia Plan.

By 1972 Nixon would reverse himself, making an attack on quotas a major theme in his convention acceptance speech. Criticizing the spectacle of the recently completed Democratic convention, Nixon said "we can have an open convention without dividing Americans into quotas. . . . Dividing Americans into quotas is totally alien to the American tradition. . . . Americans don't want to be part of a quota—they want to be part of America."

The second part of Nixon's effort to address the problems of the ghetto involved a massive and complicated proposal to reform the nation's welfare system, called the family assistance plan (FAP). FAP was the product of a partnership of Moynihan, Finch, and Shultz, who developed it over the strong opposition of Nixon's first economic counselor, conservative Arthur F. Burns. The Nixon plan was radical in three respects. First, the federal government would guarantee and finance a minimum welfare payment to eligible families (in 1969, $1,600 for a family of four). The idea was to replace a system that permitted the southern states to set welfare payments at a sub-subsistence level. Second, families with children headed by workers earning poverty level wages would receive a supplementary family allowance. Third, all FAP recipients, except for the disabled, elderly, or the parents of preschool children, would be required to register for job training and employment—Nixon's "workfare."

FAP was too complicated for its own good. The impact of the program was different from state to state, depending on the levels of public assistance, the earnings of the family (if any), and the presence or absence of the father. Under FAP, some people could work and still receive welfare, depending on how much they earned; others would lose benefits for working. States were required to add unemployed fathers to the welfare rolls (if they had not already done so) and to extend Medicaid eligibility to their families. Moreover, at a time when welfare appeared to be losing its stigma in ghetto neighborhoods, when the number of recipients had doubled in just five years, and when public opposition to welfare was rising, a "conservative" Republican president offered a program that would increase the number of welfare recipients from 10 to 24 million overnight. Conservatives were appalled.

Nixon presented the family assistance plan in a thirty-five-minute television address on August 8, 1969. From all the charts and tables that accompanied FAP's introduction, one very large and certain consequence of its enactment was brilliantly visible: the lives of millions of southerners, most of them black, would be materially improved. A contemporaneous study found that more than half (two million) of the families receiving increased benefits under FAP resided in the South, where 53 percent of all black Americans lived.[23] The study found that the typical black family receiving benefits would realize a 47 percent increase in annual income. A family of four in Mississippi, receiving $46 a month in 1969 ($190 in 1994 dollars), would, under the worst case, triple its cash income were FAP to be enacted. FAP represented an opportunity to ease the sting of poverty for the poorest families in the poorest states and, thereby, bring about a government-sponsored social revolution in the rural South. Within a five-year span, poor black southerners, living lives little changed since Reconstruction, would have won the vote and could have been lifted out of abject poverty.

Although FAP's potential effect on the rural South was vast, it was not without impact in the North. Here, the greatest benefit would go not to families already receiving welfare, but to poor families where the father was living at home. Under FAP, such poor families would receive a family assistance payment from the federal government, plus supplementary payments from the state, up to the level of the 1970 Aid to Families with

Dependent Children (AFDC) payment or the poverty level, whichever was lower. The biggest impact would have been in states where families with unemployed fathers were not previously eligible for AFDC. In these states, a family of four with no earnings would move from zero assistance to $2,200; a family in which the father earned $1,000 would go from a total annual income of $1,000 to $3,013. In a state with AFD-CUP—the unemployed father program—the family income would have increased much less, from $3,753 to $3,813, but the federal government would have picked up a slightly larger share.[24]

FAP passed the House of Representatives by the impressive margin of 243 to 155 in April 1970. Southern representatives voted overwhelmingly against it. Of the seventeen southerners who did support FAP (out of 102), most were from big cities, such as New Orleans or Miami, or were Republican loyalists. But Wilbur Mills of Arkansas, the chair of the Ways and Means committee, was the southerner who counted most. He cosponsored the bill and guided it largely untouched through his committee, through the Rules Committee, and onto the floor of the House. Seventy-two Republicans voted against their president, almost all of them conservatives. Northern Democrats supported the Nixon plan by the lopsided count of 126 to 19. There was no clear pattern to the opposition: New York City's most liberal representative, Shirley Chisholm, and its most conservative, Mario Biaggi, united to vote against FAP. Chisholm was the only black representative to oppose FAP in 1970; when it came up a year later, only one black supported it.

The Nixon proposal died in the more liberal Senate. It was killed by southern Democrats and western conservatives, with the connivance of liberal Democrats. Liberal Democrats were churlish and defensive in the face of a dramatic proposal from a long-standing and detested foe. Caught off guard, they had no ready counteroffer. Senator Harris, who would run for president a year later rather than run a losing campaign for reelection to his Senate seat in Oklahoma, proposed the National Basic Income and Incentive Act, which more than doubled the federally guaranteed minimum income, from $1,600 to $3,740, and expanded the number of eligible beneficiaries from 24 million to 75 million. Under the Harris plan, mothers with dependent children of any age would not be required to work, and childless couples would be eligible for the guaranteed income. The price tag for the Harris plan was $20 billion, versus $5 billion for FAP.[25] Eugene McCarthy introduced the plan proposed by the National Welfare Rights Organization (NWRO), then at the peak of its power. Called the Adequate Income Act of 1970, the NWRO proposal called for a floor of $5,500 for a family of four ($21,629 in 1994 dollars), but with no work requirements and a marginal "tax" rate of 67 percent on earnings, the plan was an antiwork program. More than one-half of the American population would have been covered, at an additional cost of $71 billion. In short, it was not a proposal that could be taken seriously. As Moynihan noted, however, the NWRO succeeded in moderating the support of some groups favoring FAP (such as Common Cause), and in eventually swinging black politicians and some civil rights organizations, such as the Urban League, into hard opposition to FAP.[26] The Harris and NWRO proposals were irrelevant, except for the fact that both McCarthy and Harris were on the Senate Finance Committee, and their votes were essential if FAP was to reach the Senate floor. As sponsors of alternative proposals, Harris and McCarthy joined southern Democrats and conservative Republicans in opposition, and a revised FAP proposal was killed in a ten-to-six vote in 1971.

McGovern, who was already planning his campaign for the Democratic nomination, also opposed FAP. In January 1970 he responded to the Nixon plan with a far-reaching proposal for an allowance of between $50 and $65 a month for every child, regardless of family income (a family with three children would receive up to $9,100 in 1994 dollars). He estimated the cost of his allowance at $10 billion in the first year. In combination with a public service employment guarantee, Social Security benefit increases, and a federalized welfare system, McGovern's cost increase estimates grew to $35 billion.[27]

But in contrast to Nixon, McGovern was not serious. He introduced no legislation, and his proposal, advanced as a major innovation in social policy, died from a lack of persistence by its architect. In September 1970 McGovern appeared before the Senate Finance Committee to testify on FAP and did not even mention his January proposal. Instead, he argued against FAP's mandatory work requirement, preferring incentives in the form of an increase in the minimum wage and guaranteed public service jobs. He recommended combining FAP with free food stamps, at an additional cost of $1 billion to $2 billion. He also wanted to federalize the administration of welfare, but did not provide any estimate of the additional cost.[28]

McGovern displayed both imprecision and inconsistency in formulating successive proposals for America's poor. These habits of mind would return to sting him badly in the presidential campaign in his advocacy of a program to pay $1,000 to every American—including the Rockefellers—regardless of need. In a primary debate with Hubert

Humphrey, McGovern suggested: "There is no way to estimate the cost of this program other than to say that there is no net cost to the Treasury at all."[29] Presumably, the cost could have been obtained simply by multiplying the estimated population of 207 million in 1971 by $1,000 to yield $207 billion—$778 billion in 1994 dollars! In his memoirs, he claimed that his program was, really, not so different from the FAP proposal.[30] McGovern was hammered for his scheme—first by the Democrats, then by Nixon and his surrogates in some of the most effective television commercials of the campaign. In late August, reeling from the mishandling of Eagleton's brief tenure as his running mate, McGovern abandoned the $1,000 idea. In its stead, he proposed government-guaranteed jobs for three and one-half million un- or under-employed people and a federally financed $4,000 allowance for families of four headed by nonworkers.[31]

McGovern's wanderings reflect the intellectual condition of liberal Democratic politicians and academics who had drawn back from any serious thinking about America's lower class following Moynihan's censure by black and leftist critics. There was only one point of consistency in the several schemes he advanced: no one was required to seek work in return for income payments. In truth, he demonstrated no thoughtful or consistent perspective in the problem of racial inequalities and poverty. He acted as if his first obligation was to avoid criticism from the Left and black leaders. McGovern's political timidity and intellectual weakness signified the lowest point of liberalism and Democratic politics.

5»

THE COSTS OF BLACK UNITY:
POLITICAL ISOLATION

Black political unity is a relatively new concept in American politics. Although the Fifteenth Amendment gave blacks the right to vote in 1870, generations of black citizens found themselves disenfranchised by poll taxes, phony tests, intimidation, and violence; that is, until the passage of the Voting Rights Act of 1965. Seen by many as the crowning glory of the civil rights movement, the Voting Rights Act led to the registration of black voters on an unprecedented, massive scale. As the black voting bloc solidified, black political leadership explored the new terrain in search of a voice.

MARTIN LUTHER KING, JR.

Dr. Martin Luther King, Jr., led black Americans out of the wilderness. He smashed American apartheid, liberating black southerners. During his lifetime, no one could match the respect and adoration accorded King by black Americans. A 1966 Harris poll of black Americans asked how they rated the job various groups and leaders were doing in the fight for Negro rights. A nearly unanimous 88 percent rated King as doing an "excellent" (75 percent) or "pretty good" (13 percent) job. No other individual or group was even close.[1] In Gallup's year-end survey determing the nation's "most admired men" in 1964, Americans ranked King ahead of everyone save President Johnson, former President Eisenhower, and Winston Churchill.[2]

Today, Martin Luther King's legacy is appreciated even by conservatives—even if they never honored him in life—as representing the "good" civil rights movement. They romanticize his devotion to the ideal of a color-blind America, his adherence to the tenets of the American creed, and his advocacy of integration rather than separatism. For example, in justifying the rise of white-rights organizations, writer Jared Taylor explained, "What they call for is exactly what Martin Luther King called for: equal treatment for all races."[3] But conservatives have been quicker than liberals to emphasize one of the distinguishing characteristics of King's leadership: his appeal to the promise of American life, the call to animate the words of the American dream for all Americans. Glenn Loury, a self-defined black conservative, wrote:

> King constantly evoked an image of Americans as decent, magnanimous, moral, righteous—as a freedom-loving people whose great fault lay in failing to achieve in reality the nobility implicit in their civic creed. His task was showing them how profoundly wrong were the exclusionary practices against which he fought. This America of King's, of course, was deeply flawed, but he chose to emphasize its potential for redemption.[4]

Many black leaders remind white Americans of their shameful heritage of racism. King did it in his time, but he was able to combine lamentations about past sins with a spirit of optimism that white Americans would redeem the nation's pledge of racial justice. He gave whites an escape that did not require humiliation: "Just give us the respect you know we are owed," he said.

A second, critical element in King's leadership was his unswerving devotion to nonviolence. Although he characterized black riots as demonstrating the full extent of black discontent, he regarded them as mob actions. After Watts exploded, he called for the extension of nonviolent demonstration on a massive scale as the best antidote to the threat of more riots.[5] King never advocated "self-defense," the euphemism employed by radical leaders such as Rap Brown and Malcolm X to explain, excuse, or encourage black violence.

King reflected the black leaders' historic ambivalence between liberty and equality, between encouraging black self-help and demanding recompense from whites, between color-blindness and racial consciousness. He understood the appeal of black separatism. King's leadership was distinguished by its ceaseless search for white allies, for a coalition that could push civil rights, of course, but that could shift to economic issues once racial equality was encoded. For all the visible frailties of white liberals, King never suggested throwing them out of the movement:

> We [Negroes] band together readily; and against white hostility, we have an intense and wholesome loyalty to one another. But we cannot win our struggle for justice all alone. . . . I believe there is an important place in our struggle for white liberals.[6]

Instead of political separatism, King urged black Americans to "become intensive political activists," and to "master the art of political alliances." He advocated working with, and learning from, organized labor and American Jewry. King told blacks to emulate Jewish Americans with their emphasis on family, education, social action, and political involvement.[7]

In pushing for political coalitions, King accepted that new programs must be race-neutral, because initiatives intended to benefit only black Americans could not muster sufficient consensus. He understood what conservatives would not acknowledge: black Americans, as poor Americans, required preferences in jobs, education, and housing:

> The closest analogy is the GI Bill of Rights. Negro rehabilitation . . . would require approximately the same breadth of program. . . . Just as was the case of the returning soldier, such a bill for the disadvantaged and impoverished could enable them to buy homes without cash. . . . They could negotiate loans from banks to start businesses. They could receive . . . points to place them ahead in competition for civil service jobs.[8]

But even here, King thought his GI Bill should be for people who were poor—black or white—unlike his successors who would press for preferences defined by race alone.

King, however, had no convincing strategy for dealing with the problems of the northern poor. He searched and hypothesized; he defended Moynihan; he talked about the weaknesses in black family life; he pushed housing integration and expanded job opportunities; he led demonstrations and conducted negotiations with mayors and corporate executives.

But he had no clear answer to either the subtle obstacles erected by northern whites or the problems of lower-class blacks concentrated in northern ghettos.

Martin Luther King was the only black leader who possessed enough moral authority and visibility to contend with the complexity of the "next, most profound step in civil rights"—full participation by black Americans in American society. And he understood clearly that black Americans could not prosper on their own, that black-white comity was a necessary condition for realizing the movement's objectives.

After Dr. King's death in April 1968, no one emerged who could mobilize the black community and sustain the vision of a racially cooperative society. Even before King's assassination, the media were emphasizing the divisions between King and the more militant black leaders. By 1967 these militants had enunciated a sharply different vision for American blacks—the vision was called Black Power.

BLACK POWER AND THE SEEDS OF RACIAL ISOLATION

A spirit of racial comity, the hymns celebrating "black and white together," and the hopes for full integration were at the core of the civil rights movement in the early 1960s. That view was challenged by a very different set of ideas during the second half of the 1960s. The rationale for black political isolation was set forth most coherently in the 1967 book written by Stokely Carmichael and Charles Hamilton called *Black Power: The Politics of Liberation in America*. Ironically, they finished the book the month of the Detroit riots, offering "the politics of Black Power as the only visible hope" to avoid "prolonged destructive guerrilla warfare."[9]

The Black Power movement may have been inevitable, even necessary for its time. Its influence was greatest with the black intellectual and political elite. Black Power succeeded in building racial pride in a people who had endured centuries of white supremacist propaganda. It stimulated scholarship to challenge the received wisdom about the African roots of black Americans, their reactions to enslavement, and the role of black Americans in the Union cause during the Civil War. Black Power focused attention on the overlooked and forgotten contributions of black writers, inventors, scholars, and other gifted individuals. Black Power, in short, helped check the overweening arrogance of white Americans who contentedly assumed that the black contribution to American prosperity and culture had been limited to strong backs, good rhythm, and achievements in music and sports.

But Black Power also was a direct challenge to King's leadership, personally and philosophically. Carmichael and Hamilton outlined the priorities of Black Power as follows:

> To [challenge the majority society], we must first redefine ourselves. Our basic need [is] to reclaim our history and our identity from what must be called cultural terrorism, from the depredation of self-justifying white guilt. We shall have to struggle for the right to create our own terms through which to define ourselves and our relationship to the society, and to have these terms recognized. This is the first necessity of a free people, and the first right that any oppressor must suspend.[10]

The authors of Black Power attacked the fundamental premises of Martin Luther King's approach to civil rights: integration, individual rights, nonviolence, and coalition politics. In their place, Carmichael and Hamilton emphasized group progress, group rights, "self-defense," and political separatism. On nonviolence, they wrote:

> Those of us who advocate Black Power are quite clear . . . that a "non-violent" approach to civil rights is an approach that black people cannot afford and a luxury that white people do not deserve."[11]

On integration:

> "Integration" as a goal today speaks to the problems of blackness not only in an unrealistic way but also in a despicable way. It is based on complete acceptance of the fact that in order to have a decent house or education, black people must move into a white neighborhood or send their children to a white school. . . . Such situations will not change until black people become equal in a way that means something, and integration ceases to be a one-way street. Then integration does not mean draining skills and energies from the black ghetto. . . .[12]

On group rights and action:

> Black people have not suffered as individuals but as members of
> a group; therefore, their liberation lies in group action. This is
> why . . . Black Power . . . affirms that helping individual black
> people to solve their problems on an individual basis does little
> to alleviate the mass of black people."[13]

On America's middle-class values:

> The values of this society support a racist system; we find it
> incongruous to ask black people to adopt and support most of
> those values. We also reject the assumption that the basic insti-
> tutions of this society must be preserved. The goal of black peo-
> ple must not be to assimilate into middle-class America. . . .
> The values of the middle class permit the perpetuation of the
> ravages of the black community.[14]

Black Power reflected the temper of the 1960s: America was diseased; middle-class values were materialistic and hollow; the "system"
was not worth preserving. Black Power followed its condemnation with
a call for racial separatism.

In the late 1960s two groups emerged from the separatist movement
that fed the fears of suburban middle-class whites who worried that black
America was spinning off in dangerous, radical directions. The Black
Panthers were established in Oakland, California, with the announced
purpose of organizing black "self-defense" teams in major cities. They
were masters at attracting media coverage, through such tactics as an
armed march into the halls of the California legislature. They practiced a
sophisticated menacing of white society in general and of the police in particular. Romanticized for their black berets, military titles, and revolutionary rhetoric, the Panthers spread to major ghetto cities, extorted
money from local merchants for breakfast programs, and, with clenched
fists, talked of "power to the people." Liberal elitists could not bring
themselves to criticize the glorification of violence and the racial separatism of the Panthers. Instead, some turned to fund-raising for the
Panther's legal costs, the ironies of which were captured in Tom Wolfe's
Radical Chic.[15]

The second group was the National Welfare Rights Organization
(NWRO), which was established by a black college professor, George

Wiley. Wiley relied on the intellectual constructs of two Leftist professors at Columbia University, Frances Fox Piven and Richard Cloward. NWRO was biracial in theory, but very black in practice. The Piven-Cloward-Wiley goal was to push the Democrats to enact a guaranteed income. They wanted to establish welfare as an entitlement and to organize the urban poor to overload the welfare rolls, driving up the costs to states and cities until mayors and governors would force Congress to provide fiscal relief in the form of a guaranteed income for everyone. NWRO organized protests and sit-ins, filed law suits, and trained welfare recipients to press for every authorized benefit. The idea was to bring down the welfare system and to rewrite the rules of American capitalism. But when a guaranteed income plan was proposed in the form of Nixon's Family Assistance Plan, the NWRO opposed it as too parsimonious, thereby contributing to its defeat.

During the period of Black Power's maximum impact, between 1967 and 1973 or so, most black Americans were living lives unrecognized by the advocates of Black Power. Civil rights and federal lawyers were litigating to bring about a rapid and comprehensive end to the South's dual school systems and to extend desegregation to northern cites. Between 1968 and 1972 southern schools were transformed from the most segregated in the nation to the most integrated (or at least, the most desegregated).[16] By 1970, just five years after the voting rights law was signed, black southerners were registered to vote in about the same proportion as white southerners (in just two years, black registration in Mississippi shot up from 6.7 percent to almost 60 percent of eligible registrants), but they were voting in Democratic primaries, not setting up the separatist parties consistent with Black Power.[17] And black Americans were taking advantage of new opportunities for higher education and for white-collar employment. No one, it seemed, could wait for a radical abstraction like Black Power to catch up to real life.

UNEASY ALLIES: WHITE LIBERALS AND THE BLACK ELITE

The term *white liberal* came into fashion during the civil rights struggle as a label for those who favored the aims of the movement but who were queasy about the pace, manners, or tactics of its leadership. James Baldwin called liberals the black's "affliction"—"someone who thinks you're pushing too hard when you rock the boat, who thinks you are bitter when you are vehement."[18] King wrote his famous "Letter from the Birmingham City Jail" to sympathetic white clergymen who urged an end to nonviolent confrontations as "untimely." "I have never yet engaged in a direct action," King wrote, "that was 'well-timed' according to the timetable of those who have not suffered unduly from the disease of segregation."[19]

The heart of the white liberal-black relationship was not mutual interest—but disrespect. White liberals patronized blacks; in private they clucked about the latest horror story of quotas and double standards for minorities, and in public, they acted as if black people would wither if their ideas were debated seriously and openly. And so, issues such as affirmative action, crime, welfare dependency, male idleness, and family instability were not subjected to the normal give-and-take of political discourse. Driven by guilt, timidity, or hypocrisy, liberals wanted to prove that they were not oppressors, that they understood, they sympathized, they wanted to help. And because dealing with a black person was, for many sheltered liberals, an exotic experience, the black person came to be treated as an ambassador from another land: a Black Person, not an American who happened to be black.

One consistent exception to the white liberal rule should be noted: many Jews were willing to engage in sharp debate when the issue was anti-Semitism or quotas. After black Americans, American Jews are the most reliable Democratic voters. They were prominent supporters of the civil rights movement and, more than other whites, many Jews have been in regular contact with blacks as landlords and shop owners in ghetto neighborhoods. As a group, Jews understand discrimination and persecution. And they are quick to jump on any hint of anti-Semitism, as Jesse Jackson learned following his reference to New York City as "Hymie town" and his pledge of support for the Nation of Islam leader, Louis Farrakhan.

But since the late 1960s, liberal Democrats have been hurt in presidential politics by their silence in the face of radically alien ideas on racial issues. Afraid to argue with either the Left or blacks, liberals ended up supporting or, at least, abetting crazy ideas. The collapse of the liberal discourse on issues of family stability, welfare dependency, and illegitimacy, and the abandonment of the concept of personal responsibility for crime and riots, left no position for liberals other than as apologists for extreme black views. Liberals went beyond explanations for black misbehavior to excuse actions that almost all Americans—black and white—considered to be outside the basic social contract. (Liberals found other ways to offend moderate voters by deprecating traditional patriotism, showing naivete about the Soviet threat, and appearing to favor libertinism and drugs.)

None of this should have been altogether surprising. After all, before the 1960s, white Americans routinely refused to consider black Americans as human beings, treating them instead as social oddities or inferiors. The small, brief opportunity that liberals had in the mid-1960s to agree on the scope of the problems facing black Americans was lost when Moynihan was told to shut up. Any remaining hope was smashed with Martin Luther King's assassination.

Robert Kennedy was one politician who could speak effectively to black Americans, working-class whites, and liberal reformers. He was almost alone in speaking out early and plainly about the political implications of Black Power. In 1966, for example, he chastised Floyd McKissick, the head of the Congress of Racial Equality (CORE), saying, "you are turning your back on Negroes and whites working together and if people can't meet your definition, you read them out."[20] The deaths of Martin Luther King and Robert F. Kennedy, just two months apart, created a vacuum that has never been filled.

The new black militancy was not warmly received by most Americans, black or white. But the Left embraced the spirit of insurgency and the revolutionary rhetoric. White liberals carelessly incorporated much of the black militant program as their own. Effectively, it was as if white liberals said, "We'll handle foreign policy, national security, macroeconomics, and the environment; why don't you blacks fill in the crime, welfare, civil rights, and city stuff." The only major disagreement between Black Power and the McGovern Democrats was over integration and school busing, which McGovern insisted be supported in the platform.[21]

Thus, the public agendas of the black and white elites were conveniently joined in the Democratic party. As has been noted, the result was an electoral slaughter of historic proportions in 1972, the alienation of working-class Democrats, and the takeover of the national party machinery by ideologues and zealots determined to shut out the party's elected leaders in Congress and state capitals.

RACIALIZED THOUGHT AND THE SUPPRESSION OF DIVERSITY

After the suppression of the Moynihan report, black leaders and white liberals stopped arguing in public. Outspoken black critics could "blame whitey" for all the ills afflicting black Americans. The orthodox solution invariably came down to a combination of racial preferences under the rubric of affirmative action and massive public programs. When these "demands" were not fully met, the allegation of racial insensitivity and insufficient commitment was leveled. Disagreement with the ideas of any "brother," however outrageous, was discouraged. Black unity, when organized around such radical ideas, made coalition politics impossible.

This orthodoxy continued to hold sway in the 1990s, despite increasing criticism. In writing about the confused response of black leadership to the nomination of Clarence Thomas to the U.S. Supreme Court in 1991, Cornel West, the provocative scholar of Afro-American studies, identified the trap of "racial reasoning:"

> Most black leaders got lost in this thicket of reasoning and hence got caught in a vulgar form of racial reasoning: black authenticity [leads to] black closing-ranks mentality [leads to] black male subordination of black women in the interests of black community in a hostile white racist country. Such a line of racial reasoning leads to such questions as: "Is Thomas really black?" "Is he black enough to be defended?" "Is he just black on the outside?". . . .
>
> Unfortunately, the very framework of racial reasoning was not called into question. Yet as long as racial reasoning regulates black thought and action, Clarence Thomases will continue to haunt black America—as Bush and other conservatives sit back, watch, and prosper.[22]

The "closing-ranks mentality" means that any truth-telling that could possibly feed the arguments of opponents must be condemned. So if the CCNY pseudo-scholar Leonard Jeffries assails Jews for "financing the slave trade," he is spared criticism by black scholars who privately mock his scholarship. When Marion Barry was tried for crack cocaine use, he was cited as a victim of "racist prosecution," cheered by fellow black mayors, and defended by the national president of the NAACP. Meanwhile, any discussion touching on reviving the tradition of black self-help, which had preserved strong black families through the unspeakable horrors of segregation and racial oppression, is criticized as giving comfort to conservative victim-blamers.

In 1978 the black sociologist William Julius Wilson broke with the orthodoxy when he published *The Declining Significance of Race*. A liberal, respected scholar, Wilson could not be dismissed as an "oreo" or "conservative." He argued that the deteriorating conditions in northern ghettos could be best explained by the deindustrialization of the American economy, which had eliminated high-paying, semiskilled jobs in and around cities, and by the progress and subsequent flight to the suburbs of the black middle class. Children in these ghetto neighborhoods grew up without the example of successful blacks to emulate; institutions such as lodges, churches, and clubs, which provided the glue for a sense of community, had been drained of their leadership. Ignoring the arguments on racism and separatism, Wilson advocated black participation in coalitions that would push economic reforms to benefit all poor people, not programs targeted to the black poor alone. He concluded:

> The challenge of economic dislocation . . . calls for public policy programs to attack inequality on a broad class front, policy programs . . . that go beyond the limits of ethnic and racial discrimination by directly confronting the pervasive and destructive features of class subordination."[23]

Wilson's book was immediately denounced by black academics and activists. Wilson was charged with four major violations of black orthodoxy. First, he had sinned by drawing attention to the expansion and progress of the black middle class. Second, Wilson had claimed that affirmative action had helped primarily those who, by reason of family background, education, and luck, would have found good jobs anyway. Third, he had argued that the great disparities in black income and employment status could not be blamed on any pervasive, contemporary white racism. Fourth, citing W. E. B. DuBois and King, Wilson had proposed that black Americans would be better served by joining ranks with white, Latino, and other groups advocating race-neutral policies.

The attack on Wilson illuminates the process by which black insularity has hindered the development of a broader progressive coalition. First, by insisting that all blacks are victimized by "the system" of pervasive racism, liberals surrender ground to the conservative explanations for a growing black middle class: that systemic racial oppression has ended and that black people who study and work hard frequently succeed. Not only is the conservative explanation more credible as a matter of fact and observation, but it is more optimistic, appealing to the nation's uncritical belief in the American creed.

Second, the rhetoric of professional blacks and their white allies offends the rules of American society. For example, liberal Democrats aver that white racism is so endemic that black Americans must be offered guarantees for income, jobs, and college placements—that if left to compete with others they would certainly fail. Third, there is no room for white Americans who believe in equal opportunity and racial justice. The political arithmetic is simple and inarguable: if Americans are encouraged to group together by color and to think that society's ills are color-generated, then whites will win every time.

MULTICULTURALISM, AFROCENTRISM, AND OTHER HEIRS TO BLACK POWER

Although the Black Power movement has waned, the ideas that gave birth to the movement have been relabeled. Advocates of "multiculturalism" and "cultural diversity" push for heightened racial and ethnic consciousness and a new kind of intellectual balkanization. Adelaide Sanford, a member of the New York State Board of Regents who strongly advocated compulsory adoption of multicultural curricula, argues that each race and ethnic group must have the freedom to define themselves and determine what their children will be taught.[24] Multiculturalists reject the idea that the American republic is supported by a strong foundation of individual rights and opportunities. Scholar Derrick Bell goes so far as to suggest that civil rights laws are born of the same spirit that sanctioned slavery and segregation: "At best, the law—protecting blacks from blatant racist practices and policies, but rationalizing all manner of situations that relegate blacks to a subordinate status—regularizes racism."[25]

The drive for racial unity among black scholars and activists is not an intramural game of the black elite. While the urgings of the Afrocentrists influence curricula decisions in city schools and on university campuses, they also give rise to a much graver threat by lending intellectual respectability to racial separatism. What is noteworthy is that such a radical proposal—one that challenges the core values of American society—is so tamely viewed by black and white Americans who purportedly believe in the idea of one nation.

The views frequently expressed by black leaders assert that racism is the best or sole explanation for the unhappy plight of black Americans. A black leader who advances the notion that a white conspiracy aims at the genocidal elimination of black males through police murders and imprisonment will be cheered by many black audiences and challenged in practically none. Similarly black leaders blame much black crime on government's effort to flood ghetto neighborhoods with drugs. (In one poll, 60 percent found such an explanation true or plausible.[26]) Gaps in educational performance between black and white students are frequently presented as the consequence of uncaring school systems, suburban-controlled legislatures, and "Eurocentric" curricula and teachers. Higher rates of black infant mortality are explained as the consequence of the deliberate withholding of health services to black mothers and babies.

It is important to keep in mind the persistent focus the contemporary racialist orthodoxy has on victimization and the vehemence with which these positions are defended. The polarizing rhetoric threatens any dissenter with excommunication. When Yale professor Stephen Carter wrote of the complex and nuanced personal consequences of affirmative action programs on his life, he was pilloried, along with San Jose State professor Shelby Steele, by the Reverend Benjamin Hooks, president of the NAACP, as "just a new breed of Uncle Toms." Black Americans who recall the powerful traditions of black self-help and of strong moral traditions can expect comments such as this from Adolph Reed, Jr.: "his focus on self-help and moral revitalization [in ghetto neighborhoods] is profoundly reactionary and meshes perfectly with the victim-blaming orthodoxy of the Reagan/Bush era."[27]

OTHER VOICES

Many black Americans have resisted the more extreme ramifications of black unity. The spectrum of black thought and ideas is much richer and more textured than the usual public discourse allows. In particular, the conservative, distinctly southern, Baptist, and family orientation of black discourse is erased by the orthodoxy. A 1992 poll reported that black Americans are more likely to describe themselves as conservatives than liberals by a 34 to 28 margin![28] Only a small band of self-proclaimed "black conservatives," however, have dared a frontal attack on the orthodoxy of black unity. Their names—emblazoned in some Black Hall of Shame—include Thomas Sowell, Glenn Loury, Walter Williams, Robert Woodson, Justice Clarence Thomas, and Representative Gary Franks. These conservatives say, "Forget the legacies of enslavement, Jim Crow, and discrimination and act like the Americans you are. Individual black Americans are responsible for their lives, and you are as free as any other American to go as far your talents and ambition can take you." This kind of talk is heresy to the advocates of black unity. For black

Americans, the label "conservative" has the same appeal as "quisling" would have to a Norwegian patriot.

The ground between black conservatives and the advocates of black unity is nearly a no man's land. A few academics, such as West, Wilson, Carter, Randall Kennedy of Harvard Law School, and Julius Lester at the University of Massachusetts, explore a middle ground, one which acknowledges the powerful effects of centuries of white oppression but stops short of calling for racially determined preferences and which seeks to establish common cause with potential allies to enact programs that would be broadly beneficial but with particular relevance to black Americans. Much of this dialogue can be found in the pages of two quarterly publications: *Reconstruction,* established by Kennedy in 1992, and the *American Prospect,* started in 1990.

BLACK POLITICAL UNITY IN THE JACKSONIAN ERA

Jesse Jackson tested the theories of black political unity in his 1984 campaign for the Democratic presidential nomination, and then pushed them to the limit in 1988. Jackson's campaigns were based on three premises. The first was that a positive racial appeal to black Americans would translate into increased turnouts and Jackson votes. Although Jackson spoke of "rainbows" and frequently appeared with white strikers, white farmers, or white feminists, he would not have been taken seriously without mobilizing black voters. Jackson built his base on support from black churches. In 1984 black voters cast 18 percent of all Democratic primary votes, and Jackson received 77 percent of them. (Walter Mondale got 19 percent.)[29] In 1988 black turnout increased to 21 percent of primary votes, an astounding 92 percent of which went to Jackson.[30] This means that two-thirds of Jackson's 6.7 millions votes were black votes, and that he captured about one of every eight white votes (although many of those came in the late primaries, when Governor Michael Dukakis was "the last white man standing"). As Brooklyn Representative Shirley Chisholm demonstrated in her brief 1976 campaign for the presidential nomination, the novelty of blackness alone is insufficient to earn such support.

The second premise of the Jackson campaign strategy was that he would be treated by the press and his fellow candidates, not as someone vying for the American presidency, but as the representative of black America. In a remarkable post-convention interview, Jackson claimed to be the carrier of "the emotions and self-respect and inner security of the whole race." "Historically," he said, "we did not spiritually unify Blacks of different ideological persuasions. . . . We are molding our community together."[31] Jackson suggested that black voters supported him because he "best articulated their feelings, views and interests. . . . I represent a chance for our children to make a breakthrough to make America better. Through a lifetime of service and struggle, I have earned [black] support." In May, 1984 *Time* magazine acknowledged Jackson's special status in an effusive cover story:

> Because of his color, and because he was never given a realistic chance of winning the nomination, Jackson has been treated differently from other candidates. His rivals dealt with him gingerly, hoping not to alienate potential black support in the fall. The press concentrated on his vivid campaign style and rarely challenged his positions on the issues.[32]

The press ignored or sidestepped actions, lapses, and statements by Jackson that would have been subjected to frenzied investigation and reporting had they been associated with a potential white nominee. For example, only spotty attention was paid to Jackson's exploitation of Martin Luther King's assassination. Jackson had claimed, falsely, to have been conversing with King when he was shot and that he bloodied his shirt cradling King until the ambulance arrived. Jackson then hopped a plane to Chicago and arranged an appearance on the next day's *The Today Show* on which he wore the stained shirt. He was able to avoid close scrutiny by the press concerning the management and financial administration of PUSH and Operation Breadbasket, two organizations Jackson created and led, despite evidence of carelessness, if not nonfeasance.[33] Jackson also escaped criticism for his foreign policies, which emphasized support for notoriously unpopular figures such as Fidel Castro and PLO Chairman Yassir Arafat. He went far beyond the common Democratic opposition to Reagan-Bush support of the Nicaraguan Contras to extend enthusiastic support to the discredited Sandinista regime.

There was a consistent and important exception to the pattern of deference paid to Jackson: American Jews—individually and organizationally—were quick to criticize Jackson on two counts—that he was pro-Palestinian, if not anti-Israeli; and that he drew support from anti-Semitic black nationalists, most particularly the Nation of Islam's leader, Louis Farrakhan. (Jews on the Left, it should be noted, were among Jackson's most fervent white allies.) During the 1984 campaign, his relations with Farrakhan and Jackson's reference to New York City as "Hymie town" were the only issues on which Jackson was hammered by the press in the same way, for example, that Gary Hart was pursued on marital infidelity or Senator Joe Biden was discredited for law school plagiarism.

The third premise of the Jackson campaign strategy was that the Democratic nominating process could be used to advance his personal ambition to succeed King as the embodiment of black America. Unlike his primary opponents, Jackson was not bound by the imperatives that prevail for a candidate truly seeking the nomination. This freedom, when combined with the pervasive timidity of the party's liberal elite about race and its allied issues, gave Jackson enormous room to maneuver.

Both Walter Mondale and Michael Dukakis understood the dangers of Jackson's visibility and demands, but neither was prepared to address them in a direct and effective way. Both men tried to appear strong and "presidential" in their negotiations about the vice presidency, platform issues, and Jackson's convention role. In the end, however, they acted in ways which connoted weakness, a fatal impression for someone seeking the presidency. Jackson was given a prominent role in the 1984 convention, but then refused to endorse Mondale until after Labor Day. Although Mondale insisted that he was not negotiating with Jackson, Jackson's support did not come until after a meeting at which Mondale agreed to campaign patronage, a "black" foreign policy speech, and emphasis on certain domestic issues.[34] Mondale seemed unable to run his own party and was tarred as the candidate of special interests because of his public deals, not only with Jackson, but with feminists, unions, and Jews. Yet before the convention, a New York Times/CBS poll reported that black Americans preferred Mondale over Jackson by a 53 to 31 margin.[35]

Between the 1984 and 1988 campaigns, Jackson offered ample evidence that his political interests were better described as racial rather than Democratic. During the Reagan years, the most powerful institutional defender of civil rights laws and enforcement was the House Judiciary Committee, chaired by Watergate hero and civil rights advocate, Peter Rodino of Newark. Yet in 1986, Jesse Jackson tried to unseat Rodino, supporting instead a black county official named Donald Payne in the primary. Two years later, after Rodino retired, Payne ran but was opposed in the primary by a black city councilman. This time, Jackson's racial interests were served by neutrality—Payne was not deserving of his endorsement.

In 1988, as the Democratic National Convention drew near, Jackson put Michael Dukakis on the defensive. Jackson learned from a reporter, not from the Dukakis campaign, that he would not be the vice presidential nominee. Jackson used this slight to mount a campaign among black audiences, even though the convention was less than a week away and he stood no mathematical chance of blocking the Dukakis nomination. He replayed his rejection before the NAACP convention, and then went off on a three-day bus trip to Atlanta, during which he suggested a deal to guarantee his role in a Dukakis administration. Only on the eve of the convention did Jackson back off in a private meeting with the nominee.[36] But the damage was done. Jackson had played to a powerful emotion among black Americans by "dissing" a powerful white man and getting away with it.

The fervent and enthusiastic cries that rang out from black churches on Jackson's preannouncement crusades matched those words fervently spoken by Republican strategists for Ronald Reagan and then George Bush: "Run, Jesse, run!" Jackson's high-profile campaign and his mobilization of black voters, particularly in the South, were a perfect prelude for sweeping Republican victories in November. Black political unity at its height under Jackson was one more "gift" from the Democrats that helped to ensure the Republican hold on the White House and the election of two presidents hostile to the politics and policies favored by most black voters.

BLACK VOTER PREFERENCES

Jesse Jackson's attempt at harnessing the black vote is only to be expected: As a whole, blacks tend to vote uniformly more than any other group. Many speak easily of the "black community," as if one could generalize about 30 million Americans of color. However, an HBO/Joint Center for Economic and Political Studies poll found 73 percent of blacks identifying themselves as Democrats, while only 4 percent said they were Republicans.[37] In presidential elections since 1964, black support for the Democratic candidate has ranged from 82 percent for Clinton to 96 percent for Johnson, who was the only Democrat to carry a majority of white voters. In comparison, white Americans are just about evenly split between Democratic (36 percent), Republican (33 percent), and independent (31 percent).[38]

The reason black Americans support Democrats is obvious: blacks are much more likely to support government activism, because black

Americans are twice as likely as white Americans to be employed by government, three times more likely to live below the official definition of poverty, and seven times more likely to be on welfare. In the 1992 election, black voters gave noticeably greater weight to education and health care issues in casting their votes than did other voters, and much less attention to the deficit, abortion, and the environment.[39] When addressing problems such as inadequate health care, joblessness, and drug addiction, black Americans are more likely than whites to favor government guarantees promising to take care of everyone seeking treatment or work.

Because of the black community's overwhelming preference for Democratic politicians since 1964, many Republicans have stopped competing for black support. Republicans assume no risk by emphasizing racially charged issues such as crime, welfare, and quotas, nor by building an all-white southern party. By contrast, until Bill Clinton's 1992 campaign, Democrats responded as if there were vigorous competition for black votes that required special attention to the issues promoted by black leaders. The result of such efforts was a net loss of votes.

GIVING AND TAKING ADVANTAGE

Politics rewards those whose interests are well organized and intensely held. For example, the National Rifle Association's 2.5 million members have regularly stopped the enactment of laws favored by four-fifths of Americans. Lyndon Johnson by contrast carried polls in his back pocket that showed 65 percent support for his Vietnam policies, but this support was passive and unorganized, while the opposition was motivated, organized, and fervent—and it brought him down. The success of organized, motivated interests is also demonstrated by the activities of ethnic, religious, and racial groups. Considering the American tradition of ethnic consciousness and exploitation, it is no wonder that black Americans have heeded calls for racial unity against a history much crueler than anything faced by American Irish or Jews. Black entry into the councils of the national Democratic party was earned in ways similar to those of other ethnic groups: appeals to unity based on shared resentments and aspirations, concentrated votes in key electoral states, control of job and contract-dispensing positions. Like politicians everywhere, black politicians bluffed about their ability to deliver or withhold crucial votes and used the bluff to extract personal and organizational advantage.

This is an old and honorable game in Democratic politics. What makes the liberal-black exchange different is that it is not based on mutual political advantage. The exchange is not based on mutual respect, because there is so little.

THE SIMPLE POLITICAL ARITHMETIC OF RACE

On April 1, 1990, the decennial census found 29,986,000 Americans who classified themselves as "black" and 218,724,000 who did not. The ratio of blacks to nonblacks was 1 to 7. In 1992, after presidential campaigns by Jesse Jackson in 1984 and 1988, and considerable public emphasis on voter registration, exit surveys of voters estimated that black Americans cast about 8 percent of the votes for president.[40] For twenty years, liberal Democrats have campaigned to increase racial awareness, to make strong and specific appeals to black Americans as blacks, and to arouse black resentments about problems visited most heavily on black families.

The political problem with this type of approach is that there simply are not enough black votes to make it worthwhile. If Americans are forced to think in terms of black and white, black will lose every time.

Presidential campaigns are decided on the issue of leadership, and this contest takes place in the center of the American political spectrum. Liberal Democratic candidates demonstrate time and again that they cannot lead their party to a strong coalition, so why should anyone expect that they could handle the much more complex challenges of leading the nation? At precisely the time they should have been healing the wounds of the primary season and building support for their platform on a national basis, they responded to demands that the losers be given a share of the victory. In both 1984 and 1988, Jackson, a far superior orator to either Mondale or Dukakis, was given his own prime-time opportunity to remind American voters vividly and memorably what American voters already knew: the Democrats were the party of the poor, the dispossessed, the homeless, the disabled, and the pressure was on the party to do even more. Just when Democrats needed to forcefully remind working- and middle-class voters that they were more likely than the Republicans to look out for their economic interests, they were instead reinforcing their appeal to people who were either highly likely to vote for Democrats or not to vote at all.

CONCLUSION

The political isolation of black America is accompanied by the rhetorical shrillness emanating from the visible black leadership, a leadership that benefits from such isolation. The dangers of the political isolation of black Americans are beginning to be appreciated by black and white progressives alike. Academics such as Wilson, Kennedy, and West have written about the need for stronger coalitions across racial lines, for greater honesty in public debate, and for recognition of the appalling costs of family dissolution. Yet, the prevailing orthodoxy of racial unity and white demonology is powerful enough that 29 percent of black New Yorkers are willing to imagine that their national government would invent and disseminate the AIDS virus to eliminate black Americans.[41]

There is an answer to the problem of black isolation: more politics; that is, better politics by white Americans and black Americans alike. The search for common ground—which is the purpose of politics— requires the honest statement of interests and differences. White liberals and black liberals need to respect the process enough to use it to mutual advantage. They need to determine which problems are best explained by racial discrimination and which are not; but most of all, they need to respect each other enough to speak directly, courteously, and seriously about the issues. The results will not be surprising, except to those who deny the purposes and efficacy of politics in the American Republic.

6»

THE HIGH COSTS OF
CONSERVATIVE RULE

Conservative Republicans were, for most of this century, a quaint group in American politics. They were tagged as the fathers of the Great Depression with telling effect by Democrats; they whined about big government and deficit spending, and terrorized the nation with tall tales about a domestic communist conspiracy. Conservatives were mostly white, Protestant residents of small towns, and they had limited political power. Even in the Republican party it was liberal Republicans who usually decided who would run for president on the GOP ticket.

Then, in 1964 the conservatives took over the Republican party and nominated Arizona's Barry Goldwater, "Mr. Conservative," as their presidential candidate. The debris was everywhere after the 1964 elections: LBJ took 61 percent of the vote and carried all but five states. Fifty-two percent of Americans identified themselves as Democrats; only 25 percent labeled themselves Republican.[1] Polls showed that the bipartisan civil rights agenda was widely supported; Goldwater, who had opposed the measures, represented a defeated, isolated minority. In the weeks following his defeat, the label "conservative Republican" seemed to move from "quaint" to "endangered." The *New York Times*'s James Reston, the nation's most influential political commentator, summarized what would quickly become the popular wisdom: "Barry Goldwater not only lost the Presidential election . . . but the conservative cause as well. He has

117

wrecked his party for a long time to come."[2] Not quite. The Republicans
went on to take the White House in five of the seven subsequent elections.

Moreover, in 1980, conservative Republicans demonstrated their
mastery of coalition politics with the election of Ronald Reagan. His
landslide reelection in 1984 and George Bush's victory in 1988 proved
that, in sixteen years, conservatives had progressed from laughingstock to
unbeatable. The 1994 midterm elections, which gave the GOP control
of Congress for the first time in forty years, suggested that Bill Clinton's
1992 presidential victory was an aberration that would not be repeated
in 1996.

THE SOURCES OF THE CONSERVATIVE RENEWAL

It is important to understand how a conservative majority was built
in such a relatively short period of time. Clearly, it could not have been
done without the complicity of the liberal elite that took over the
Democratic party in 1972. But liberal timidity and hubris, by themselves,
were not enough. The conservative ascendancy was propelled by
race-freighted issues as well as the shocks to the American economy felt
during the 1970s. Beyond that, conservatives were active intellectually,
aggressive in broadening their narrow electoral base, and well financed.

CONSERVATIVES IN THE WHITE SOUTH

In 1991 Thomas B. and Mary D. Edsall began their definitive analysis of the economic, cultural, and political forces that framed the destruction of the Democratic coalition with the 1964 Goldwater campaign.
Race—specifically a visceral defense of segregation—was at the heart of
Goldwater's sweep of the Deep South. As the Edsalls argued, however, the
Goldwater candidacy offered the segregationist southerner something
more than old-style white supremacy:

> Goldwater's success demonstrated that conservative ideology
> provided a new avenue for the Republican party into the South,
> an avenue that permitted the GOP to carry the most anti-black
> segment of the nation without facing public condemnation. For
> a substantial segment of the white South, conservatism became
> a cloak with which to protect racial segregation. At the same

time, in a development that would soon have national relevance, Goldwater demonstrated that the socioeconomic class
structure of the New Deal alignment in the deep South could be
fractured by the issue of race. . . . [T]he issue of race actually
produced an ideological conversion of poor southern whites
from a deeply held economic liberalism to economic conservatism.[3]

Goldwater set the stage for the South. Kevin Phillips laid out in
microscopic detail the blueprint for the long-term takeover of the white
South by conservative Republicans in his 1969 book, *The Emerging
Republican Majority*. He accurately observed, "Now that the *national*
Democratic Party is becoming the Negro party throughout . . . the South,
the alienation of white [George C.] Wallace voters is likely to persist."[4]
Phillips instructed Republicans on the acrobatics required for expanding
their political base in the South: "Maintenance of Negro voting rights is
essential to the GOP. Unless Negroes continue to displace white
Democratic organizations, the latter may remain viable as spokesmen for
Deep Southern conservatism."[5]

Republicans were perfectly positioned to take advantage of the large,
rapid changes in public opinion as the televised image of black America
shifted from that of prayerful victims of racist southern police to that of
rioters and looters.

CONSERVATIVES VERSUS THE GREAT SOCIETY

Outside the South, conservatives began their climb out of the hole
dug by the Goldwater debacle simply by showing up. In the 1966 elections, twenty of the forty-seven Democratic freshmen who had been elected on LBJ's coattails were defeated in traditionally conservative districts
by generally conservative Republicans. The pattern was national, with
Democratic losses particularly heavy in Iowa, Michigan, and Ohio.[6]
Daniel Moynihan said the 1966 elections indicated that "the recent period of accelerated, intensive innovation is over," and that the elections
were a "clear instruction to elected officials everywhere that the country
has gone about as far as it wishes in providing social welfare and economic assistance to the Negro masses."[7]

In opposing Great Society experiments such as the War on Poverty,
conservatives appealed to white working-class Democrats who wanted to

keep black northerners "in their place."[8] Conservatives never promised to maintain segregation, but they vociferously opposed any Democratic efforts to orchestrate a new political balance of power in northern cities. Liberals had sought to break down the barriers to high-paying unionized construction jobs for blacks (although never with the enthusiasm of Nixon's labor secretary, George Shultz), to protect young black men from arbitrary arrest and harassment by white cops, to bus black kids into schools in other neighborhoods, and to build houses for poor families in working-class neighborhoods. These policies ran headlong into the interests and strongly held beliefs of many working-class Democrats. Conservatives opposed LBJ's "social engineering," expanded procedural rights for criminal defendants, "forced" school busing, and expanded public housing. Conservative views paralleled those of whites who feared or disliked black Americans.

CONSERVATIVES AND LAW AND ORDER

Rising crime rates that coincided with the Great Society strengthened the conservative appeal to fearful whites. As liberals tried to excuse and explain rising crime rates and ghetto riots, conservatives talked about law and order and "bleeding heart" judges. As it turned out, conservatives knew what to say about crime, but not what to do about it. They blamed liberal judges for freeing criminals on technicalities and succeeded over time in stripping judges of sentencing discretion. Republicans declared one war after another—against crime in Washington, crime in the streets, drugs every place—and lost them all. Ironically, they opposed federal programs to help police departments add patrols and new technologies and steadfastly opposed control of handguns. Conservatives celebrated the return of capital punishment; they spent billions on futile attempts to close the nation's borders to drugs but showed little inclination to expand drug treatment opportunities. Republican presidential candidates emphasized crime-fighting as if they were running for police commissioner or mayor.

The conservatives' failed policies and false promises did not hurt them with the voters, however, because liberals gave them a free ride on the issue of crime. As seen in Chapter 3, liberals initially denied that crime was increasing and then suggested that crime could not be fought directly until the "underlying causes" had been removed. They claimed that anyone who even brought the subject up was a fear-mongering race-baiter. By the time liberals realized their error, their credibility on the issue was badly damaged.

POPULAR PERCEPTION OF CULTURAL TURMOIL

Along with the breakdown in law and order, conservatives were helped by the growing debate about social and cultural standards. As the various baby boom revolutions—civil rights, sexual freedom, drug experimentation, educational freedom—erupted, matters that heretofore were considered within the preserve of private conduct became raging public issues. The situation on college campuses was intense. Universities were physically occupied, professors and presidents shouted down with obscenities from the children of the prospering middle-class. When S. I. Hayakawa, the professor-president of San Francisco State College, insisted that the free speech rights be preserved for all persons, not just antiwar protesters and Black Power advocates, he rode his fame to a seat in the United States Senate.

Women rebelled. Feminists fought for the cause of college-educated women whose careers were blocked by male stereotyping and conventions about a woman's "place." Housewives went to work to preserve their family's standard of living. Lawsuits opened "men's work" to women in construction, policing, sales, and management.

The most personal territories became legal battlegrounds: the U.S. Supreme Court granted constitutional protection to abortion and restricted the powers of states and towns to suppress pornography. States liberalized divorce laws, reducing legal separation periods and expanding the grounds for divorce. Homosexuals came out of the closet, demanding protection from police harassment and discrimination. Feminists, homosexuals, and abortion rights' advocates lined up with the Democrats; traditionalists and antipornography, antiabortion, "pro-family" advocates went with the Republicans.

The cultural revolution drove millions of Americans who had previously allied their economic interests with the Democratic party to see the Republican party as the protector of stability, civility, and good sense. Because the Democrats offered no coherent or credible vision for curbing inflation and ending stagnation, the transition to the Republican party was made easier. Author Charles Morris summarized the 1960s this way:

> The revolution had become tawdry and, even worse, boring. . . .
> Blacks were still an underclass, and the war was raging. . . .[M]ost
> of the country was tiring of the revolutionaries' antics. One of
> the few political achievements of the radicals, in fact, may have

been twice to ensure the election of Richard Nixon as President of the United States.[9]

Liberals were warned. In 1967 Moynihan, then a director of the Americans for Democratic Action, spoke to the ADA's annual conference, urging liberals to make league with conservatives who shared an interest in the "stability of the social order," and who recognized that "unyielding rigidity is just as much a threat to the continuity of things as an anarchic desire for change."[10] Unfortunately, most liberals were afraid to acknowledge that a problem even existed. Richard Scammon and Ben Wattenberg criticized Democrats in 1970 for confusing the cultural revolution with political opportunity:

> In all: [the electorate is] unyoung, unpoor, unblack. Furthermore, the young and the poor are unmonolithic in their Presidential voting behavior. Six in seven voters are over thirty. Nine out of ten are unpoor. Nine out of ten are white. Because there is some duplication . . . a fair guess is . . . that seven of ten American voters are neither young, nor poor, nor black.
>
> Lesson: Talk about building a powerful "new political coalition" whose major components are all the young, all the poor, all the blacks doesn't make much electoral sense.
>
> Reprieve: That the electorate is unyoung, unpoor, and unblack does not mean they are antiyoung, antipoor, or antiblack.[11]

Scammon and Wattenburg were dismissed as "neoconservatives."

THE BATTLE OF IDEAS

William F. Buckley started the *National Review* in 1955 as an organ of conservative commentary and letters—a *New Republic* of the Right— and quickly established himself as the leading voice of American conservatives. His was a lonely voice, however, because most respected political analysis and commentary came from liberals.

With the quickening changes of the 1960s, Lyndon Johnson used financing approaches that had not been tested to try to solve problems that had not been well defined. In 1965 a group of northeastern intellectuals—most of them Democrats—began the *Public Interest,* a lively quarterly journal that concentrated on the domestic issues that swirled around the Great Society. In its infancy, there was nothing particularly conservative about the journal's editors or contributors, except their willingness to debate questions that liberals shunned. They wrote convincingly about the place of family and community values, the demographics of crime, standards of civility, and the limits of government guarantees. James Q. Wilson opened the issue marking the journal's twentieth anniversary with these words: "The most important change in how one defines the public interest that I have witnessed . . . over the last twenty years has been a deepening concern for the development of character in the citizenry."[12] By 1985 such sentiments were owned by conservatives.

The neoconservative provocations went largely unchallenged by liberal Democrats. One could argue that neoconservatism's purpose was not to oppose liberalism, but rather to reinvigorate it with a moral purpose that would strengthen America's great innovation—self-government. Irving Kristol, a founder and co-editor of *Public Interest*, put it in these terms:

> Our revolutionary message . . . is that a self-disciplined people can create a political community in which an ordered liberty will promote both economic prosperity and political participation. To the teeming masses of other nations, the American political tradition says: To enjoy the fruits of self-government, you must first cease being "masses" and become a "people" attached to a common way of life, sharing common values, and existing in a condition of mutual trust and sympathy as between individuals and even social classes.[13]

The nation's business leadership had always been conservative, and its public philosophy was easily stated—lower taxes, less regulation. Free market advocates, however, were badly underrepresented in Washington policy debates through the 1960s. This began to change with the emergence of the American Enterprise Institute (AEI), under the leadership of William Baroody. One of the original "policy entrepreneurs," Baroody understood that ideas had to be packaged and marketed, and he knew the Washington market. AEI attracted conservative stars such as Irving Kristol, Melvin Laird (a former Wisconsin representative who became President Nixon's defense secretary), and, in 1977, former President Gerald Ford. AEI became a center of policy discussion aimed at demonstrating the inefficiencies and costs of government regulation to opinion leaders and legislators. By the early 1980s, Baroody had succeeded in providing a forum for what writer James Allen Smith called "a conservative counterelite."[14]

The idea that federal regulation was hindering economic growth and job creation and adding needless costs became so powerful by the mid-1970s that the Carter administration initiated the deregulation of the airline, energy, banking, and trucking industries.

In the early 1970s, the conservative base was widened after the emergence of the self-described New Right, led by Paul Weyrich, the founder of the Committee for the Survival of a Free Congress; Edwin Feulner, the founder of the Heritage Foundation; Richard Viguerie, George Wallace's direct-mail wizard; and Kevin Phillips, the political geographer from Nixon's 1968 presidential campaign. The New Right sought to convert the economic, racial, cultural, and social resentments of working- and lower-middle-class whites into votes for a conservative revolution. Weyrich and Feulner saw the Heritage Foundation as the source of ideas for militant conservatives dedicated to overturning the social revolutions of the 1960s and defeating the liberal "elite."

While free market and libertarian conservatives pushed to "get government off people's backs," a strident and energetic New Right argued for government intrusion on the most personal decisions. In 1973 New Right leaders enlisted the support of a Virginia preacher, Jerry Falwell, and persuaded him to mobilize evangelical Christians who were angered by the 1973 Roe v. Wade decision legalizing abortion.[15] The Moral Majority was born. It advocated prohibition of abortion and contraception and government scrutiny of libraries, newsstands, record stores, and cinemas.

The New Right wanted prosecutorial powers used to ferret out violators of long-forgotten sodomy and fornication laws. They opposed feminism, homosexuality, and pre- and extramarital sex, and campaigned to require state-sanctioned prayer in public schools. By 1992 the New Right was strong enough to dictate the Republican platform on abortion, school prayer, family values, and illegitimacy.

By 1975, then, conservative thinkers and activists were pushing their ideas on a broad front. What they lacked was a cohesive economic policy that went beyond support for free markets, lower taxation, and deregulation and that could be sold to middle-class voters as an antidote to lagging productivity, high inflation, and high jobless rates.

REAGANOMICS

Since the 1920s, conservative Republicans offered a consistent and unappetizing economic philosophy. Its most noticeable feature was a tiresome whine about the dangers of deficit spending. Even as the American economy dominated the world and created history's largest middle class, conservatives persisted in their dour sermonizing. The conservative view was shrunken, negative, and considered irrelevant by most voters—until the 1980 presidential campaign of Ronald Reagan.

Reagan's campaign had several enormous advantages. The incumbent president, Jimmy Carter, was fumbling, unpopular, and immobilized by the Iranian hostage crisis and a stagnant economy with record-high inflation. Reagan offered an economic plan that promised a sharp reduction in taxes *and* a balanced budget. Republicans had somehow squared the circle: everyone would receive a 30 percent reduction in their federal income tax rate and—not to worry—federal deficits would be eliminated by 1984. That was the promise, one that George Bush labeled "voodoo economics."

The salesman for supply-side politics was Jack Kemp, a retired professional quarterback and New York congressman. He convinced Reagan to adopt it as the economic centerpiece of his 1980 campaign. Supply-side's publicist was Jude Wanniski, an editorial writer for the *Wall Street Journal,* which turned its op-ed pages into a continuous billboard for radical tax-rate cuts. The problem facing the supply-side enthusiasts was obvious. If tax collections declined by $150 billion, while military expenditures shot up, a large, recurring budget deficit would result. Coming to supply-side's rescue, Wanniski produced a heretofore unknown California economist, Arthur Laffer, who had the solution: the Laffer Curve. Based on flimsy theory and little documentation, the Laffer Curve postulated that marginal tax rates were so high and smothering of enterprise that their sharp reduction would set off economic growth; in turn, this growth would generate tax revenues sufficient to offset the revenue loss from the tax cuts.

Few liberal economists attacked supply-side theory. Walter Heller, the economic advisor to Kennedy and Johnson, documented that Kemp's frequent references to the favorable impact of the 1962 tax cut on federal revenues conveniently ignored the stimulative effect of the Vietnam buildup.[16] Inexplicably, no one joined his attack. Thomas Edsall described the shell-shocked Democratic party: "[The] economic crisis was the essential factor in the ideological and intellectual collapse of the Democratic party, creating substantive problems that the party was both unequipped and unprepared to address."[17]

THE DELETERIOUS EFFECTS OF DEFICIT SPENDING

The real objective of the radical supply-siders was to cripple the broad consensus about the role of government in American society. Cautious supply-siders opposed large deficits, proposing sharp reductions in government spending. Radical supply-siders saw structural deficits as the best means to bring government to heel: First, slash taxes; then, exploit the dangers of the resultant deficits to constrain and even dismantle federal domestic programs. The radicals won. In Reagan's eight years, the national debt tripled from a little more than $900 billion to almost $3 trillion.

Once again, it was Daniel Patrick Moynihan who most clearly stated what was being tried. Even though he voted "yea" as New York's senior senator on the 1981 tax cuts, Moynihan was quick to see the implications of the Republican program. In September 1981 he said of the zealots in the new administration: "This new group . . . is like nothing we have seen. They are to conservatives as anarchists are to liberals."[18] And, he asked: "Do we really want a decade in which *the* issue of public discourse, over and over and over, will be how big must the budget cuts be in order to prevent the deficit from being even higher?"[19]

The intentions of the radical supply-siders are a matter of public record: David Stockman, Reagan's first-term budget director, confessed all—first to William Greider of the *Washington Post*, and then in his 1986 memoirs. Stockman knew that the only way Reagan could deliver on his promise of tax cuts, huge increases in defense spending, and a balanced budget was to moderate Pentagon increases, shave Social Security and Medicare benefits, and "zero out" a variety of other domestic programs. But Reagan refused to go along with anything but symbolic cuts in the military. And, as Greider observed, "one politician who scurried away from the President's proposed cuts in Social Security was the president."[20] Reagan's retreat was encouraged by the 96 to 0 vote in the Republican-controlled Senate against his proposal to cut Social Security. Similarly, when Stockman proposed reducing or eliminating subsidies for timber, farming, manufacturing, and energy—in the interests of eliminating "weak claims," not "weak clients"—he lost every fight to conservative Republicans.

Stockman was desperate to cover the huge gap opened up by the tax cuts and military spending increases. He resorted to wildly unrealistic economic assumptions, phantom spending cuts (Stockman called these "reductions to be determined later"), and blind faith in the willingness of politicians to act against the interests of their constituents. Stockman confessed to Greider: "None of us really understands what's going on with all these numbers."[21] The budget of the U. S. Government was out of control! In his memoirs, Stockman characterized Reaganomics in these terms:

> The Reagan Revolution was radical, imprudent, and arrogant. It defied the settled consensus of professional politicians and economists on its two central assumptions. It mistakenly presumed that a handful of ideologues were right and all the politicians were wrong about what the American people wanted from government. And it erroneously assumed that the . . . inflation-swollen U.S. economy . . . could be instantly healed when history and most professional economists said it couldn't be.[22]

The radical supply-siders were unrepentant (and still are). Paul Craig Roberts, a supply-side purist, blamed Stockman for exaggerating the deficit to aggrandize his role as budget director.[23] Stockman was also accused of being a mole for the "balanced budget Republicans" who had flailed for decades against deficits. Ten years later, when the federal debt had ballooned by $2.6 trillion, Kemp accepted no blame for the deficits and worried little about what to do about them. In a memo to Bush's campaign managers, excerpts of which found their way to the *Wall Street Journal*, Kemp and his six congressional colleagues had a number of startling recommendations:

▲ Reduce income tax rates on all working families. The . . . rate should be cut across the board, dropping the 15% rate to 12%, and capping the top rate at 28%.

▲ Phase in an increase in the personal exemption . . . to help relieve the tax burden on families. Our ultimate goal should be to restore the exemptions to the Truman levels, which in current dollars would be over $6,000.

▲ Reduce the capital gains tax to a maximum of 15% [from 28] and to zero for long term investments.

▲ Index the capital gains tax . . . to end the confiscatory practice of taxing illusory gains caused by inflation.[24]

Kemp's proposals were astounding for their audacity. The Kemp package would have reduced federal revenues by scores of billions, just as the deficit was approaching the $300 billion mark, but Kemp bet that a promise of debt-financed prosperity was good politics.

Recently, the "miracle" of such Reaganomics has trickled down to the state level. I was elected to the New Jersey State Senate in 1993 along with a new Republican governor, Christine Todd Whitman, who won a narrow victory over an unpopular Democratic incumbent, Jim Florio. She attributed her 26,000 vote plurality to her proposal for a Reaganesque 30 percent cut in the state's income tax rates. By proceeding in her first year to implement her promise, she attained celebrity status among Republicans. Like Reagan, Whitman refused to finance her tax cut with offsetting reductions in state spending, but instead deferred contributions to public employee retirement funds—thus putting off the pain until after she would be safely out of office.

ALTERING THE GOVERNMENT COMPACT

America elected revolutionaries in 1980. The Reaganites were as blindly committed to laissez-faire economics as any Great Society bureaucrat ever was to the efficacy of government initiatives. To be sure, in many cases regulation had gone too far: manufacturers of waffle irons had to warn buyers against closing the lid on their hands; the Interstate Commerce Commission ordained how many truckers could serve the Fort Wayne-Atlanta market, what they could haul, and what they could charge.

True, government was a nettlesome intruder at times, but it had always represented the compact among Americans regarding the balance that should be struck among competing interests. Politics before Reagan reflected a broad consensus that prosperity required both private and public investment. For most of the twentieth century, that consensus favored taxes that were based on ability to pay. Americans wanted government to protect bank depositors; to make home ownership affordable and higher education accessible; to ensure safe water and clean the air. Part of the compact was that government would help the striving poor and take care of those who could not work because of disability, age, or other incapacity. These were the tenets that most Americans subscribed to before Reagan's election, and their implementation helped explain the breadth of the postwar prosperity.

President Reagan wanted to alter the compact. He sought to trim Social Security, cut back on help to poor mothers, reduce aid for colleges and college students, eliminate government employment as a last resort, end general assistance to local governments for transit and crime control, cut back food stamps and nutrition programs for the near-poor, and charge "users" for many government programs. Ultimately, the American people said "no" to many of his proposed cuts. Interestingly, the Republican-controlled Senate was less accommodating to Reagan's cuts than the Democrat-controlled House. David Stockman concluded that there was no such thing as a "conservative Republican" in Congress, and that the American people were opposed to the antigovernment ideology of Reagan's friends:

> The actual electorate . . . is not interested in this doctrine; when it is interested at all, it is interested in getting help from the government to compensate for a perceived disadvantage. Consequently, the spending politics of Washington do reflect the heterogeneous and parochial demands that arise from the diverse, activated . . . electorate across the land. What you see done in the halls of the politicians may not be wise, but it is the only real and viable definition of what the electorate wants.[25]

Reagan's free-market, antistatist doctrine was not accepted by Republicans advancing the interests of timber companies and Boeing. The defenses mounted to protect opportunities for poor and working class Americans, however, were less effective.

THE REAGAN REVOLUTION AND THE STRUCTURE OF OPPORTUNITY

The tension between liberty and equality, between individual enterprise and community need is the classic dynamic in American democracy. Alexis de Tocqueville observed in the 1830s:

> Although private interest directs the greater part of human actions in the United States . . . it does not regulate them all. I must say that I have often seen Americans make great and real sacrifices to the public welfare; and I have noticed a hundred instances in which they hardly ever failed to lend faithful support

to one another. The free institutions which the inhabitants of the United States possess, and the political right of which they make so much use, remind every citizen, in a thousand ways, that he lives in society. They every instant impress upon his mind the notion that it is the duty as well as the interest of men to make themselves useful to their fellow creatures.[26]

Tocqueville noted strong support for public education. He observed that even the backwoodsman "is acquainted with the past, curious about the future, and ready for argument about the present; he is, in short, a highly civilized human being." Tocqueville concluded that "the instruction of the people powerfully contributes to the support of the democratic republic."[27]

This is the essential spirit that Reagan and his zealots deprecated. They saw government not as a compact among citizens and their representatives regarding what needed to be done together for the future of the nation, but as an alien force run by elitist conspirators. Two minutes into his presidency, Reagan said "government is not the solution to our problem; government is the problem." As John Kenneth Galbraith noted, this premise is the first of three supporting what the economist termed the "culture of contentment": "there must be a doctrine that offers a feasible presumption against government intervention." Second, he argued, the culture requires a "social justification for the untrammeled, uninhibited pursuit and possession of wealth." The third need, Galbraith contended, is to "justify a reduced sense of public responsibility for the poor. Those . . . members of the . . . underclass, must . . . be seen as the architects of their own fate."[28] And, of course, conservative intellectuals were inspired to demonstrate the latter point, first by casting doubt on the efficacy and thoughtfulness of antipoverty programs; then by arguing that government assistance actually made the problems worse. The chief proponent of this latter view was Charles Murray, author of the 1984 best seller, *Losing Ground*.

Conservatives rationalized their agenda, an attack on the structure of opportunity, with a logic as follows:

> *Whereas* (Affirmative action) (Job Training) (Head Start) (Any tax-supported antipoverty program) has not helped the very poor escape poverty; and
> *Whereas* the striving poor seem to escape the worst indignities of poverty without tax-supported assistance; and

Whereas there is no reliable way to distinguish the persistently poor from the striving poor in any lower-class neighborhood; now, therefore be it

Resolved that the waste of taxpayer funds going to antipoverty programs should halt immediately; and

Further resolved that the poor be informed that the only escape route lies in their individual qualities of self-reliance, perseverance, labor, and thrift.

Neither conservatives nor liberals have convincing explanations for the significant economic progress made by black Americans after 1960. In 1959, 52 percent of black Americans were poor; by the early 1970s the proportion was less than a third. Cities with large black populations suffered the greatest population losses as black families became suburbanites. What happened? The economy had continued to grow and to create jobs, but the government also had a great deal to do with black progress. Employers were forbidden to discriminate against applicants or employees by race; courts interpreted the law in an expansive way, which led many employers to protect themselves by aggressively seeking minority employees; hundreds of thousands of black Americans finished high school and used federal and state government support to attend college, while others joined the military. Conservatives tout these achievements as evidence that black Americans do not require special assistance to move upward, ignoring the role played by direct public employment (black Americans are twice as likely as whites to work for government), higher education aid, and affirmative action. Liberals act as if no progress has been made, lest the will to help those remaining behind should disappear.

Millions of black Americans joined the middle class by taking advantage of opportunities (affirmative action excepted) available to all poor Americans. Blacks are more likely to live in cities, (by 1991, 25.7 percent of whites lived in central cities compared to 56.3 percent of blacks). Blacks are therefore more likely to rely on public services, play in public parks, and take public transit to school or work. They are also more likely to attend public schools, rely on public libraries, and attend public colleges and universities with public scholarships or guaranteed loans. They might live in public or publicly subsidized housing; they rely disproportionately on Medicaid and public hospitals for their health care. These services and programs are open to all poor. Together, they make up the "structure of opportunity": investments in the services and facilities that give poor Americans a fighting chance to escape poverty.

The Reagan and Bush administrations withdrew from the federal-state partnership required to maintain the structure; successive Republican budgets reduced or eliminated federal funding. In no case did federal funding keep pace with inflation, increased demand, or new problems such as the impact of AIDS on public hospitals.

Reagan laid out his vision in his first budget, prepared for the 1983 fiscal year. Building on the $40 billion or so of cuts he achieved in 1981, he proposed a three-year plan that increased military spending by 54.4 percent, while eliminating assistance for public transit, school milk programs, CETA (Comprehensive Employment and Training Act), the Job Corps, work incentive programs, legal services for the poor, acquisition of urban parkland, and family planning. Major reductions in other aid programs were also proposed: Pell Grants—scholarships for poor students—were to be cut by 54.2 percent, work-study aid by 60.9 percent, and funds for education for the disadvantaged by 39.5 percent. Reagan's own inflation assumptions for the three years would have reduced the real value of these programs by another 15.5 percent. With the exception of federal housing programs, however, Congress refused to approve Reagan's drastic reductions.

The ghost of budgets past is alive and well in the Republican Congress that was elected in 1994.

HIGHER EDUCATION

The Republican animus to higher education opportunity—apparent during the Reagan-Bush years and in the Republican-controlled Congress elected in 1994—deserves special attention. A college degree is increasingly what separates Americans who "make it" from those who do not. Accessible and affordable higher education relies on a partnership between the federal government, which provides student grants, guarantees student loans, and supports the high costs of research universities, and state governments, which organize and finance the institutions of higher education that educate about 80 percent of all students. Beginning with the Great Society, the federal government facilitated college education for all Americans who aspired to it. Before then, the national government helped only veterans and those competent in science, engineering, and foreign languages—disciplines connected to national security.

During the 1960s and 1970s, government responded to the baby boomers' growing demand for higher education with new funding, institutions, and flexible admission standards. More than one of four American colleges was established in the decade of the 1970s, including 43 percent of all two-year colleges. At the time, higher education was still affordable for middle-class families. In 1980, for example, the costs of attending a public four-year college represented 7.3 percent of median family income; by 1988 the cost had risen to 12.7 percent. Private colleges and universities also became more inaccessible. In 1980, tuition and residence at a private university took 19.7 percent of median family income; by 1988, it was 39.9 percent.[29]

As higher education costs rose more quickly than family incomes, the policies of the Reagan-Bush administrations contributed to the squeeze in two important ways. First, direct federal support to colleges and universities and to students did not keep pace with inflation. Federal aid to private institutions declined from 18.8 percent of current revenues in 1980 to 15.9 percent in 1989; students were forced to make up the difference through higher tuition and fees. At public institutions, the federal contribution fell from 12.8 percent to 10.3 percent of revenues; tuition funds took up the slack, increasing from 12.9 percent to 15.5 percent.[30]

Congress resisted the cuts Reagan advocated, particularly for student aid; nonetheless, the Reagan and Bush administrations successfully tilted federal aid from grants and direct federal loans to federally guaranteed loans. The effect of this shift was greatest for working- and lower-middle-class families, whose credit capacity became badly strained by borrowing for college. In 1991 the Bush administration went so far as to propose limiting Pell Grants to families with incomes under $10,000. If adopted (it was not), 400,000 recipients would have been eliminated. Meanwhile, the maximum Pell Grant covered less and less of a poor student's tuition costs (the average fell from 41 percent to 26 percent) as the 1980s progressed.[31]

The second, more important shift was President Reagan's success in transferring the pain of his inflated deficit strategy to the states. While ostensibly moving decisions to the "governments closest to the people," Reagan walked away from many traditional federal-state partnerships. Congress attempted to slow the pace and magnitude of devolution, but the combination of reduced federal financing and local tax revolts put most state governments one recession away from serious fiscal trauma. For example, between 1983 and 1991, states responded to federal cuts by increasing funding for need-based scholarships by 68.4 percent (above median family income increases of 43.8 percent). During the 1980s states increased their spending for higher education by 90.7 percent, well ahead of either inflation or comparable federal spending. More students, higher costs, reduced federal assistance, straitened state finances, stagnating family incomes; in this climate, something would have to give. The 1991 recession accelerated trends that were already heading in the wrong direction. The American Council on Education reported with a despondent air in 1992:

> For much of the public sector, basic funding has been cut back abruptly, often despite continuing enrollment increases.
>
> ▲ The majority of colleges and universities in the public sector have had to deal with mid-year budget cuts. . . .
>
> ▲ Taking inflation into account, two-thirds of public institutions lost ground in the last year.
>
> ▲ The most frequently cited effects of recent budget cuts. . . . increased tuition and fees . . . increased class size and fewer sections of courses . . . [and a] freeze on hiring for regular faculty positions.[32]

California, long the global model for access to affordable, high quality post-secondary education, was particularly hard hit by a deep recession, higher demand, higher fees, and fewer course offerings.

A 1991 study by Thomas Kane tried to untangle the discouraging trends in college enrollment and graduation rates for black Americans in the 1980s, particularly the sharp fall-off in the early years of the decade. Kane found (as Adam Smith would have predicted) that higher college costs, matched by lower federal grants and perhaps the increased auditing of family financial information by the Reagan administration led to a decline in the college enrollments of eighteen- and nineteen-year-old, low-income students, both black and white. By 1986 the portion of black high school graduates going on to college had declined to 26.1 percent, from a high of 33.5 percent in 1976; for Latinos it dropped to 26.9 percent, from 35.5 percent (before turning back up in the late 1980s). Meanwhile, white enrollment rates climbed steadily to 41.7 percent in 1991.[33] Moreover, higher costs seem to have discouraged middle-income black students, but not white ones. Kane reports, "The average public tuition at a 4-year university rose by 45% in real terms between 1980 and

1988, while the maximum Pell Grant declined by 13%."[34] Kane concludes that the rebound in black enrollment rates that occurred in the late 1980s was a function of the improved educational backgrounds of black parents, reflecting the sharp increases in high school graduation and college attendance beginning in the 1950s.[35]

As a parenthetical note, one explanation for the fall-off in black college enrollment can be found in the decreasing inclination of black male high school graduates to attend college. A milestone was reached in 1976, when the same percentage of white and black male graduates went onto college (35.4 percent). By 1991 the attendance rate for white males was 42 percent, versus only 32 percent for black graduates (and that was up from a low of 25 percent in 1988).[36] Put another way, whereas white and Latino women made up about 55 percent of white and Latino student body in 1991, black women represented 62 percent of all black college students, a proportion that has grown since the mid-1970s.[37]

The same dynamic that made a college degree more difficult to obtain also affected home ownership. The American dream is not lived out in a rented apartment: the Federal National Mortgage Association confirmed that 80 percent of Americans identify a single-family, detached home with a yard as the ideal place to live and that only a secure retirement ranks higher than owning one's own home as a life goal.[38] Following World War II, the federal government stimulated home ownership: the Veterans Administration (VA) and Federal Housing Administration (FHA) guaranteed mortgages that carried low down-payments and interest rates. The national policy guaranteed accessibility by stimulating supply and subsidizing demand. The effort worked, although because of discriminatory practices by the FHA and real estate agencies, it worked primarily for white families.

In 1970 the median price of a new house was 2.3 times median family income, and the FHA and VA guaranteed 37 percent of all mortgages. By 1990, however, a new house cost 3.4 times median family income, and federal guarantees fell to 18 percent of mortgages. Harvard's Joint Center for Housing Studies found that the median price of a first home for families in the 25-to-29 age range increased by 21 percent between 1970 and 1990, while median income declined by 7 percent (from $28,500 to $26,700). While about one in four married couples under age 25 owned their own house in 1970, the proportion was less than one in six by 1990; for those where the head of household was between 25 and 29 years of age, ownership declined from about 44 percent in 1973 to 35.9 percent in 1990—an 18 percent drop.[39]

The Reagan revolution put both home ownership and higher education out of the reach of an increasing number of Americans.

PRIVATIZING THE PUBLIC SCHOOLS

The Reagan revolutionaries did not confine their efforts to higher education. The previous chapter described the threat to the unity of American society of "multiculturalism." But radical conservatives have been much more effective at diluting the nation's sense of common purpose and shared sacrifice than any multiculturalists. They worship the workings of the marketplace and cast ordinary consumption and investment decisions in the light of high religious purpose. In the hands of radicals such as Reagan, the conservative philosophy confuses the essential nature of government with those of the private corporation or investor. Conservatives do not accept that government exists to do what private enterprise cannot or will not do and to moderate the unacceptable consequences of free market forces. No recent effort better captures this threat than the conservative urge to privatize the common school.

Public education has come under increasing attack from conservative intellectuals for "dumbing down" educational standards and expectations. A national survey by the Reagan administration—"A Nation at Risk"—found American students falling behind the country's economic competitors in their preparation for the global marketplace. The radical Republican solution to this problem is to deflect tax dollars from public schools to parents. "The key to educational reform is greater parental choice," wrote William Kristol, Vice President Dan Quayle's chief policy adviser, "giving parents the ability to choose the schools their children attend by making public schools compete for students and by publicly subsidizing students who choose to attend private schools."[40] Kristol wants to end the monopoly status enjoyed by public schools by helping private and religious schools with public money.

Ironically, parental choice was first proposed by progressives during the Great Society. The Ylvisaker Task Force recommended that "bounties" should be put on the heads of low-income city students—black and white—to make them attractive to private and suburban public schools. Theodore Sizer, then dean at Harvard's education school, wrote: "The children of the poor would be sought by schools, indeed competed for, in that they would bring with them significant additional funds to provide for special and exciting programs." Sizer estimated the cost of the bounty program to be about $16 billion a year (about $71 billion in 1994 dollars), limited as it was to poor children. The proposed bounty would be $6,550 in 1994 dollars.[41] The theory was that poor city kids would benefit educationally by being scattered to schools where upwardly mobile middle-class kids were in the majority.

Conservatives, on the other hand, evince great interest in the problems and prospects of lower-class children only as a means to subsidize private schools. William J. Bennett, the former drug czar and secretary of education, is a particularly visible proponent of privatization and quick to side with poor black kids:

> The strongest case for overhauling the current education system is the lousy education the underclass are [sic] receiving. The underclass are [sic] least able to afford a bad education, since a good education is still the best way out of poverty. . . . I believe that quality education is the central civil rights challenge facing us today. And the best way to improve American education is to support a reform agenda based on parental choice, accountability, merit pay, alternative certification and a solid core curriculum.

Bennett concluded with the tantalizing thought that "poor minority students deserve the same kind of education that upper-class white kids get."[42] When Benno C. Schmidt, Jr., explained his resignation as Yale's president to chair the Edison Project, a venture by Whittle Communications, which plans to open one hundred proprietary schools by 1996, he insisted that poor city kids would be included. The Edison Project, he said,

> . . . will operate at roughly the same per-pupil costs as public education, and will be open to all. It will accept 20% of its students on full scholarship. It will operate in every type of community—rich and poor, urban, suburban, and rural. In inner cities, most students may be on scholarships; in the suburbs few.[43]

The campaign for choice received a major boost when the Brookings Institution published a tract by John Chubb and Terry Moe in 1990. Hailed as "path-breaking" by the Heritage Foundation, their book received extraordinary attention because of its publisher. For most of the

1960s and 1970s, "liberal" was The Brookings Institution's first name, even though its board was bipartisan and mainstream establishment and its publications decidedly nonideological. Brookings's reputation was shaped by the back-and-forth service to successive Democratic administrations by the prominent economists on its staff. The publication of the analysis by Chubb and Moe by an institution of the liberal establishment seemed like an endorsement for a key tenet of the conservative ideology—that government services should be subjected to marketplace tests.

Chubb and Moe's prescription for privatization rested on their view that educational reform will never work if attempted through public school boards because the boards are relentlessly democratic and democracy is untidy. Here is their principal argument:

> Our guiding principle in the design of a choice system is this: public authority must be put to use in creating a system that is almost entirely beyond the reach of public authority. Because states have primary responsibility for . . . education, we think the best way to achieve significant, enduring reform is for states to take the initiative in withdrawing authority from existing institutions and building a new system in which most authority is vested directly in the schools, parents, and students. The restructuring cannot be construed as an exercise in delegation. As long as authority remains "available" at higher levels . . . it will eventually be used to control the schools . . . . [A]ll higher-level authority must be eliminated.[44]

The utter failure of educational reform, according to Chubb and Moe, is not the fault of scholars or reformer-activists, both of whom know what needs to be done. "Reformers are right about where they want to go, but their institutions cannot get them there," Chubb and Moe wrote.[45] The solution follows quickly from their analysis: employ the people's power to rid the public schools of the people's power. For, as Chubb and Moe noted, "as long as . . . [public] authority exists and is available for use, public officials will come under intense pressure from social groups of all political stripes to use it."[46] And the solution is choice. According to Chubb and Moe,

> We think reformers would do well to entertain the notion that choice is a panacea. This is our way of saying choice is not like

the other reforms and should not be combined with them. . . .
Choice is a self-contained reform. . . . It has the capacity *all by
itself* to bring about the kind of transformation that . . . reformers have been seeking in myriad other ways.[47]

For those readers who do not chase after footnotes, it is important to
note that Chubb and Moe provided the emphasis in the above passage.
After years of frustration, with nearly everyone complaining that today's
employees cannot write or think clearly, that television is deadening our
minds, that lower-class parents do not know what to do to help their kids
along, that politics has been hijacked by Gucci-shod, fast-talking lobbyists,
there is finally a solution—indeed a panacea—offered with confidence.

THE POLITICS OF PRIVATIZATION

Privatization is a way to exploit poor city kids and their parents in
order to subsidize upper-income families with tax dollars. It is not offered
as a way to break down racial and class barriers in private and suburban
schools, because its proponents know that middle-class white families
will not sacrifice the educational opportunities of their children to accommodate the educational needs of poor, minority kids. According to conservatives, the market will take care of poor kids either by improving
city schools or by providing private alternatives in the cities.

In the mid-1990s only about 5.5 million, or 12 percent, of elementary and secondary students attend nonpublic schools. Of that number
about 85 percent go to religious schools—particularly Catholic schools,
which reported about 2.5 million students in 1991. This is important
information, because choice proponents oppose a "choice" that is limited to public schools (as Bill Clinton proposed during the 1992 campaign).
Therefore, in the early years of any new school choice program proposed
by conservatives, the effective choice for most parents would be between
public schools and religious schools. (The independent schools tend to
charge tuitions that are higher than typical public school costs, which
would effectively put them out of reach for most poor parents unable to
supplement their tax-paid vouchers.) Wisconsin's choice program, the
most extensive to date, is available only to low-income families, and their
choice was initially restricted to public or nonsectarian private schools; the
program has attracted only a few hundred students of the 92,000 in
Milwaukee's public system.[48]

Conservatives know that religious schools are the primary nonpublic choices available to city parents. In fact, they have argued for some time that parochial schools do a better job educating low-income students than do the city schools that spend much more money. Yet, practically no attention has been paid to the fundamental question of constitutionality. One would expect to read constitutional arguments under which parents could choose religious schools, but few proponents even mention that there might be a problem. Chubb and Moe dismiss the question in one parenthetical sentence in a 318-page work: "Our own preference would be to include religious schools as well, as long as their sectarian functions can be kept clearly separate from their educational functions."[49]

If choice is to have any practical effect, religious schools must be available on the school menu. Whether public funds should be channeled into religious programs is something the Supreme Court must decide. So far, the Court has blocked all but special, student-centered public assistance to religious schools, such as bus transportation, school lunches, or textbooks.

THE COSTS OF PRIVATIZATION

What about other alternatives to public schools? Benno Schmidt has been vague as to whether the Edison Project assumes the existence of tax-paid vouchers for its financial viability. Edison "will not rely on public funding, and it takes no position on the wisdom of vouchers," he has said.[50] Assuming that religious schools are not eligible to participate in publicly financed choice programs—and that is the most reasonable assumption—then the only "choices" would be existing or new private schools, which presently serve fewer than 2 percent of all students (and only 15 percent of students attending nonpublic schools). Presumably, existing nonpublic schools would be able to expand their enrollments if vouchers were available, but not enough to meet the anticipated demand for nonpublic schools.

As in any market system, one can anticipate new schools springing up to meet this new demand; some of those new schools might be proprietary. This scenario strongly, however, suggests that the major rationale of privatization advocates—to give poor minority kids the same kind of education available to upper class whites—will not be met. Schools organized to take the money of low-income families will not have the ability nor the inclination to provide high quality education for average revenues.

Chubb and Moe accept the popular view that a student's achievement in school is influenced by the student's cohort and the parents' education.[51] Schools directed at low-income families are not likely to draw the cross-section of class and income idealized by choice proponents. The evidence from magnet schools offers little encouragement in this regard. Taking into account that income and education are highly correlated in American society, it does not seem likely that school choice, as proposed, will advance the standing of lower-class children at all.

Even with universal vouchers that carry average per pupil costs, the Edison Project does not seem likely to provide an alternative for substantial numbers of parents. Whittle Communications and Schmidt have scaled back their initial claims for the scope of the project: planned start-up investment dropped from $2.5 billion to $750 million, and expected first-year enrollment fell from 200,000 to 65,000.[52] Journalist Sara Mosle points to two major burdens that it must face as a nonprofit competitor: it must return a profit (say 15 percent of "sales" before taxes are paid), and facilities must be purchased or constructed with borrowed funds. If Edison receives $5,600 for each of its 65,000 students, it will generate $364 million in revenues; about $80 million of this would be directed to interest and investor returns, and about $73 million would not be realized because 20 percent of the students would be on full scholarship. This leaves only about $3,200 per pupil a year for direct educational costs, not even half of what independent elementary schools spend on each student.[53] Because the heaviest education costs are for teacher salaries, the Edison Project would appear to have to rely either on a very high student to teacher ratio or on a major expansion in the role of technology. But technology is expensive.

If proprietary and religious schools are not the answer, then the taxpayer can assume that most of the costs of a voucher program would, initially at least, end up being reshuffled among public school districts. Moreover, there is an additional cost question that choice proponents avoid altogether. If universal vouchers are available, then they must be available to parents whose children presently attend nonpublic schools. As a practical matter, it would be a simple step for the parents of any private school child to enroll their child in the local public school to establish voucher eligibility. Affluent Americans would take advantage of this "entitlement" if offered, just as they have taken advantage of their Social Security benefits even when they have substantial pensions.

Assuming that only the parents of children in nonreligious schools were included, the additional costs would be roughly $5 billion and would represent a pure income transfer from the working and middle class to the upper-middle and high-income classes.

CHOICE AND THE LESSONS OF THE FREE MARKET

We know a lot about how the marketplace operates in education, particularly when dealing with the poorest and least sophisticated "consumers."

The federal government has financed a voucher program for post-secondary education for three decades. Through a variety of loan and grant programs, any qualified student can receive assistance to attend any accredited institution. Although most aid goes to students attending conventional four- and two-year colleges and institutions, a curiously disproportionate amount goes to students who attend proprietary trade schools. In 1990 these students accounted for only 6 percent of 12.6 million undergraduates, yet they accounted for almost 25 percent of the guaranteed student loans and Pell grants. Their default rates have been almost five times those of students attending four-year institutions, so that, by 1990, trade school graduates accounted for almost half of the $2.4 billion in defaults.[54]

In marginal commercial districts in any large city, one can frequently find a "college of beauty culture" or "computer institute" or "school of the secretarial sciences." These places exist to harvest money from the unsophisticated poor who are eligible for federal grants and guaranteed loans. In fact, almost 80 percent of all students at proprietary, nondegree schools rely on federal aid, compared with 30 percent of other undergraduates. These proprietary schools are "accredited" by a national accreditation council that is controlled by the owners of the proprietary schools, who act to keep out potential nonprofit competitors. A 1990 Senate report likened the accrediting agency to "putting the prisoners in charge of running the prison."[55]

Democrats and Republicans alike have overlooked the scandal of trade schools (in fairness, the Bush administration did more to discipline the worst offenders than any of its predecessors). Trade schools aim their advertising and recruiting at low-income people who are "guaranteed" a "free" education and a glamorous job after training; some schools even recruit in homeless shelters. (This tawdry story is but one sad part of our national failure to provide effective training for the majority of adults who do not go to college.) Nothing suggests that these "market-driven" proprietary trade schools produce results justifying the enormous public investment in them. For example, Katherine Boo reported that in 1990, "New York . . . officials warned that the market was glutted, [but] *more city residents used federal funds to study nail sculpting and hair cutting than any other vocational subject.*"[56]

Because there are no federal requirements that trade schools actually provide their students with marketable skills, and there is no penalty for consistently low placement rates, the schools put their emphasis on recruitment and packaging federal loan and grant applications. Boo noted that a "mid-eighties General Accounting Office study of 1,600 schools counted up an orchard's worth [of bad apples], charging that more than two-thirds of trade schools 'misrepresented' their placement rates, curriculum, or student aid."[57] In 1989 the U.S. Department of Education found that half of the $1.8 billion in student loan defaults came from proprietary school students;[58] just a year later, the amount of such defaults had increased to $1.06 billion.[59] The double shame is that, not only do trade schools rarely deliver on their promises of jobs, they further pauperize their students when, without a decent job, the "graduates" are forced to default on their loans, ruining their credit standing.

Privatization advocates ignore the results of this substantial, long-term, expensive failure in school choice as they wring their hands over the plight of the city poor.

OVERCOMING CONSERVATIVE INDIFFERENCE

American politics has come to a curious watershed. In the 1992 elections, the radical notions of the Reagan Revolution seemed to have been largely rejected amid talk of a "decade of greed." But the paralysis of Clinton and the Democrats in the wake of their failed health care reform effort gave new life to the Reagan coalition. Once again the tensions among conservatives have been smoothed over by the ferocity of their opposition to Clinton personally and to his policies. Republicans were united for the 1994 campaign by a "Contract with America," which offered a neo-Reaganist formula of reduced taxes, increased military spending, a balanced budget amendment, and a continuation of the cultural war on issues such as abortion, illegitimacy, and idleness. The Republicans successfully appealed to antigovernment sentiments without having to specify how they would slash spending to achieve a balanced budget. Clinton and the Democrats lost their voices and failed to offer any off-setting vision to guide the nation's future.

The costs to American society of the triumph of Reagan's radical brand of conservatism have been high. The basic compact between the people and their government has been shredded. The role of the national government in mobilizing and directing public investment to transportation, colleges and universities, libraries, open spaces, and clean water, air, and land has been denigrated and marginalized. In truth, the fundamental idea that underlies capitalism—that current sacrifices in the form of savings and restrained consumption are necessary for future prosperity—has been endangered. Instead, government is held up as the source of economic stagnation and moral decay, even as the popular will mandates Social Security, Medicare, scholarships and loans, parks, and health research, none of which can be supplied by the marketplace.

The conservative ascendancy feeds on, and contributes to, growing divisions in American society along racial and class lines. The civic culture is increasingly stratified, and the opportunities for mingling and mixing across lines of color and status have been reduced. Conservative politics benefits from this sense of "us versus them." Indeed, conservative policies heighten this outlook by demonizing issues such as crime and welfare.

The Clinton administration has abetted the Republican resurgence by failing to pursue policies that are consistent with the priorities of his election campaign. He has been irresolute in his earlier opposition to racial quotas and undisciplined in pushing a consistent vision that responds to the growing economic fears of most Americans. Clinton has failed to argue for a national effort that strengthens the structures of opportunity.

The costs of conservative rule open opportunities for progressives to rebuild their standing and to forge new coalitions that cross not only racial and economic class boundaries, but partisan ones as well.

Given this context, we need to return to the questions that motivated this book: How can a progressive center be restored, and what can be done about the legacy of racial discrimination and inequality?

7»

REBUILDING A PROGRESSIVE VISION

Liberal was a proud label in the middle third of the twentieth century, when it described those who fought to expand opportunity to poor and working-class Americans by guaranteeing any qualified student the chance to attend college and graduate into the middle class.

Liberal was a proud label when it was attached to those black and white Democrats who stood up for disenfranchised southern black citizens against the Democrats' staunchest and most reliable supporters in presidential elections, white southerners.

Liberal was a proud label when it described a generation of pragmatic and thoughtful politicians who guided public investment to research, infrastructure, transportation systems, and housing in sufficient amounts to sustain prosperity and create the first truly middle-class society.

Liberal was a proud label for those who introduced Social Security, Medicare, and other programs to lend dignity to old age and assistance to the helpless.

Then, as we have seen, liberals stopped thinking and talking sensibly about issues freighted by race, which, in turn, impaired their credibility on basic questions about the role of government in sustaining prosperity and in assuring all Americans of access to middle-class opportunities.

By now, the word *liberal* is so compromised that I retain it only as a political pejorative. I use *progressive* to describe my preferred vision and politics.

Progressives need a vision—not an ideology and not a catalog of federal programs, but a vision. Without one, progressives will be left with only the daily demands of politics to guide them, and when there is no progressive vision, ideological conservatives set the terms of the public debate, leaving progressives to react defensively and aimlessly. By the early 1990s, liberal nomads ended up supporting proposals such as balanced budget amendments and regressive taxation, which run directly counter to a progressive posture.

SOME REASONS FOR OPTIMISM

Progressives have a fighting chance. The 1992 election results demonstrate that the electorate has great doubts about Reaganonomics and that Republicans are now on the wrong side of the cultural wars with their alliance with the Right. What is less clear right now is whether the progressives have a plan to achieve sustainable economic growth and to move the public debate off the no-win issue of deficits. The 1994 election results suggest that they do not. Not yet.

Beyond Bill Clinton's 1992 election, progressives can find several sources for optimism. First, most Americans no longer support the notion that the surest route to economic growth is to increase the after-tax income of the wealthiest Americans. Although this repudiation of Reaganomics represents progress, it does not mean that Americans now support the traditional Democratic enthusiasm for government activism. But as budget cuts cramp well-liked services, doubts about further cuts are growing. The current state of public opinion is jumbled, but there appears to be a policy majority being built that looks to the federal government to restructure health care, reform welfare (again), make the tax system more progressive, and protect Social Security and Medicare.

A second reason for optimism is that progressives seem to be waking up, albeit slowly. The signs of stirring are too tentative to constitute a "school" or a "movement," but the number of progressives willing to take a fresh look at previously taboo subjects has increased. Daniel Patrick Moynihan never went to sleep: an advocate of social insurance, welfare reform, and tax incentives for families and workers, he has been a *provocateur* and tormenter of ideologues on the Right and Left. For his efforts, he has been labeled a Rightist by the Left, a misogynist by feminists, a racist by black nationalists, and a brother by neoconservatives.

After the suppression of the Moynihan Report in 1965, only a few liberal scholars would speak out: William Julius Wilson broke the silence in 1978 with his book *The Declining Significance of Race*. Gary Orfield kept pushing school integration, Christopher Jencks investigated racial and class inequality; David Ellwood and Mary Jo Bane concentrated on welfare and the family. Moreover, as the 1990s began, two important journals were launched. Randall Kennedy, a black Harvard law professor began *Reconstruction* to provide "a forum for uninhibited commentary on African-American politics, society, and culture." Paul Starr, a Princeton sociologist, and Robert Kuttner, the liberal columnist, launched the *American Prospect*, which described itself as "a Journal for the Liberal Imagination." (Both journals are headquartered in Cambridge, Massachusetts.)[1]

Charles Peters and the group of prominent writers he has attracted to the *Washington Monthly* have been an important source of provocation and common sense among progressives since 1978. The *Washington Monthly* has provided critiques of the most damaging assumptions of McGovern liberalism. Self-described "neoliberals," Peters and his friends have attacked government "waste, fraud, and abuse," while also advancing ideas for fostering social equality, enhancing military effectiveness, and supporting selective deregulation.

New Jersey Senator Bill Bradley began to make race, politics, and poverty a matter of consistent personal attention in July 1991 by challenging President Bush's personal and political views on race. He has persisted by focusing on crime and the Los Angeles riots and by seeking longer-term program ideas. Barney Frank, a U.S. House member from Massachusetts and a certified liberal, published a harsh criticism of the liberal left wing of the Democratic party, in which he wrote: "For a variety of reasons, some strategic, some ideological, some attitudinal, and all of them wrong, many in our party object to an effort to demonstrate that liberals are patriotic supporters of the free enterprise system who think that hard work should be rewarded and violent criminals severely punished."[2]

Journalists have helped set the stage. Nicholas Lemann offered a sweeping analysis of the great migration of black sharecroppers to northern ghettos; the Edsalls recounted the changes in the economy, the cultural conflicts of the 1960s and 1970s, and the building of a conservative policy majority; Jim Sleeper, a *New York Daily News* columnist, traced the unchallenged rise of black street radicals and showed how their growing influence in New York City politics was abetted by white liberals and the Left; E. J. Dionne explained the increasing public distaste for politics growing out of the capture of the two parties by ideologues who concentrate on issues of little interest to most citizens.[3]

Third, Democrats speak more effectively to the economic interests of working- and middle-class Americans, a constituency that makes up the electoral majority. They support social insurance for the jobless and universal health insurance coverage. Democrats protect wage earners when tax bills are written and unions when collective bargaining is the subject.

Progressives also stand to gain now that the politics of cultural issues are shifting to favor those who stand for values such as choice and privacy concerning personal rights, particularly abortion. It is the Republicans who are the extremists because of their involvement with the Religious Right, antiabortion activists, and homophobes. They favor government interference with family decisions about appropriate care for the terminally ill, and they are intolerant on issues of religious freedom. Republicans, in short, are on a narrow-gauge track not dissimilar to the one that led the national Democrats nowhere after 1972.

A fourth reason for progressive optimism is that the reality of race relations is better than racial nationalists have led Americans to believe. Integration may have died as a widely publicly stated goal in the 1970s—precisely at the time that it became a realistic possibility—but watch noontime crowds on city streets or in office cafeterias or drop by an after-work softball game to find examples of easy black-white relationships. At a Democratic convention or a gathering of Teamsters or Planned Parenthood, integration appears vibrant. A 1991 *Newsweek* survey found that two-thirds of white respondents and four-fifths of black respondents said they knew "many members of another race well," and 47 percent of the whites and 63 percent of blacks said they "socialize regularly with members of another race."[4] A New Jersey poll reported that 78 percent of white and 88 percent of nonwhite respondents reported having "made friends with someone of a different race," and 64 percent of white and 71 percent of black respondents said they had invited someone of another race to their homes.[5] Even allowing for exaggerated responses, Americans are not a people who seem divided into "two nations—separate, hostile, unequal" as suggested by the title of a best-selling book by Professor Andrew Hacker.[6]

American culture is increasingly mottled. Bill Cosby, Michael Jordan, and Michael Jackson are among the "hottest" definers of popular culture as well as the promoters of soft drinks, soups, shoes, juice, and cereals; Toni Morrison, Maya Angelou, and Alice Walker are important voices in American literature; Denzel Washington and Danny Glover are major film stars; Spike Lee and John Singleton are highly regarded young movie directors. American music—from gospel, jazz, rhythm and blues, and rock and roll to classical interpretation—has been heavily shaped by black Americans. Louis Armstrong, Marion Anderson, Leontyne Price, Ella Fitzgerald, Duke Ellington, and Paul Robeson are true legends.

Even though conditions are more hospitable for rebuilding a progressive vision than they were in the 1980s, formidable obstacles remain. Progressives must demonstrate that they are unafraid to stake out clear and sensible positions on controversial issues. In particular, to banish the term *white liberal* once and for all, progressives of both races need to discuss their visions for a harmonious, multiracial society frequently, openly, and candidly.

THE FAILURE TO DISCUSS RACE

Liberals on the Senate Judiciary Committee set a new standard for timidity during the hearings on the nomination of Clarence Thomas to the Supreme Court. Thomas was the head of the Equal Employment Opportunity Commission in the Reagan administration, and he had presided over a radical shift in policy from seeking agreements with large employers and major institutions to correct *patterns* of discrimination to adjudicating *individual* complaints. The Thomas hearings were the perfect opportunity to probe his judicial philosophy about racial preferences, but Thomas received not one question about racial matters. By contrast he was asked about abortion sixty-eight times.

Representative Frank, a sassy Boston Democrat, defines the "notsaposta" (as in "you're notsaposta talk about that") as a "truth that members of a political party are told by ideologues that they cannot acknowledge, lest they give aid and comfort to the enemy." Frank writes:

> Notsaposta is the . . . grievously mistaken view that acknowledging a troubling truth will weaken a party's ability to resist the conclusions that its political opponents might draw from those truths. What happens, in fact, is almost always exactly the opposite. The failure to join your political enemies in affirming some beliefs that are strongly and widely held by voters weakens your ability to win them over to your side because you effectively concede these issues to your opponents. The Democrats' silence makes us suspect.[7]

Frank has said that the two most damaging notsapostas are crime and for-eign policy. But the notsaposta list is, unfortunately, much longer, with most of the issues framed by race.

Progressives cannot have a useful conversation about race without a willingness to agree with "conservatives." The polarization of dis-course—the Left blaming racism and "the system," the Right blaming black behavior and values—freezes the debate at a point that gives the political and moral advantage to the conservatives. Conservatives make sense when they discuss the advantages of two-parent families, the essen-tial role of individual and family responsibility, the need for uniform standards of civil behavior, and the primacy of the work ethic. These are not conservative ideas but broadly accepted American ideas. It is outra-geous for black and white progressives to allow their silence on such mat-ters to be interpreted as opposition to them.

A 1992 poll of black Americans received considerable attention because it found that black public opinion closely mirrored American public opinion.[8] Eighty-four percent favored mandatory job training and schooling for welfare recipients; 90 percent favored tougher measures to track down fathers who had abandoned their children. (Bill Clinton understood these black-white similarities, as evidenced by his 1992 cam-paign. During the southern primaries, in which black voters enjoyed max-imum leverage, the Clinton campaign ran campaign ads on welfare reform more frequently than ads on any other issue.)[9] Yet, the rhetoric of the black leadership shows no recognition of the views held by the 30 million Americans who are black. Any attempt to take up the middle ground regarding racial issues—preferences in particular—is countered with instant criticism-by-label: "Black conservative."

Thus, William Julius Wilson can find himself lumped with self-pro-claimed conservatives for his recommendation that black Americans pur-sue policies that produce "universal" benefits rather than concentrating on race preferences. Responding to Wilson's advocacy of race-neutral programs and coalition politics, the black activist-scholar Kenneth Tollett wrote:

> I am sad to observe that the views expressed by . . . Wilson are barely, if at all, distinguishable from those of so-called liberal . . . whites. . . . But I would like to see better represented the views of blacks who are more supportive of a race-conscious approach. . . . Although Wilson is surely not a Glenn Loury, Thomas Sowell, or Shelby Steele, his views . . . carry considerable

force and persuasiveness and give aid and comfort to whites
who resist race-conscious policies for reasons . . . inimical to the
interest of blacks.[10]

The same pattern of guilt-by-association practiced by Moynihan's
assailants can be seen in Tollett's criticism. Wilson was harshly criticized
for endorsing coalition politics, an unremarkable suggestion for any
minority that casts about 9 percent of the national vote.

College campuses are particularly tough places to have candid conversations about race. Stephen Carter, a Yale law professor, makes a simple observation that is almost always avoided in debates about race
preferences: "If one supports racial preferences . . . one must be prepared
to treat them like any preference in admission and believe that they make
a difference, that some students would not be admitted if the preferences
did not exist."[11] This fact cannot be stated on most campuses, however,
without calling down rancor and recriminations for drawing suspicion to
minority students. A Georgetown University law student who published
an article reporting significant differences between black and white students in their scores on the law aptitude test and college grade point aver-
ages was threatened with dismissal. The reaction of the law school's dean
was not unusual for such cases: copies of the offending paper were seized
and the dean declared that race "was not a part of the school's admission
process."[12] Unfortunately, selective universities that covertly employ preferences in admissions make no effort to contend with the inevitable consequences of those preferences: black students, on average, will be at a
disadvantage.

Just as liberals have failed to openly discuss racial preferences, so
too have they ignored one of the results: white resentment. It may be that
upper-middle-class liberals, who are typically unaffected by a policy of
racial preferences, do not appreciate how common the phenomenon of
white resentment has become. Moreover, professional blacks and the Left
explain white resentment as just one more manifestation of racism. When
Senator John Kerry suggested that "we can no longer simply will away the
growing consensus . . . within America's white majority . . . [that it] is they
who have borne the burden of compliance with the [affirmative action]
law," he was attacked for even bringing up the subject.[13] *Boston Globe*
columnist Derrick Jackson advised: "White resentment over 'reverse discrimination' should be recognized. But only as a fraud."[14]

Another key issue that liberals have managed to avoid is the disap-
pearance of the two-parent black family. Black male abandonment of the

newborn is now the norm, a fact of enormous economic consequence: 51.2 percent of female-headed black families had income below the poverty level in 1991, compared with 11 percent of black two-parent families. Liberals pretend that schools can magically substitute for the limited parental attention and nurturing given during the first five years of the home life. When CBS aired "The Vanishing Black Family," the National Black Leadership Roundtable, which represents most national civil rights organizations, attacked it as "unbalanced, unfair, . . . salacious" and challenged the implication that "the only legitimate . . . family form is nuclear and patriarchal." It went on:

> One was left with the impression that black families generally do not have fathers in the home, but there was no serious examination of the reasons. . . . The unconscionable high levels of unemployment . . . imprisonment, drug addiction and mortality among black men . . . all play a role. Single-parent families . . . are not as implied . . . the result of "immorality" or promiscuity, but rather are *adaptive responses to economic and social forces.*[15]

This is the kind of rhetoric that liberals have chosen to ignore. The intuition that children do better when raised by two parents, that divorce creates instability and poverty, that abandonment by their fathers is harmful to children economically and emotionally, is substantiated by research, yet liberals continue to act as if these facts are in themselves harmful.[16]

Why, when low-income families live mostly in relative peace and comfort in high-rise public housing in New York City, are similar buildings across the Hudson River in Newark abandoned or razed? Why do low-income students attending parochial schools treat their teachers courteously, while low-income students in public schools do not? Liberals do not talk about behavior; they do not make judgments even when basic rules of society are breached. Consequently, appeals for civility are identified as "conservative" issues and considered distractions from the real business of restructuring society. Micaela Di Leonardo put it this way:

> Of course we have to love, control and enlighten all our children. Street crime and drug addiction are terrible things. Early childbearing isn't great. People, including poor people, ought to be kindly and sensitive to one another in public and private. But prior to all these considerations are public policies that have created and maintain poverty and racial stratification.[17]

The four crucial issues that liberals have failed to address carefully and respectfully—racial preferences, white resentment, the black family, and lower-class behavior—are mandatory for any thoughtful approach to the nexus of race and poverty. This call for truth-telling is not a call for valor. When Senator Bill Bradley talked about crime in public in the way that whites talk about it in private, no one called him a racist, and he did not speak in euphemism:

> Today, many whites responding to a more violent reality, heightened by sensational news stories, see young black men . . . cruising the city, looking for trouble, and they are frightened. Many white Americans, whether fairly or unfairly, seem to be saying of some black males, "You litter the street and deface the subway, and no one, black or white, says stop. You cut school, threaten a teacher, 'dis' a social worker, and no one, white or black, says stop. You snatch a purse, you crash a concert, break a telephone box, and no one, white or black, says stop. You rob a store, rape a jogger, shoot a tourist, and when they catch you, if they catch you, you cry racism. And nobody, white or black, says stop."[18]

Bradley spared no one, criticizing politicians for the paralysis that afflicts liberal and conservative alike:

> What most politicians want to avoid is the need to confront the reality that causes the [white] fear. They don't want to put themselves at risk by speaking candidly about violence to both blacks and whites and saying the same things to both groups. Essentially, they're indifferent to the black self-destruction. And violence only hardens their indifference—not only to the perpetrator, but to all African-Americans.[19]

Editorialists and columnists gushed. The *Bergen* (N.J.) *Record* wrote: "It took Bill Bradley to raise the thorny questions that the presidential candidates won't touch."[20] The *New York Times* editorialized that Bradley "raised the issue [of fear] with . . . bravery and candor."[21] Bradley, by reporting on America's kitchen-table conversations, enriched the effort to find some ground between conservative indifference and relentless racialism—and was not publicly criticized for his remarks.

The Progressive Vision of a Multiracial Society

Integration and equal opportunity are at the heart of the progressive vision for a multiracial society. Advocates of separatism and "equal results" are vocal, but so sweeping is the consensus on these points that pollsters have stopped asking questions about equality of opportunity—because it is what defines the United States.[22] As we have seen, much that has been espoused since 1965 by racial nationalists and their chorus has directly challenged this defining idea. Contrary formulations—that all persons are created as members of racial, ethnic, or religious groups—might entertain some academics, but these ideas are treated as un-American by the public, both black and white. Arthur Schlesinger, Jr., a proud progressive and distinguished historian, recently described this age-old American ideal:

> The genius of America lies in its capacity to forge a single nation from peoples of remarkably diverse racial, religious, and ethnic origins. It has done so because democratic principles provide both the philosophical bond of union and practical experience in civic participation. The American Creed envisages a nation composed of individuals making their own choices and accountable to themselves, not a nation based on inviolable ethnic communities. The Constitution turns on individual rights, not on group rights. Law, in order to rectify past wrongs, has from time to time . . . acknowledged the claims of groups; but this is the exception, not the rule.[23]

The shame for many Democrats is that Republicans understand the primacy of this idea better than they do. Republicans say they support equal opportunity and oppose racial discrimination. They might not *do* anything about unequal opportunities or discrimination, but they do not oppose the visceral views of 98 percent of the nation's citizens. Democrats, by placating black leadership with talk about guaranteeing "equal outcomes," fly in the face of the American ethos.

No matter what terms are used, politically it makes sense to emphasize equal opportunity and integration. Make no mistake: as soon as someone proposes specific ways and means for the ideals of equal opportunity and integration to come alive for black Americans, white American enthusiasm flags, quickly and precipitously. For example, 76 percent support "affirmative action programs that help blacks get ahead," but only

9 percent favor "giving blacks preferences in getting jobs over equally qualified whites because of past discrimination."[24]

There was a time between John Kennedy's assassination and the 1966 elections—the Second Reconstruction—when a majority of Americans were supportive of special efforts to make good on America's promise through integration. In the face of Black Power and white resentment, black and white liberals came to speak less and less of integration. The separatists see integration as a false promise. Derrick Bell, a law professor at New York University, calls equal opportunity a "new, more subtle, but no less effective subordinating technique," in the same spirit as slavery and segregation.[25] Equal opportunity has been dismissed by Jesse Jackson as a "bumper sticker" slogan that is either "nonsense or racist."[26]

TAKING ON THE MULTICULTURALISTS

Supporting integration means opposing multiculturalism, the current variant of the old theme of racial and ethnic nationalism. Multiculturism has an innocent ring: "Respect diversity so we can all get along," as if multiculturalism is little more than appreciating differences in cuisines and customs. In fact, multiculturalism collides with the American ethos that assumes individual worth is not defined by race, ethnicity, religion, or national origin.

The appeal to tribal, racial, and religious hyphenation is dangerous stuff. Multiculturalists answer the question, Are we all Americans? in the negative. They encourage Americans to think of themselves as members of a group—especially racial, ethnic, religious, or gender groups—which heightens the sense of victimization when confronted by a society dominated by white males.

Multiculturalists emphasize "authenticity," but what they mean is adherence to their definition of what constitutes the group's "culture." Lani Guinier, the University of Pennsylvania law professor whose nomination for the top post at the civil rights division of the Justice Department was clumsily withdrawn by President Clinton, defines "authentic" black officeholders as "authentic because they are elected by blacks *and* [her emphasis] because they are descriptively similar to their constituents. In other words, they are politically, psychologically, and culturally black."[27] Guinier, herself a product of a well-educated and high-income family (her father was a graduate of Harvard College in 1926), recognizes no diversity within black America: "Authenticity reflects . . . the group perspective of a disadvantaged and stigmatized minority."[28]

However one delves into the citations and footnotes of multicultur-alist theory, and however poised and "mainstream" its proponents—like Guinier—appear once challenged, there is no way to reconstruct their views so that they accept either integration or equal individual opportu-nity as important organizing principles for American society.

Multiculturalists explain the lower achievement of black American students by the "theft" of their African heritage. Professor Leonard Jeffries, an unpublished pseudo-scholar at the City University of New York, avers that Europeans fear tracing civilization's "roots to Africa because the truth will . . . knock them off their feet," because they have "stolen" the African civilization that developed the foundations of mod-ern mathematics, architecture, philosophy, science, and political theo-ry.[29]Adelaide Sanford, a member of the New York Board of Regents, argues that multiculturalism is the vehicle by which black Americans can "self-define their culture," just as other hyphenated Americans have been free to define theirs. She also suggests that opposition to multicul-turalism is explained by the profits earned from prisons, welfare, and spe-cial education programs that begin with the academic failure of minority children.[30]

Multiculturalism is a growth industry on college and university cam-puses. Louis Menand, who teaches English at Queens College, observes that most college students are in college to get a better job or to gain admission to a professional graduate school and are little influenced by the canonical wars raging at a few elite campuses.[31] The battle is really two battles: one that focuses on admissions and scholarship decisions in selec-tive universities; a second on curriculum and intellectual standards.

Not surprisingly, many black students find themselves at a substan-tial disadvantage in competing with better prepared students, a factor that contributes to a discouraging college dropout rate for blacks. A study of 1980 high school graduates found only 30 percent of full-time black students had graduated from college after five and one-half years, com-pared with almost 56 percent of white students.[32] Increasingly, black stu-dents have been responding to academic pressure with self-segregation. They press for their own dining and living facilities, cultural societies, and even yearbooks and graduation ceremonies. Often, they demand sep-arate ethnic studies departments, increased minority faculty, and a cur-riculum freed of "dead, white males." University administrators are more likely to give into such demands than to offer intensive help in addressing the underlying academic deficiencies. Schlesinger warns against this new intolerance among minority students:

Ethnic ideologues . . . have set themselves against the old American ideal of assimilation. They call on the republic to think in terms not of individual but of group identity and to move the polity from individual rights to group rights. They have made a certain progress in transforming the United States into a more segregated society. . . . They have imposed ethnocentric, Afrocentric, and bilingual curricula on public schools, well designed to hold minority children out of American society. . . . They have encouraged minorities to see themselves as victims and to live by alibis rather than to claim the opportunities opened for them by the potent combination of black protest and white guilt. They have filled the air with recrimination and rancor and have remarkably advanced the fragmentation of American life.[33]

Stressing similarities over differences, Professor Cornel West urges a greater emphasis on unity between blacks and whites:

To establish a new framework, we need to begin with a frank acknowledgement of the basic humanness and Americanness of each of us. And we must acknowledge as a people— *E Pluribus Unum*—we are on a slippery slope toward economic strife, social turmoil, and cultural chaos. If we go down, we go down together.[34]

Despite such obvious appeals to the vision of a united, integrated society, liberals have failed to acknowledge the basic "humanness" and "Americanness" of black Americans. Instead, they have "helped" black Americans by going along with race-driven preferences, supporting spending on programs of dubious efficacy, and trying to protect black people from the daily competitions of American life. In addition, liberals have degraded black leaders and, indeed, the black community by refusing to accord their positions the same vigorous debate accorded other issues.

INTEGRATION MEANS FIGHTING DISCRIMINATION

Integration and opposition to racial discrimination are a matched pair. Americans believe that racial discrimination should not be tolerated, but disagree on the extent of discrimination that is practiced.

Americans also disagree on the extent to which differences between black and white Americans are best explained by discrimination or by other forces. And Americans certainly disagree about what to do regarding discrimination: the majority of blacks favor preferential treatment, but they are joined by only a small minority of whites.[35] The consensus opposes race preferences.

Black Americans believe that they encounter much more discrimination than white Americans believe exists. A 1989 survey found that more than half of black respondents believed discrimination was prevalent in both housing and employment (compared with 20 and 15 percent, respectively, among whites).[36] Only 30 percent of black Americans believe that antidiscrimination laws are sufficiently strong, compared with 58 percent of whites. Black Americans report encounters that suggest widespread prejudice—stares from sales clerks, taxis that do not stop, unwarranted license and registration checks by police. Most blacks also believe there is a "glass ceiling" that limits their opportunities for promotions in most jobs.[37]

Unfortunately, the evidence suggests that a great deal of racial discrimination still exists. A 1990 Federal Reserve study of 6.3 million mortgage applications found that black applicants were twice as likely as white applicants with the same income to be denied loans. Although the study did not include information on credit histories, debt levels, or other criteria pertinent to loan approvals, the disparate treatment stands out.[38] The Urban Institute's 1991 study reported that one of eight black renters was denied information about housing that was shown to white testers presenting the same financial profile. Overall, black and Latino testers encountered some form of discrimination in more than half of their encounters with realtors.[39] Anyone living near a significant black population can testify to the existence of racial boundaries. For example, Harrison, New Jersey, a blue-collar town abutting Newark, reported 45 black residents out of 11,743 in the 1960 census; thirty years later, there were 74 out of 13,425. Hillside, also contiguous to Newark, went from 35 black residents out of 22,304 in 1960 to 8,578 of 21,044 in 1990.

Republicans—who worship an unfettered marketplace—display no enthusiasm for fighting racial discrimination, which so clearly distorts free markets. In 1991, the Wednesday Group, made up of moderate Republicans in the U.S. House, issued a fifty-eight page "opportunity agenda" without mentioning housing discrimination.[40] The same was true for the Heritage Foundation's "conservative agenda" for black Americans, most of which dwelt on the need for restoring traditional moral and family values.[41] William J. Bennett, a Reagan-Bush cabinet officer and conservative author, urged a new "market-oriented" emphasis on "empowerment" in his "new civil rights agenda," but ignored discrimination.[42] Jack Kemp, the conservative most sympathetic with the urban poor, had the authority as HUD secretary in the Bush administration to move against housing discrimination, but he gave highest priority to initiatives to keep black Americans in ghettos by selling them the public housing units they occupied. Moreover, his frequent speeches on urban problems never emphasize discrimination.

Progressives seem no more inclined to fight discrimination than conservatives, however. Civil rights groups concentrate their litigation on racially proportionate remedies. Suburban progressives find fair housing less fashionable than preserving open spaces, supporting abortion rights, or helping battered spouses. Even the victims seem to have lost interest in actually combating discrimination; complaints to civil rights agencies do not reflect the level of discrimination that blacks say they encounter.

Progressives should hold conservatives accountable for their rhetoric about free markets by building a bipartisan coalition to fight housing discrimination. Criminal penalties should be imposed on those who practice discrimination; real estate agents should lose their licenses for refusing access or information to minority home-seekers, and—like embezzlers, forgers, counterfeiters, and others who rob by stealth—persistent discriminators should be imprisoned.

Since the 1960s, the American workplace has been increasingly open to black Americans, yet many believe that they are subjected to discrimination in jobs and promotions. Some unions and employers persist in freezing out qualified black applicants.[43] During New York City's building boom in the 1980s, the number of black construction workers actually declined by 15 percent, while white workers were imported from other cities as well as Ireland.[44] In cases like these, court-administered quota plans appear to be the only remedy.

REPAIRING THE SOCIAL FABRIC

American mythology insists that we are all in the same boat. Television and movies celebrate a classless America: the World War II infantry platoon became the cinematic metaphor for a civic culture that prizes a vibrant, unpretentious egalitarianism (as long, presumably, as blacks were segregated, as they were in World War II). But in fact, the social fabric is fraying. Most white children are raised in two-parent suburban families; most black children in single-parent city families. The public school is under attack by those who want tax funds diverted to private and religious schools. The best jobs and the safest and nicest places to live are found farther and farther from central cities. The easy, daily mixing of Americans by class, race, and worker status that marked a draftee-filled Army, a public school system, public libraries, and mass transit is disappearing. Three-quarters of Americans drive to work alone; only 5 percent take public transit. Even the ball park, once the symbol of "America's pastime," has become segregated, with valet parking, super boxes, and supper clubs separating the affluent from those in the bleachers. From university campuses, the reports of self-selected racial and ethnic segregation are discouraging for their frequency.

Cities are no longer the epicenters of political or social life. There are now almost twice as many voters in suburbia as in cities. Fewer and fewer suburban residents work in cities. Only a few center cities can compete with their suburbs for culture, night life, and recreation. One does not hear a lot of suburban folks saying, "Let's go to downtown Paterson Saturday night." The Lions play football in Pontiac, not Detroit; the Jets in East Rutherford, not Queens, and the Cowboys in Irving, not Dallas. The long-standing belief that American civilization is inextricably tied to the fortune of central cities is now questionable to most Americans.

Increasingly, education and class—not race, language, or religion— are the real dividers in American society. Those with advanced educations and skills valued in a globalized economy do well, and they are quietly, but effectively distancing themselves from the rest of society. Robert Reich, President Clinton's secretary of labor, has observed: "As Americans continue to segregate according to what they earn, the shift in financing public services from the federal government to the states, and from the states to cities and towns, has functioned as another means of relieving America's wealthier citizens of the burdens of America's less fortunate."[45]

Conservatives do not worry about social equality. Moreover, they want the marketplace to allocate public services such as safety, health care, university education, recreation, and transportation. They want federal assistance for social services and health care in cities halted, preferring instead that towns and cities "take care of their own"; they would contentedly see public schools disappear.

Through their semiofficial organ, the *Washington Monthly*, neoliberals have proposed strengthening institutions that bring Americans together across racial, class, and ethnic lines. With military personnel needs declining, neoliberals push for a mandatory national service program that would impose a one- or two-year community service requirement to tutor, teach, build public facilities, and provide social services, *and* to bring diverse persons together in common effort.

Restoring the Instinct to Citizenship and Civility

Alexis de Tocqueville found an America in which the instinct to civility was the foundation of citizenship and the antidote to the excesses of fierce individualism. As this "instinct" weakens, however, the quality and genius of the American system is imperiled.

Citizen is a proud title. American citizenship is more avidly sought than any in the world. Citizenship means more than voting or jury duty, more than the voluntary payment of taxes or separating clear from green glass for recycling. Citizenship is what makes our society work; it is what lends civility to our dealings with one another, and what glues together practitioners of tenacious American individualism in pursuit of communal interests.

The need to codify citizenship is evidence that citizenship has broken down, yet when it's codified, it doesn't work. Citizenship is one of the "unenforceable obligations" that Martin Luther King, Jr., had in mind, and the form those obligations take is a decent measure of the health of our republic. The more cities pass ordinances against horn blowing, public urination, street litter, loud music, and drinking in parks, the greater the evidence of our fraying compact. Civility cannot be enforced with the threat of $200 fines.

During the late 1960s, the city of New York picked up garbage in ghetto neighborhoods nine times a week during the summer and six times during the rest of the year. In the boroughs of Queens and Staten Island, garbage was picked up twice weekly year-round. Sanitation inspectors found that the dirtiest neighborhoods were those that received the most service; the cleanest, those that received the least. The popular explanations for these results focused on absentee landlords, inadequate building maintenance, corrupt garbage collectors, and racial discrimination. After a three-week survey, the *New York Times* arrived at a more plausible explanation: "where shopkeepers, landlords, homeowners and tenants seriously attempt to keep their environs clean, they are clean."[46]

It is painful, again, to write such truisms, but government cannot work unles citizens exercise the rights and repsonsibilities of citizenship. Progressives need to be very clear about the minimal obligations that citizenship entails. Citizenship and civility are locked together, and progressives should be unafraid to offend the boors and the purveyors of public obscenity and disorder in making the connection.

ECONOMIC GROWTH AND GOVERNMENT'S ROLE

Neither Republicans nor Democrats have dealt squarely or clearly with the primary economic fact of American life: 80 percent of American families are working without improving their standard of living, and the prospects that this will change in their favor are weak.

During the 1992 presidential campaign, Clinton promised a "laser focus" on the economy. "It's the economy, stupid," read the sign in his headquarters. His platform called for revamping the health care system, expanding job training, modernizing the infrastructure, targeting tax incentives to create better paying jobs, and reducing budget deficits.

But Clinton and the Democratic Congress were soon stuck on the question radical conservatives want them stuck on: What public expenditures will be cut to reduce the deficit? Senate Republicans successfully filibustered the administration's omnibus budget and tax plan, singing the Reagan-Bush anthem of "No new taxes; cut government spending." Senator Ernest Hollings's advice to President Clinton encapsulated the challenge: "By defining himself as the Daddy Rabbit of Deficit Reduction, Clinton can clean up the mess left by the Republicans, lay claim to the Perot vote and win the credibility he needs as a Democrat to pursue a progressive agenda."[47] Trapped by years of stories about the government buying $600 coffee makers, savings and loan scandals, and a sense of pervasive bureaucratic ineptitude, Democrats found their argument that the nation needed to do more, not less, about transportation, research, higher education, housing, and health care was hardly heard.

One point on which a strong post-Reagan consensus prevailed was that the wealthy were not paying their fair share. The Citizens for Tax Justice reported that "the *average* pretax income of the richest one percent . . . zoomed from $314,500 in 1978 . . . (in 1992 dollars) to $675,000 . . . a 115 percent increase."[48] Even Republicans were reluctant to attack President Clinton's proposed marginal rate increases on families with incomes higher than $200,000. Restoring a more progressive tax schedule was easy compared with winning the argument that long-term economic vitality should precede deficit-reduction as a national priority.

Deficit reduction is no-win politics. There is little credit, but much pain, to be gained from cutting deficits. Populists argue that because Congress has no discipline "the people" must take charge, by enacting a balanced budget amendment to ensure the further shrinking of government. Horror stories about lazy bureaucrats and stupid government programs feed deficit politics.

"[P]ress for a Balanced Budget Amendment," writes Martin Gross, a best-selling author and fraud-and-waste-detector. "Most states. . . have it and it works," he notes, ignoring the fact that states separate capital and operating expenses, require voter approval for long-term borrowing, and cannot print their own currencies.[49] Gross also recommends an "independent" national inspector general, without specifying how its independence would be maintained, and a rule that forbids members of the House of Representatives from supporting any expenditure in their home districts.[50]

Deficits may or may not be an economic problem. Instinctively, people assume that government borrowing will increase the costs of borrowing for everyone else, thus "crowding out" private investment. The truth is more confusing. During the 1980s, as deficits mounted, interest rates began a steady decline, reaching a twenty-year low in 1993. The enormous increases in corporate and household debt during the 1980s suggest little crowding out. Moreover, as Professor Robert Eisner of Northwestern University has noted, in contrast to conventional accounting principles, federal budgeting makes no distinction between capital and operating expenses; if the government's investments in buildings, highways, equipment, weapons, and land were depreciated like private investments, the deficit would be de minimus.[51]

But deficits are, in author Charles Morris's term, "moral hazards. They are fundamentally antidemocratic," he wrote, "they allow government to increase spending without the implicit referendum of a tax increase."[52] According to Morris and others, it is immoral for this generation to pass along to its children and grandchildren the obligation to repay debts incurred because of its own lack of discipline. In 1980 the per capita national debt was about $4,000; by 1992, it had quadrupled! Deficits of this magnitude violate strongly held principles regarding deferral of current satisfaction for long-term gains. They are also regressive, as Kevin Phillips explained in his 1990 indictment of Reaganism:

Funding this huge deficit further realigned the nation's wealth. Under Reagan, annual federal expenditures on interest would climb from $96 billion in 1981 . . . to $216 billion in 1988. No other major expense rose so sharply. . . . Not only were upper-quintile Americans collecting 80 percent of the federal interest payments made to persons, but the top tax rate applicable to these receipts was falling steadily (70 percent in 1980 . . . 28 percent in 1988).[53]

The distinction between economic and moral arguments is important. Morally, it is offensive to burden our kids with massive debt to pay for national parks, farm subsidies, Social Security payments, or Coast Guard patrols. If we think we need these services and entitlements, then we should pay for them. What we should not do, but have done since Reagan's first budget, is to borrow the money to finance tax cuts for ourselves.

The nation does not need a balanced budget amendment to the Constitution; such an amendment is a simplistic scheme of antigovernment ideologues. The obligation to balance the budget is easy to evade in practice and questionable as either political or economic theory. The government needs the option of running a deficit in order to pursue sound economic policies. Deficits may be required not only by national emergencies, but also by the need to stimulate the economy. In fact, the best explanation for the business expansion after the 1982 recession was the enormous kick given the economy by unprecedented peacetime borrowing along with a runaway increase in defense spending.

Progressives need to connect their support for public spending to the well-being of the economy and our prospects for the future. If Democrats do not take the lead in restoring the opportunity structure, then it will not be done. Sure, they can learn from the mistakes of earlier efforts. Washington functionaries should not control local programs; ineffective programs should be shut down, and taxpayers should not be expected to support those who can take care of themselves. The "striving poor," so admired by conservatives, rely on a network of public facilities and services, from schools to buses to libraries to public colleges to fight their way into the middle class. This network needs freshening and strengthening, without apology.

But everyone benefits from investment in major capital expenditures such as public transit, water and sewer projects, highways, airports, and flood control. And everyone benefits from a federal government that works in concert with the private sector in sponsoring basic and applied research that has no immediate or perceptible commercial applications. In fact, Americans have a national economic and security interest in maintaining the network of private and public research universities that are the envy of the world. In the same way, everyone benefits from providing talented students with the opportunity to receive a college education.

These are the kinds of public investment in which the United States is falling further behind other industrialized nations. It is no accident that the nation's period of maximum investment following World War II coincided with its longest period of sustained prosperity, which was enjoyed by the broadest cross-section of families.

If federal spending is heavily concentrated in these forms of investment where the payoffs are long term and benefit future generations, then there is no compelling moral or economic reason why those investments should not be financed by borrowings. Families do the same thing when they borrow to buy a house or to put a child through college. The pain is spread out over time and inflicted on those who benefit from the investments.

At bottom, the very idea of government itself must be reargued. Many Americans feel that the public interest is no longer defined by congressional enactments; instead, congressional decisions are viewed as manipulations of the political system designed to benefit special interests that are corruptly represented by Washington insiders. Alan Wolfe, a political scientist, characterizes this suspicion as a "contractual breakdown," and argues that "until one or both political parties begins the difficult task of renegotiating the contract between citizen and state, our political system will continue to generate alienation and withdrawal."[54]

However, before negotiations can begin, progressives must determine what kind of multiracial society they want to live in. With a display of forthrightness and thoughtfulness, progressives might even advance a clear, credible, and effective vision for dealing with the American dilemma and its most pernicious and discouraging contemporary manifestation—the black lower class.

8»

SOLVING PROBLEMS IN POOR CITY NEIGHBORHOODS

No serious discussion of American society can avoid the tangle of pathology found in poor city neighborhoods. Places such as East St. Louis, North Philadelphia, Camden, and Chicago's South Side suffer from a dangerous concentration of violent crime, drug and alcohol abuse, and dependency. This array of afflictions, combined with an absence of jobs, continues to discourage and baffle any attempt at a solution.

RACE, CLASS, AND POVERTY

For thirty years, bold national initiatives and comprehensive schemes have been offered to relieve poverty—drug wars, education reforms, welfare reforms, years of the child, and tough anticrime talk. Withal, the quality of life in ghetto neighborhoods has worsened to the point that they are now among the most dangerous places in the world. It is true that marginal, ameliorative, and preventative programs have created jobs for some people and have moderated the problems for some poor families. But such programs have been insufficient to slow the deterioration in the quality of life of poor neighborhoods. The national search for a conceptually coherent, efficacious, practical, and broad-ranged "Answer" has failed.

I have spent much of my professional life contributing to this failed search. My first "real" job was with Trenton's community action program in 1965 where I worked with community leaders and groups and non-profit and public agencies developing funding proposals. I worked with the staff of the White House Task Force on Cities during Lyndon Johnson's presidency. Returning to New Jersey, I was the special assistant to a reform-minded education commissioner before moving over to the governor's office as Governor Richard J. Hughes was responding to the 1967 riots in Newark and Plainfield. For eight years I ran a foundation that searched for effective answers to city problems. I visited scores of pro-grams and people with ideas in the poorest neighborhoods of some of America's poorest cities. I have consulted with community organizations and foundations, served on boards and task forces and attended more meetings about city poverty than I thought possible.

Through these efforts, I have met hundreds of bright, serious, ener-getic, motivated, tough-minded, effective human beings who were focused on what to do about poor people in poor places. Some endeavors "worked"—some poor people moved out of poverty and their lives were filled with more and better choices. Many of these efforts did not work. But there was nothing that worked so well and so consistently that it could be packaged as *the answer*.

Actually, one idea comes close to qualifying as a solution: jobs for all who seek one. The best way to liberate the lower class is a macroeco-nomic policy that sustains enough growth that labor shortages reach poor cities. Then, employers would have to reach down into the labor pool to train the poor. Harvard economist Richard Freeman found that the employment and earnings of young black males benefited disproportion-ately from the tight labor markets of the mid-1980s.[1]

Economic growth as the national urban policy benefits everyone. It avoids the divisiveness of racial preferences, the inefficiencies of social service bureaucracies, and the hysteria of tax increases. Its sole disad-vantage is that no one knows how to pull it off.

Lyndon Johnson was the last president to preside over an economy in which unemployment and inflation rates were both around 4 percent or less. American economic policy shifted from striving to reach and maintain low unemployment (3 percent) to tolerating a much higher job-less rate (no president seems much threatened by even a 6 percent rate) in preference for a lower inflation rate. Most economists and all Federal Reserve chairmen have warned that the fiscal and monetary actions that might create a tight labor market would act as gasoline on inflation's fire. Meanwhile, among the patchwork of programs aimed at helping the striving poor are some that work consistently well at reasonable cost. Prenatal and well-baby care, vaccinations, and family planning have been effective in improving the health of the poor. Public libraries, parks, affordable public transit, and a range of public institutions of higher education that connect opportunity to educational potential are services that benefit all levels of society, but provide life-changing opportunities for the poor. These programs are not dramatic or inventive, nor are they "antipoverty" programs (a virtue), but they are essential for giving concreteness to the American promise of educational and economic opportunity.

Such programs help some people escape the cycle of poverty even in the worst city neighborhoods. The Census Bureau found that 25 percent of poor people in central cities exited poverty in 1988—60 percent of them had gotten married and 50 percent had improved their employment situation.[2] Terry Adams and his colleagues at the University of Michigan found annual exit rates around 30 percent in the 1970s.[3] Much of the poverty policy debate ignores these complex dynamics and successes, nor does it acnowledge that lasting solutions to the conditions in ghetto neighborhoods must be contemplated across generational spans, not in four year election cycles.

DRAWING FROM PROGRESSIVE AND CONSERVATIVE STRENGTHS

As shown in Chapter 2, liberals retreated from sensible debate about race and poverty in the mid-1960s. Until the late 1980s or so, liberals spoke as if all black Americans were poor, subject to systematic racial discrimination, and victims of brutalizing police. The liberal position was that nothing short of an "urban Marshall Plan" or hard quotas for blacks in selective universities and jobs would work. Anyone who saw it differently was, in liberal eyes, guilty of racism or victim-blaming.

In 1970, Edward Banfield, then a Harvard political scientist, wrote an important book, entitled *The Unheavenly City,* in which he countered that the explanation for durable poverty was to be found in *class behavior,* not racial discrimination or stunted opportunities:

The lower-class forms of all problems are at bottom a single problem: the existence of an outlook and style of life which is

radically present oriented and which therefore attaches no value
to work, sacrifice, self-improvement, or service to family,
friends, or community. Social workers, teachers, and law-
enforcement officials . . . cannot achieve their goals because
they can neither change nor circumvent this cultural obstacle.[4]

While Banfield despaired about the efficacy of any government intervention in "curing" poverty, in his 1984 book, *Losing Ground*, Charles
Murray, a fellow at the conservative Manhattan Institute, concluded that
government programs only make the situation much worse:

The most compelling explanation for the marked shift in the
fortunes of the poor is that they continued to respond . . . to the
world as they found it, but that we, meaning the not-poor . . .
had changed the rules of their world. . . . The first effect of the
new rules was to make it profitable for the poor to behave in the
short term in ways that were destructive in the long term. Their
second effect was to mask these long-term losses to subsidize
irretrievable mistakes. *We tried to provide more for the poor
and produced more poor instead.*[5]

Murray's ideas provided the Reagan extremists with the intellectual cover
to justify their persistent attacks on any kind of social spending.

Antipoverty policy discourse is really parallel monologues: liberals
call for more public programs and higher spending, while conservatives
claim that the poor will ever be with us until they personally transform
themselves. Meanwhile, millions of poor Americans graduated from high
school, borrowed from the government to go to college, found jobs, and
entered the middle class. As they moved out of their old neighborhoods,
the quality of life there worsened.

Faced with the contradictory trends of a growing black middle class
and an increasingly pathological lower class, conservatives argued that
public programs were pointless—the middle-class aspirants did not need
them, and they only to made things worse for the poor. Liberals countered
that the government was not doing enough to reach the remaining poor.
So, where is the common ground? E. J. Dionne has suggested that it lies
in promoting traditional family values *and* providing social services.

In the 1990s, Americans are seeking a politics that restores a
sense of public enterprise and mutual obligation. . . . With

conservatives, Americans accept the idea captured in an apho-
rism coined by James Q. Wilson. "In the long run," Wilson
declares, "the public interest depends on private virtue."
Liberals are often right in seeing "structural problems," such as
the changing labor market, as primary causes of social decay.
But designers of social programs need to be clear about values—
and "virtues"—they are seeking to promote. Value-free social
policy is a contradiction in terms.[6]

As we've seen, some progressive politicians and academics are promoting
the unremarkable idea that efforts to aid the poor must be race-neutral
and consistent with basic American values. But that does not mean that
the poor should be expected to generate—spontaneously and by themselves—the means of ascent. Everyone has a stake in a common effort.

WELFARE AS THE TESTING GROUND

In the late 1980s, dissatisfaction with the welfare system drew conservatives and progressives closer together for a time. Congressional liberals acquiesced to the idea that welfare should impose a work
requirement, that there should be a time limit on benefits, and that fathers
should be financially responsible for their children. Conservatives agreed
that tax dollars should pay for transitional assistance. In response to the
Welfare Reform Act of 1988, many states enacted reforms that reinforced
society's ethos about work and family responsibility, including more generous tax credits for earned income, a "marriage bonus," and financial
penalties for children conceived while on welfare.

Up until the Clinton administration announced its welfare reform proposal in June 1994, congressional Republicans agreed that reform would
have to include funds for day care and transitional health coverage for
recipients moving into the labor force. Once in control of Congress, however, the new majority quickly abandoned support for transitional assistance
and adopted a sharply punitive tone. Republicans now go so far as to suggest that a child living in a family without means is no longer entitled to
public support. Instead, they propose a freeze on federal welfare payments
at the 1994 level; each state would have to decide if children causing the
1994 roll to be exceeded would be supported with state funds or not.

President Clinton's welfare reform proposal was a conceptually solid,
but badly underfinanced measure. He was handcuffed by the 1993

budget reconciliation deal, which required the administration not only to design a work-oriented reform, but to identify programs to be cut or revenues to be increased to cover any additional costs. The result was a proposal to impose the work requirement and a two-year benefits limitation only on recipients under the age of twenty-four and for modest new spending of $9 billion over five years.

If the Republican-led 104th Congress adopts President Clinton's plan, and it is implemented fully and effectively, it will not make a dent in the character and magnitude of the problems afflicting the underclass. It is important not to confuse "underclass" with "welfare recipient." Most recipients rely only temporarily on welfare (70 percent are off the rolls within two years). A hard core of remaining recipients, however, exhibit many characteristics of the underclass: no affinity for work, no expectation of marriage or of paternal support for their children, little capacity to inculcate educational values.

For welfare reform to cut into the underclass problem, its incentives need to be stronger and more automatic, and an unprecedented number of public service jobs must be created. This is the approach *The New Republic's* Mickey Kaus urges—"replacing AFDC [Aid to Families with Dependent Children] and all other cash-like welfare programs that assist the able-bodied poor. . . with a single, simple offer from the government—an offer of employment for every American citizen over eighteen who wants it, in a useful public job at a wage slightly below the minimum wage for private sector work."[7] Once someone was working full time, the government could supplement their income through the earned income tax credit to bring the family above the poverty line.

Kaus is unsentimental about those who can, but will not, work. He proposes no government backup for them. But he understands that a work mandate means that the parents of young children must be provided child care, an expensive entitlement. Like Newt Gingrich, he proposes public orphanages for the children of parents who refuse to work and lack the means or will to support them. How can Kaus justify proposing such high-cost ideas at a time of public stinginess?

> The best estimate I've been able to come up with . . . puts the total bill at between $43 and $59 billion a year more than we're spending now. That's not counting the value of any of the public service work performed by the neo-WPA workers. Still, it's expensive. So? *This isn't a cost-cutting program. It's a solution*

to the underclass problem. In the long run, if the welfare culture
is absorbed into the working, tax-paying culture, the budgetary
payoff will be enormous—not to mention the payoff for social
equality.[8]

To put Kaus's estimates in perspective, the 1993 federal bill for AFDC was
about $23 billion, while food stamps (which would be discontinued under
Kaus's approach) and Medicaid (which Kaus would replace with a national health scheme of some kind) added another $40 billion. But consider
that the expansion approved in 1993 for the earned income tax credit—
a tax refund program that increases the income of the working poor—
adds $26 billion to federal spending.

Kaus is right. Mostly. Importantly, he puts the nature and magnitude
of the welfare problem in a realistic context. He spares neither the liberals for their condescending efforts to protect welfare clients from life's normal tests nor conservatives for their rote invocation of traditional values
and failure to support transitional programs welfare recipients need to
have a fighting chance. But work incentives and sermons about personal
responsibility may not be enough for many members of the underclass.

FAMILY DIFFERENCES

The most obvious problem with ghetto life is that poor families tend
to be weak families, and overwhelmingly they are headed by a single parent. Public programs cannot supplant the nurture, comfort, discipline,
and preparation for learning supplied by a strong family. David Ellwood,
then of Harvard University, concluded that "the vast majority of children who are raised in a two-parent home will never be poor during
childhood. By contrast, the vast majority of children who spend time in
a single-parent home will experience poverty."[9]

Raising children is demanding, difficult, tedious, and time-consum-
ing. Good parents teach their children not to cheat or steal, to accept
responsibility, and to say "please." The difference between one- and
two-parent families is not necessarily in parental motivation, love, or
belief in education, but in the sheer capacity to attend to child-rearing in
the limited time available.

But all families are under increasing stress. Most American mothers
now work; parents have less time for their kids and for each other. Each

year, more than a million children see their parents divorce. Television-watching has increased, drawing children away from homework and the educational achievement that goes with it. Barbara Dafoe Whitehead wrote of the consequences:

> If we fail to come to terms with the relationship between family structure and declining child well-being, then it will be increasingly difficult to improve children's life prospects, no matter how many new programs the federal government funds. Nor will we be able to make progress in bettering school performance or reducing crime or improving the quality of the nation's future work force—all domestic problems closely connected to family breakup.[10]

Senator Daniel Patrick Moynihan is even more emphatic:

> The institution of the family is decisive in determining not only if a person has the capacity to love another individual but . . . whether he is capable of loving his fellow men collectively. The whole of society rests on this foundation for stability, understanding and social peace.[11]

The way children are raised in lower-class families is very different from the desired norm—in fact, differences in child nurture help define the lower class. Most underclass kids are conceived by unmarried parents and born into broken families. All the risk factors for a child are heightened by lower-class life: during pregnancy, lower-class mothers are more likely to drink, smoke, and take drugs, resulting in much higher probabilities of low-birth weights, which, in turn, leads to higher rates of retardation and chronic illnesses. The father is usually absent, and takes no financial responsibility for his child. As children grow up, the streets, with their magnetic and dangerous allure, too often win the competition for their time and energy. Eventually, the tone and quality of life in lower-class neighborhoods is determined by young males—immature, undisciplined, and dangerous.

Public programs cannot easily correct for these disadvantages, yet there is no credible evidence that abandoning such families to marketplace forces and to homilies about personal responsibility will work. We cannot abandon the search for solutions nor relieve the federal government of a central role.

SOURCES OF HOPE AND THREE SIMPLE RULES

There are a few reasons to be hopeful—very few. A respectful, open dialogue about race and poverty has started among black and white progressives. But the legacy of disrespect and white patronization is great and progressives must reestablish their credibility before the Left-liberal ideological warfare is settled. However, even the limited progress to date presages an end to easy Republican exploitation of the cultural "wedge" on the Left and suggests an opportunity to build a broader consensus on welfare and family issues.

Progressives need to be reminded of three simple criteria in developing new approaches to urban poverty. First, the approaches must be consistent with basic American values, such as work, family, individual responsibility, and community. Second, without a growing economy there will be neither enough jobs nor the political support to fight poverty. Third, policies and standards must be universal; that is, they cannot be seen as providing special deals for minorities.

The earned income tax credit and Pell Grants for higher education are examples of race-neutral programs that attract broad support (now even these popular programs are under attack by the Republican congressional majority). The argument that society must help blacks in particular because of past injustice simply does not carry—not in a nation of immigrants whose ancestors were more likely to have been serfs in Galway or Galacia than slave owners in Georgia. However, most of us believe that the striving poor need a helping hand. Society's expectations about family and personal responsibilities, the role of work, and the place of civil behavior cannot be compromised for poor minorities, nor should we assume that their potential for learning or their capacity for work is less.

Ignoring these simple truths is to invite failure, political folly, or both. Beyond these criteria, there are three rules that must be followed in order to reverse the trends in urban poverty.

RULE ONE: RESTORE THE STRUCTURE OF OPPORTUNITY FOR ALL AMERICANS

The phrase "structure of opportunity" has a sloganeer's taint. I mean it to refer to those investments by society that help create a sense of community and reduce the odds against the unprivileged. The structure of opportunity includes the public square where, theoretically, we mingle regardless of color, class, or income, in places such as parks, libraries, museums and concert halls. But it is more than these. Most importantly for the city poor, the structure of opportunity includes public schools, public institutions of higher education, public transit, and job training programs.

Conservatives ignore the essential place of these public investments in helping generations of the poor realize the American Dream. Oh, they love the success stories of heroes like Colin Powell, who grew up in an immigrant Bronx family, attended the New York City schools, and took the subway to the City College of New York (CCNY). But in today's conservative vision, any future Colin Powells will just have to do without the school, subway, and CCNY part. Conservatives want to end the federal governments assistance for public transit, and seriously reduce it for schools and higher education. They also want to privatize government by selling off some of these public assets and subjecting the remaining services to the whim of the market. "User fees" are called for, as if public services were typified by the Coast Guard rescue of millionaire yachtsmen.

I represent one of the wealthiest and most Republican counties in the nation, where taxpayers pay for local parks, public golf courses and equestrian centers, and open space. The quality of our public schools ranges from good to among the best private schools; the county's two-year college enjoys a strong academic reputation. Morris County exemplifies the Republican vision: local taxpayers pay for a high standard of amenities and security, but when it comes to national and state politics, they make plain their interest in keeping their tax dollars at home. It's what the Edsalls describe "local liberalism."

Progressives support the structure of opportunity, just not very effectively: they need to distinguish between programs that work and those that do not. For years, liberals ignored the abuses of proprietary trade schools, the sloppiness of compensatory education projects, and the failures of public housing. The case needs to be made that all of us rely on the programs that Reagan and Bush and the 1994 "Contract with America" sought to scuttle: public higher education, public schools and libraries, job training, and public transit.

RULE TWO: THINK LONG-TERM

The radio ads promise that "you can be speaking a foreign language like a native in just thirty days" by listening to some tapes while driving to and from work. Conservatives and liberals are about as credible in their ideas about the lower class. The 1994 "Contract with America," with its shameless gimmick of enacting of sweeping constitutional changes in "100 days," raised short-term, simplistic silliness to a new art form.

Conservatives do not worry much about the lower class, regarding it largely as a useful symbol of Democratic failure. The conservative constituency is increasingly spatially isolated and largely unaffected by the underclass. Jack Kemp, one of the few conservative who demonstrates a concern for city problems, recommends subsidizing businesses that locate in poor neighborhoods and public housing tenants who buy their own apartments. His schemes, however, disguise their true costs and, in effect, subsidize ghettoization; they also beguile us with the idea of a simple solution to the complex problem of urban poverty.

When Moynihan warned in his 1965 report that many black Americans were not well prepared for the competitions opened up by the passage of civil rights laws, liberals ignored the evidence, choosing to believe instead in the efficacy of quick-fix scenarios. They pursued proposals for massive income transfers to the poor, "empowerment" through tax-supported community organizing, comprehensive social services, or the reform of public institutions like schools, welfare, and police departments. Each approach reduced the goal of transforming lower-class families into middle-class families to one of either improving the physical environment of poor neighborhoods or of getting bureaucrats, teachers, and social workers to change their behavior. Liberals, too, accept easy answers to hard questions.

Unfortunately, the nation quickly lost its patience with the poor, and a generation has come and gone since the national consensus last favored, however briefly, a full-scale effort to end poverty.

RULE THREE: RESPECT SMALL VICTORIES

Discussion about urban poverty has been driven by ideology: conservative thinkers have laid the blame on the poor while the liberals have taken to blaming society itself. Both overlook the practical lessons of those programs that have proved effective and, especially, the role of strong leadership and long-term dedication.

The first time I attended a staff meeting of the North Ward Center, a community service organization in Newark, I was embarrassed by the sternness, flamboyance, and length of Steve Adubato's lecture over a gum wrapper he had picked up on the front steps. True, the center was quartered in a particularly dramatic setting, a baronial Victorian mansion that had been painstakingly restored to museum quality. But why should its staff be berated for fifteen minutes over a gum wrapper? Because, as I learned, if the staff first allowed the presence of a gum wrapper, then soon it would tolerate a few minutes' tardiness, the loss of a file, or the failure to follow through on a case.

The premises of any effective school or program will be clean and welcoming; the program staff will show respect for the people they work with; they will offer a warm, orderly, supportive, and purposeful atmosphere. Small mistakes are not ignored. Such examples are necessary to provide participants with the guidance, assistance, and incentives to act differently from the examples provided by a lower-class culture.

Successful programs are usually those that serve limited objectives in a narrowly defined community. For example, the North Ward Center does not run programs for delinquents even though it has the funds and facilities to do so and crime is a major problem in its neighborhood. Why? Because it doesn't know how to transform poor, adolescent males. The center offers day care services, job training, nutrition and transportation services for elderly residents, and sports for boys and girls. It buys and rehabilitates housing. Another successful program, the South Shore Bank in Chicago, concentrates its lending and related activities on three neighborhoods, even though many other Chicago areas could use its expertise and commitment.

Limited scope means limited victories; unfortunately, many consider limited victory to be un-American. We seek resolution within a thirty-second commercial or a two-minute news report. Popular movies portray a world that, without the heroic efforts of one smart white guy, is moments away from total destruction. For messy and complex problems, we trust the quick, technological answer. Slogans have replaced thoughtfulness; we "fight wars" against drugs or crime and expect to win.

Small victories are dismissed as idiosyncratic, trivial, or "creaming." For a generation, we have ignored the truth of how hard it is to intervene successfully in the lives of persons who do not grow up in families with middle-class values and aspirations. Well-run programs provide services, but also offer a structured introduction to the norms of the classroom or workplace. Some program participants gain much from these programs because they use them as a window to understand "how the world works"; for example, they learn how personal relations and performance can increase their options. Others—many of whom may be personable and enthusiastic—fail, not because they are lazy or immoral, but because old habits are too strong; the gap is simply too large to be filled with training or educational programs.

ILLUSTRATING THE RULES

Examples of programs that honor these rules can be found in many cities. Some of these model programs provide job training, others housing, some prepare poor kids for college, and others are broad-ranged community development corporations. Most are run by nonprofit organizations, not government agencies. Voluntary organizations avoid cumbersome procedures, inefficient work rules, and close political oversight. Moreover, effective programs usually benefit from the efforts of a strong leader who is dedicated to working in a tough neighborhood. They act with flexibility, compassion, and careful attention to the particular needs of each client.

The public education system in Newark, New Jersey, serves as a good example of the empty search for grand strategies and the facile acceptance of quick-fix solutions. In 1967, I worked for Carl Marburger, New Jersey's newly appointed "reform" education commissioner. The year before, Governor Richard J. Hughes had bested the educational establishment, splitting off higher education from the control of the "lower" educationists. I started work the week after the Newark riots. My boss was determined to make a difference in the lives of poor city kids.

In the late 1960s, there were two principle approaches to bring the minority poor up to standard: integration and supplementation.

Policy enthusiasts, including some educators, were analyzing the conclusions and implications of the Coleman report, the most comprehensive survey of student achievement ever conducted.[12] Advocates of federal financing for public education had pushed for the report, anticipating a conclusion that poorly performing students came mostly from schools too poor to provide the amenities and support typical of suburban schools. Instead, the Coleman report concluded that low-performing students tended to come from poor, undereducated families and usually attended school with kids from similar backgrounds; school spending and facilities had no measurable impact on achievement. The report fed the conclusion that it made most sense to send kids from lower-class families to schools with a clear majority of middle-class peers. Since most black kids were then both poor and concentrated in schools with other poor black kids, the clear implication of the report was that racial integration should be pursued for educational as well as constitutional and social reasons.

The competing answer in 1967 was to provide poor kids with compensatory education. In 1965, Congress enacted the Elementary and

Secondary Education Act; Title I funneled significant new funding to school districts based on the number of poor kids enrolled. The rationale was intuitively appealing: schools would make up for what was not provided by the family. The problem was that compensatory education meant radically different things to different people. Conventional thinking focused on improving the reading and math performance of poor kids by providing after-hours schooling, smaller classes, enriching activities such as field trips, and tutorial help. Others proposed, in the words of Diane Ravitch, that "poor children would do better in school if the school would respect their culture and values, rather than trying to impose middle-class culture and values on them."[13] Many Title I programs hired "paraprofessionals" from poor neighborhoods and established advisory committees to give the poor a voice in their children's educations. The two approaches to improving education for the poor—integration and compensation—were pursued simultaneously.

By 1967, the drive for integrated schools had headed north. Carl Marburger had gained his reputation by integrating the Detroit schools as assistant superintendent in the early 1960s and then running the reservation schools for the Bureau of Indian Affairs. In New Jersey, in the wake of the 1967 Newark and Plainfield riots, the question was focused on how the state was going to educate large numbers of poor minority kids in the older cities. Task forces were established, buildings were inspected, pleas for more money were heard—there was even a recommendation that the state takeover the Newark schools. Marburger explored the takeover idea, but received little encouragement from the governor or Democratic legislators.

School integration was already proceeding in many smaller New Jersey communities. Princeton had come up with a plan that paired predominantly black and white elementary schools so that children from each neighborhood would spend first through third grades at one and fourth through sixth at the other. The New Jersey Supreme Court authorized the commissioner of education to prevent one district from withdrawing its students from another if the result was an increase in segregation. But this would not work in the cities—Marburger had observed what simple arithmetic confirmed: there were simply not enough white students left in the city to bring about meaningful integration as long as municipal boundaries were observed. His remarks set off a political firestorm that helped the Republicans win control of both legislative chambers in the 1967 elections.

Fast-forward to January 1994: I am now a member of the State Senate education committee, interviewing the newly designated education commissioner. The main question is: Should the state take over the Newark schools? And if so, what do the educational bureaucrats in Trenton know that could be reasonably expected to improve the prospects for large numbers of poor minority students? The answer did not mention or suggest that the prospects of any student in Newark could be improved by a public policy that aimed for integration by race or class. Moreover, it was clear that nothing much had been learned in the intervening twenty-eight years to offer confidence that state operation would produce higher student achievement. In July 1995, the state took control of New Jersey's largest district without offering any plan for improved education (it already had run the Jersey City schools for six years and test results showed no improvement).

More than a quarter-century had passed between these two glimpses at education in New Jersey's largest city, and in that time, "education reform" had become an industry that employed scholars, policy entrepreneurs, corporate leaders, politicians, teacher unionists, foundations, and citizen groups. Since the mid-1960s, the industry has spawned one model and fad after another. Technologists have pushed talking typewriters, computer-assisted instruction, and interactive television; community activists have gone from integration, parental empowerment, and decentralized school boards to Afrocentric male academies and "multiculturalism." There have been pushes for community schools, school-based management, More Effective Schools, magnet schools, charter schools, and partnership schools. Conservatives who opposed vouchers when they were proposed to ease metropolitan segregation, now embrace them as the only answer for the poor and rich alike. In the meantime, schooling for most poor kids has been reduced to stigmatizing, remedial instruction and limp "self-esteem" projects. Plainly, something is wrong.

This discussion about how to educate lower-class children will not be a long one. My prescription is simple and unachievable on a large scale: find tough, energetic, demanding principals who believe that every kid can achieve. Good schools must be clean, inviting, respectful of students and parents, and demanding of teachers and students; they must put forward high expectations for academic achievement, and must be led by one who never loses sight of the vision while attending to the details. The shame is that this has been known for years, but politicians, policy proponents, and educators have continued their quest for grand solutions.

The public policy implications are equally simple: do whatever is possible to increase the probability that such principals can be convinced to work in tough schools for the long run. The first bill I introduced in the

New Jersey Senate would replace life tenure for principals and other administrators with three- to five-year contracts. It has set off nasty fights with powerful interest groups, which view these contracts as a first step to stripping teachers of tenure or as a way to politicize the appointment of principals. The beneficiaries of such a victory are currently unorganized, unrepresented, and frequently unappreciative, but their needs should outweigh those of the protectors of the status quo.

Two stories from New York illustrate the problem and the promise found in the public education system. In November 1988, the principal of a Bronx elementary school was arrested for buying crack. It turns out that he had, for many of his sixteen years as principal, appeared at school intoxicated and shabbily dressed. He had been suspended three times; in the year before his arrest, he had been late or absent 142 out of 184 school days. No charges had ever been filed against him for three reasons: his good friend was the chairman of the local board; his white subordinates (he is black) feared that any charges they brought against him would bring accusations of racism; and the local school board thought the process for ousting a tenured principal was too cumbersome (only one principal in a system with a thousand schools was dismissed in the 1980s; the average disciplinary proceeding took 631 days!).[14]

A few months earlier, the *New York Times* profiled P.S. 87, an elementary school (one of the 616 in New York) whose students performed well above expectations. Why did P.S. 87 have a waiting list for admission? Because it was run by a tough-minded, visionary principal who involved parents extensively, respected her students, recruited teachers who wanted to teach in a racially mixed school without separate tracks for low and high achieving students, and emphasized reading and more reading.[15] One must ask: Has the profile of an effective school ever included a bureaucratic, jargon-spewing, time-serving principal?

MOVING AHEAD

We can now glimpse the changing political conditions that offer whatever small optimism can be mustered about the prospects for dealing with city poverty. When Democrats distance themselves from ideas that offend the political and cultural sensibilities of most Americans, opportunities to find bipartisan accord on new initiatives arise. Consider, for example, the relative ease with which President Clinton secured agreement on a significant increase in the coverage and funding for the earned income tax credit as part of his 1993 budget proposal. He proposed that it be expanded so that full-time workers without children be included for the first time and that the ceiling on tax credits for workers with two or more kids would go to $27,000. The cost of Clinton's proposal was about $27 billion a year, a huge increase to the federal spending when budget deficits are the principal preoccupation of Washington.

The earned income tax credit is favored by both parties because it rewards people who work full-time. However, as the Republican congressional majority seeks to make good on its balanced-budget promise, the credit has been targeted for reductions and for an increase in the enforcement of its eligibility criteria.

The strong bipartisan accord needed to restructure the welfare system lasted only a short time. The losers in its demise are the poor and the states who administer the system. Republicans have backed off from their early support for transitional child- and health-care for recipients taking training or low-wage jobs. Instead, Republicans now see welfare as a way to reduce federal spending by capping it at the 1994 level in the form of a block grant to states. This would remove the federal partnership and dollars from any increases in the welfare rolls, leaving to the states to pick up the slack (or not).

What cannot be envisioned is a federally financed and coordinated second war on poverty. Leadership on poverty issues will have to come from the states as they grapple with welfare, education, housing, and health issues. This is as it should be in an area where the policy choices are so clouded and the resources so pinched. Progressive Democrats in New Jersey, by way of a brief example, took the lead in revising welfare laws to eliminate payments for additional children born while the mother is on welfare, and to reduce the incentive for mothers under eighteen from moving into subsidized housing.

The deterioration of conditions in poor city neighborhoods over the last generation should warn us off grand designs. The problem is not that nothing works; the problem is that what works requires a degree of diligence and patience that is uncommon in the contemporary merchandising of public issues. Liberals have been slow to acknowledge failure; conservatives exploit the failures for political advantage. Neither posture moves the debate to a point where solutions can be the focus of bipartisan effort. We don't need another round of program proposals with catchy acronyms, lofty objectives, and doubtful leadership.

What works are programs with fidelity to basic American principles, programs that favor work over idleness and personal responsibility over escape, programs that demonstrate respect for the dignity and competencies of the poor. Misfortune, disadvantage, and poverty should determine the universe for such programs, not race or ethnicity. Standards for everyone—staff, parents, and kids—must be high. Programs that work emphasize cleanliness, order, civility, and good citizenship. They take a long-term view of the investments required before payoffs are delivered. They accept small victories as sufficient recompense. And most often, they are programs that, while largely financed with tax dollars, are run by nonprofit organizations, not civil servants.

9»

PROGRESSIVE RESTORATION:
WITH OR WITHOUT CLINTON

No country without a revolution or a military defeat and
subsequent occupation has ever experienced such a sharp
shift in the distribution of earnings as America has in the last
generation. At no other time have median wages of American
men fallen for more than two decades. Never before have a
majority of American workers suffered real wage reductions
while per capita domestic product was advancing.

—Lester C. Thurow,[1] MIT economist

THE ENDANGERED MIDDLE CLASS AND
THE OPPORTUNITY FOR PROGRESSIVES

The American Dream is threatened for most Americans. Since 1973,
nearly one-half of American families have seen their standard of living
decline! The fortunes of about 60 percent of the remainder have stagnated. Only the top 20 percent of households have seen any improvement in
income and wealth. These sobering facts animate the idea of building a
new progressive coalition.

The extremists who have taken over the Republican party ignore the stagnation or deterioration in living standards for 80 percent of American families. Any economic problems are blamed on government or on the failure to abide by the family values prescribed by the divorced white men who lead the Republicans. To the extent that a vision for broadened prosperity is detectable from extremists, it is this: trust the investor class to invest the funds Republicans make available to it through new tax deals in ways that will eventually benefit those who work for salaries and wages.

Progressives do not have much of an answer, either. They have been too busy fighting a rear-guard action in the cultural wars, trying to convince voters that they really do favor punishing rioters and violent criminals, that they are true patriots who believe in a strong national defense, that they endorse the American passion for work (even for welfare recipients under certain circumstances), and that they are not all that enthusiastic about bigger government and higher taxes.

Much of this book has argued that progressives got sidetracked from the main business of politics and government because they were afraid to argue sensibly on a tangle of issues freighted by race. Before they can rebuild a political majority, progressives must both shore up their coalition and come up with an answer to restoring the American dream.

STRESSES IN THE PROGRESSIVE COALITION

Progressives can take no one for granted, least of all black Americans. Going along with racial preferences and appearing weak-willed on welfare reform and crime has produced little enthusiasm among black progressives and has opened the door to the permanent flight of Reagan Democrats to the GOP. When the shared interests of white and black Americans and of working—and middle-class Americans are emphasized, progressives can win.

Black and white Americans hold unremarkably similar views about work, personal responsibility, patriotism, crime control, and the importance of education. Both worry about good jobs, health care, safe neighborhoods, and the future of their children. Black Americans tend to be more conservative on social issues than black leaders.[2] For example, they are slightly more likely than whites to favor prayer in public schools and restrictions on abortions.[3] Moreover, most blacks perceive much less animosity and much more amiability from whites than is suggested by the dire and divisive language of professional blacks.[4]

If white progressives do not lead the public discussion about racial bias, the shared interests of black and white Americans, and the exaggerated claims of professional blacks, then interracial differences will grow and with them the hopes of a new coalition. But public discussion is terribly difficult, as I discovered when I helped arrange a series of forums on racial and ethnic issues for the New Jersey Democratic State Committee. There is no simple or quick way to break down patterns of speech and expectation that have been built up over thirty years. Nor is it realistic to expect black political leaders to agree to coalition approaches on issues such as racial districting or set-asides without a demonstration of good faith by white politicians, and of alternative, race-neutral programs that give promise to black Americans.

There are important voices for biracial politics who should be heeded. John Lewis, a U.S. House member from Atlanta and a hero of the civil rights struggle, has never given up on the idea of an integrated society. Hugh B. Price, the president of the national Urban League, noted in his 1994 inaugural address:

> For all our suffering, we cannot become so fixated on our problems that we ignore our commonality of interest with others. All of the problems I've addressed . . . inadequate schooling, idle and alienated youngsters, and chronic unemployment—cut across racial lines. If we're ever to deal with them on a scale remotely equal to their size, we must coalesce with people of other complexions who feel the same pain, even if it isn't yet as acute.[5]

Obviously, both black and white Americans would benefit from policies that lead to sustained economic growth (the migration of poor black families into the middle class stagnated in the late 1970s). Black and white progressives share the belief that government plays a crucial role in stimulating and sustaining economic growth, by prescribing the rules for fair and open markets, financing infrastructure investments, and guaranteeing educational opportunity. If, however, progressives emphasize bailing out society's most troubled members, they squander the chance to incorporate increasingly anxious working- and middle-class white Americans into the coalition. Democrats do not need to prove again that they care about poor people, nor must they apologize for going after the votes of white suburbanites.

BLACK AND ʹHITE (PROGRESSIVES) TOGETHER?

The U.S. S reme Court may force black and white progressives to get together. In series of decisions at the end of its 1994–95 session, the Court came clos to abolishing racial preferences in all federal programs. In *Adarand Constructors v. Pena,* a 5-4 majority ruled that the federal government may use racial classifications even for "benign purposes" (such as to increase minority participation in government contracts) only when "narrowly tailored" to further "compelling governmental interests" that can withstand the "strictest judicial scrutiny." Racial classification is "a highly suspect tool." Justice Antonin Scalia wrote: "In the eyes of the government, we are just one race here. It is American." Underrepresentation of women and minorities is no longer, by itself, evidence of gender or racial discrimination.

In *Miller* v. *Johnson,* the Court ruled that legislative districts that are drawn where race is the "predominant factor" are suspect, notwithstanding the Voting Rights Act of 1982, which directs states to use race to draw districts in which minorities will be a majority. There is little doubt that states with significant minority populations have reapportioned using race as the "predominant," even exclusive, basis. On redistricting—as opposed to set-asides—black Democratic elected officials will receive enthusiastic support from white Republican legislators to retain such districts.

But the Court is not the only source of provocation for progressives. Republican candidates are making race preferences a key issue in the 1996 presidential elections. Governor Pete Wilson of California bet his candidacy on the issue (foolishly, as it turned out). President Clinton must look at election day in November 1996 knowing that in California—the state he absolutely must carry to have a chance at reelection—he will share the ballot with a referendum abolishing all racial, ethnic, and gender preferences in all public institutions.

If progressives think that the Court can be out-waited and the GOP outwitted, they must face the fact that rebuilding their legislative majorities is unlikely if strict racial districting persists. Democrats need look only to the results of congressional elections in the eleven southern states of the Confederacy where generally moderate white Democrats have been replaced by conservative to extremist white Republicans. The Democratic majority of 86 to 40 in 1990 shifted to a 66 to 59 Republican edge after 1994, and that was before several conservative Democrats switched parties. The number of black Democratic representatives rose from just five in 1990 to seventeen in 1994. Not all of these results can be attributed solely to racial reapportionment—Republicans have been gaining steadily in the South, and 1994 was a particularly bad year to be a Democratic incumbent.

Republicans feast on isolating blacks and Democrats on issues of race. It is not surprising that, in the round of redistricting that followed the 1990 Census, the Republican National Committee provided black and Latino activists with expensive software to help them draw up their own maps maximizing the number of safe minority seats. While it is clear that racial apportionment benefits the black politicians who are guaranteed safe seats, other beneficiaries (other than white Republican politicians) are tougher to identify. In New Jersey's 8th district, for example, a one-term Democratic incumbent ran furiously, yet lost by 2,000 votes in 1994, while in the adjoining super-majority minority district, the incumbent hardly campaigned, yet won by a 72–28 percent margin. Black progressives do have a stake in helping to elect larger number of white progressives. Moreover, black Americans may not be well served by district lines that overwhelmingly protect incumbent black legislators—everyone benefits from competition or its threat. But worse, the effort to build a biracial coalition may be thwarted by black legislators who, to represent their constituents and to avoid powerful primary challenges, must fight tooth and nail for racial policies such as quotas and set-asides that cannot be sold in majority white districts.

This discussion suggests where the black-white progressive debate might begin. It will not be an easy one for a very simple reason—most of the compromising will necessarily involve black interests. Moreover, in the absence of a clear progressive vision of what the country must do to restore real equal opportunity, there is no good reason for black elected officials to deal.

PROGRESSIVES MUST VISUALIZE AMERICAN SOCIETY WITHOUT RACE PREFERENCES

Progressives must be clear about the implications of race preferences: they so strongly counter the fundamental beliefs of American society that they should be opposed, except in cases of persistent discrimination where temporary preferences are the only solution.

Progressives should fashion alternatives to racial preferences based on the experience of the U.S. Army. The Army builds on old-style affirmative action. It accepts no one who fails its recruitment test standards (which are

only a bit lower than those of the Navy and Air Force). After basic training, screening tests identify enlisted personnel who do not possess the literacy and mathematical competencies to compete successfully for
promotions. These soldiers are put through a comprehensive and quite
expensive instructional sequence to bring them up to standard. The result
is an institution that is led by a remarkably diverse noncommissioned
officer corps and where black Americans, in particular, find true equal
opportunity to perform and lead. The Army requires officer promotion
boards to include minority candidates or justify their exclusion in writing.
No quotas are employed. The consistent attention to inclusion, a vigorous
ethic against racial discrimination (the career of any officer cited for
racially offensive language or behavior is finished), and high priority in
performance reviews to effective leadership on diversity and inclusion
issues has produced the nation's most thoroughly integrated institution—
and one of its most effective.

The military services are one of a few places in American society
where white Americans are almost certain to encounter black Americans
as superiors. The Army experience confirms the crucial role of leadership in suffusing organizations with a commitment to equal opportunity
and an intolerance of racial discrimination. It also illuminates the value of
remedial assistance for underperformers. The Army balances race consciousness with an absence of quotas. Americans—black and white—
support this old-style affirmative action by a wide margin.[6]

Consider how the Army approach might work to replace set-asides,
now endangered by Supreme Court decisions. Under existing law, fixed
percentages of government contracts are reserved for women and minority vendors on the grounds that they were subjected to prior discrimination. I have developed legislation that assumes a public interest in helping
small businesses that are started without sufficient family or personal
contacts and assets. Preferences would be based on economics, not race or
gender. If you are undercapitalized and have a relatively low net worth,
and your business is small, you would be eligible for preferred contracts
for a period of five years, whatever your color or gender. After five years,
you are either ready to compete or not.

The same standards can be applied to employment and promotion
decisions. Employers should be required to demonstrate that they had
included women and minority candidates in their search, and that there
are acceptable explanations for disproportionately low representation.
As the chairman of the board of a $300-plus million manufacturing com-
pany, I can certify that white men need to be reminded systematically

and persistently about the existence of quality candidates who are non-white and nonmale. Employers should have to document their special efforts to increase the hiring and promotion opportunities for those who traditionally have been excluded. One test is whether the corporate compensation program rewards senior executives for increasing the diversity of the workforce.

Progressives must act on the belief of most black Americans that racial discrimination is widespread. They should push clear, prompt, and vigorous enforcement of antidiscrimination laws, particularly in the area of housing. As discussed in Chapter 7, the results of matched-pair tests corroborate statistical evidence that in a significant percentage of encounters with the real estate industry, black and Latino home buyers are not given the same information or encouragement that white buyers receive. Racial discrimination distorts the market at great personal and financial cost to its victims. Those responsible for it should be treated as thieves. Just as an Army officer ends his or her career by abusing anyone because of their race, so should those responsible for housing discrimination lose their realtor licenses and be subjected to fines, even jail time.

CLINTON'S FADING OPPORTUNITY AND THE POLITICS OF REBUILDING A PROGRESSIVE COALITION

Bill Clinton's 1992 victory as a "New Democrat" provided a road map for a potential progressive coalition. He won by emphasizing the growing economic insecurity of middle- and working-class Americans, the increasing costs of health care, and the generally fading hopes of those who "play by the rules." His election coalition cobbled together "new" and "old" Democrats, environmentalists and loggers, factory hands and professional women, and black Americans and some white southerners. Bolstered by a solid stripe of farming and industrial states across the middle of the country, Clinton received a convincing majority of Electoral College votes, but only 43 percent of the popular vote. The Clinton coalition died an infant in 1994. In the wreckage, Democrats could see no bright lining: Congress ended up in Republican hands for the first time since 1952, with still a dozen of so conservative Democrats ready to switch parties, and Republicans held thirty governorships, including eight of the ten largest states. When the Republican national chairman asserted that his goal was control of all fifty legislatures by 2001, it did not sound terribly unrealistic. Worse, much worse, Democrats had nothing to say.

The 1994 election reflected Clinton's utter failure to use his presidency to respond to middle-class despair he so brilliantly identified and spoke to in his 1992 campaign. Oh, he tried, but not with a focus or persistence proportionate to the task of reversing a three-decade drift of working- and middle-cass voters to the GOP. Clinton honored his pledge to "jump start" the economy by proposing a $30 billion "stimulus" package. In the third month of his presidency, a GOP filibuster killed the plan. In truth, Clinton's package was a grab bag—proposals for capital investments, basic research, and modernization mixed with short-term spending for food aid and summer jobs. And as writer and investment banker Charles Morris pointed out, the magnitude of the plan was timid, within the statistical margin of error of the accounts for a $6 trillion economy.[7]

Clinton tried, too, with his September 1993 proposal to remake the American health care system. His plan did not recognize that there was no strong consensus about what constituted the "health care crisis." Was it the 40 million Americans without any coverage, the lack of portability of benefits, the fast-rising prices for medical care, or the billions squandered in insurance paperwork? The Clinton plan would have treated all of these problems at once by setting up a new public agency that would finance universal coverage in mysterious ways and by providing health care through a confusing tangle of "alliances" and regional functionaries. He lost, and badly. The "New Democrat" looked like an enthusiast of big government and higher taxes—proposing in Phil Gramm's words, a health system with "the efficiency of the post office and the compassion of the IRS."

Clinton deferred any noticeable or painful spending cuts and dropped his campaign message of shared sacrifice for a better future. "Sacrifice" is the dirty word of politics, for either party.

Ordinarily, a growing economy with lots of jobs and no threat of war is a boon to an incumbent president and his party. Not for Bill Clinton. Even though the economy had generated seven million new jobs since his inauguration, with low inflation and global stability, the nation reflected no sense of well-being.

Building a new coalition on this wobbling foundation must begin with the traditional progressive base. The highest concentration of Democratic support is found among black Americans, whose vote for Democratic nominees has not dropped below 80 percent since 1964. Jews and Latinos are the next most loyal supporters, followed by single working women, gays, and union households. Throw in middle-class activists such as environmentalists, and the Democrats can count on about 40 percent of the electorate (McGovern polled 38 percent).

The liberal-Left wing of the party has asserted for a quarter century that sharpening the party's message of deliverance to the "desperate, the damned, the disinherited, the disrespected" would result in an out-pouring of additional poor, minority, and youthful voters sufficient to win presidential elections. Wrong. The big Democratic losers—George McGovern, Jimmy Carter in 1980, Walter Mondale, and Michael Dukakis—all did very well among base Democratic voters, but the increased voter turnout promised by the Left never materialized. Ruy Teixeira reconstructed the 1988 election using Jesse Jackson's most brazen promise of voter mobilization: "Assuming the highest turnout scenarios (for blacks and Hispanics, 10 points higher than whites; for the white poor, 10 points higher than the white rich), the computations still show only 4,677,000 net additional votes for Dukakis."[8] In other words, with improbable and unprecedented levels of voting among poor whites and minorities, Dukakis would still have lost by more than two million votes—assuming no off-setting Republican mobilization.

PROGRESSIVES SHOULD NOT COUNT ON THE PEROTISTAS

As soon as the 1992 returns were in, pundits were suggesting that Clinton's reelection in 1996 would be assured if he went after the 19 mil-lion mostly white, mostly middle-class voters who supported indepen-dent candidate Ross Perot—the "Perotistas." The pundits drew on the parallels with the 1968 election—another three-way race—in which Nixon won with 43 percent of the vote while George Wallace received 13 percent, launching the generation-long journey of the white working class and white southerners into the Republican party.[9] While the parallel is appealing on its face, the contrasting interests of Perot supporters with other potential coalition members presage substantial difficulties.

Stanley Greenberg, Clinton's pollster, in a postelection survey of Perot voters, discovered what he called "refugees" from the Republican party, voters who were resentful of Reaganomics and uneasy about the hold of the religious right on the GOP (Perot and Clinton voters were about even in their support of abortion rights).[10] But more than anything else, Perot voters were found to be deeply antigovernment and anti-establishment, which set them apart from both Clinton and Bush voters. Greenberg notes: "These attitudes are less about ideology and more about the failure of public trust that characterizes their view of almost all big institutions from big business to Congress to big labor."[11] He found that Perot supporters are strongly convinced that the "poor are trying to get something for nothing," that "it's the middle class, not the poor, who really get a raw deal," and that "we have gone too far in pushing equal rights for different groups. . ."[12] Perot's strongest support came from white voters under age thirty and white men without a college education, precisely the groups affected most negatively by race preferences and by declines in real income.[13] Perot voters wanted government to reform health care to guarantee universal access *and* reduce costs and to clean up the welfare system.[14]

In short, the typical Perot voter was just boycotting the Republican church until it got a new preacher; most never bothered with the Democrats. The common ground between the neopopulist, antigovernment sentiments of Perot's voters and Clinton's governmental activism is too narrow for building any coalition.

Restoring Bipartisanship to the Progressive Cause

To govern, a progressive coalition must include progressive Republicans. GOP moderates such as New Jersey's former governor, Tom Kean, can see that their party is headed in a direction that is as irrelevant and as offensive to most Americans as that taken by the McGovern Democrats in the 1970s.

Republicans provided much of the leadership and many of the votes to pass the historic civil rights laws of the 1960s. Until 1964 the party was dominated by its eastern, liberal establishment. In short order, Republicans became the antiblack, white separatist party, driving out a number of progressives including New York mayor John V. Lindsay, Nixon's civil rights chief Leon Panetta, and Michigan senator Donald Riegle. By the 1980s, the Republican pattern of exploiting racial fears on issues such as crime and welfare was well established, further offending increasingly silent and impotent GOP moderates. The party of Lincoln was dead.

GOP moderates might excuse their party's abandonment of black Americans as good politics, but not so the full-scale cultural warfare that set up Bush's 1992 defeat. Under the rubric of "family values," Republican convention speakers expressed disdain not only for homosexuals, but for working mothers, single parents, and non-Christians. Republicans came across as harsh, intolerant, and self-righteous. They should have learned from the McGovern Democrats: linger in the company of extremists and one is tarred with their label, as George Bush was, thanks to Pat Buchanan and Pat Robertson.

The wheel has turned. As Kevin Phillips has noted:

> In domestic affairs, we have seen how much of the critical GOP momentum in the Nixon and Reagan years had come from social issues: rising crime, judicial permissiveness, the death penalty, riots and racial tension, welfare . . . campus radicalism, busing, quotas, patriotism. . . . Not only did these points . . . lose importance next to 1992 dislocations in the economy, but a new set of domestic and cultural issues were emerging for the 1990s: health care, education, urban problems, the environment, economic fairness, abortion and what could be called a "women's" array of concerns, including day care, parental leave, equal pay, the feminization of poverty, the glass ceiling in employment . . . and sexual harassment. Issues like these favored the Democrats.[15]

They should also favor progressive Republicans.

The fading of Republican progressives is reflected in the meager support given to moderate measures President Clinton put forward in the 103d Congress. Only 40 of 174 Republican representatives voted for the family leave act; only 35 voted for federal protection for abortion clinics. On the Senate side, the influence of progressive Republicans is hard to detect.

Progressive Republicans finally stood up in 1995, along with most House Democrats, to try to stop (unsuccessfully) congressional evisceration of environmental regulation. Speaker Gingrich's agenda includes dismantling the Environmental Protection Agency's capacity to oversee implementation of the clean air and water statutes, adoption of pro-industry standards, and a surrender of federal management of millions of acres of national forests and ranges.

A right-wing *putsch* in the Republican party would be entirely favorable for Democrats. The politics of abortion and gun control already favor progressives. I won a state senate seat in one of the most Republican counties in the nation by emphasizing my pro-choice, pro-gun control positions against a longtime antiabortion, pro-NRA incumbent. A strategy that relies on the hope of Republican extremism alone, however, provides progressives neither purpose nor durability.

EXTREMISTS HAVE HIJACKED THE REPUBLICAN PARTY

Conservative, at one time, referred to a philosophy of fiscal prudence, a long-term perspective, and a recognition that savings and investment are the engine of capitalism. Conservatives from Adam Smith to Robert Taft understood as well that government was an essential partner with the market economy to finance those public investments that the private sector can never undertake. Under these now quaint terms, I am a conservative.

As for the current leadership of the Republican party, "conservative" is a marketing term with only a fragile connection to traditional conservative standards. The term now camouflages an extremist and dangerous politics that can be stated thusly: think short-term (not past the next election); promise tax cuts *and* no-pain spending cuts; pay for this improbable combination by borrowing from the next generation; serve the investor class, trusting that its decisions to optimize *its* income and wealth will eventually translate into improved living standards for the 95 percent of society that works for a living; relieve industry by minimizing oversight of markets and winking at compliance with environmental regulations; and talk frequently about campaign reform and the "broken system," but do nothing. Unhappily, one stance the GOP leadership shares with Democrats: ignore the erosion in middle-class living standards and opportunities.

The pattern has been the same since 1980: Republicans blame government at all levels for slow economic growth. Republicans campaign against government spending and high taxes. Once elected, they fail to cut spending, but borrow heavily to finance their tax cuts and spending increases. It is worth telling the story about New Jersey Governor Christine Todd Whitman's tax cut because it shows how shortsighted politics plays at the state level and translates into national acclaim (and it is one in which I played a bit part as a minority member of the state senate).

Initially, Whitman campaigned against tax cuts: "There is no point giving an election year tax break when you have to come back . . . and hit them for two times the cut" she declared early in the 1993 gubernatorial campaign.[16] By late September, she changed her mind and proposed a 30 percent cut in income tax, despite being roundly criticized for ignoring a looming $1 billion–2 billion budget gap and not identifying how the tax cut would be financed. Whitman won a close election over an unpopular incumbent governor.

Before reliable budget information was available, Governor Whitman announced in her inaugural address a retroactive 5 percent cut to make good on her promise and to "energize" New Jersey's laconic economy. The proposal was nothing less than another supply-side miracle wherein a $300 million tax cut in New Jersey's $230 billion "economy" would propel a spree of spending and investment sufficient to set off a job-creating splurge. To pay for the cut and to maintain state aid for property tax relief, Whitman balanced the budget by borrowing almost $4 billion over three years from public employee pension and retiree health benefit funds with the argument that they were "overfunded." (One change she made left New Jersey with an *unfunded* liability of more than $30 billion for retiree health benefits.) Who benefited? The across-the-board 5 percent cut returned about $50 to the average New Jersey family, $850 to families with incomes of $300,000, and about $12,000 to the governor's family.

The revenues that were lost came from the Property Tax Relief Fund (New Jersey has the second highest property taxes in the country—by constitutional dedication the Fund receives every penny of income tax revenues). When the pension borrowings end, the lost revenues will be shifted to the property tax, the largest tax for most New Jersey families. For example, the average family of four in the middle quintile had a 1992 income of $54,000, paid $3,186 in property taxes and $1,080 in New Jersey income taxes—its "savings" of $54 in income taxes would be offset by property tax increases of about $162.

When 1994 job figures showed an increase of 65,000 jobs in New Jersey, the governor called a press conference to connect the job growth to her income tax cut. In 1995 as New Jersey unemployment rate hovered above those of her neighbors and the national average the governor was silent. The supply-siders' formulation, questionable enough for the national economy, is nonsensical at the state level.

The short-term politics of the Whitman tax cut are irresistible: spending goes up (the second Whitman budget is $16 billion—$1 billion more than her predecessor's last budget); property taxes are stabilized, and a campaign promise is kept. And in the bumper-sticker politics of the 1990s, "Tax Cut" sure beats "Yeah, but just wait," or "Our kids will pay for the tax cuts." Long-term, the picture is not pretty: borrowing has ballooned, and the pensions will have to be funded unless the bloody fight of cutting benefits is won. By the time state politicians are forced to deal with these nasty problems, Governor Whitman will be safely out of office.

If words yet have meaning, there is no way that the term "fiscal conservative" can be applied to the policies of Governor Whitman (or Ronald

Reagan, George Bush, or Newt Gingrich). The policies are not only short-sighted; they are reckless.

The extremists place unqualified faith in the marketplace. Take the Republican answers to the problems of public education. "Liberate parents, make public schools compete" is the chant of extremist Republicans who support vouchers. They want to get the federal government out of the business of setting national standards and helping states to develop and enforce them (an idea of George Bush and his education secretary, Lamar Alexander). But nowhere do the extremists give the intuitive explanation for declining educational achievement: children spend most of their time watching television, less of their time on homework, and their parents are not around to enforce the standards prevailing in Europe and most of Asia. The absence of mothers from the home and the growing appetite for entertainment over education are both market-driven developments that better explain America's mediocre performance than the existence of a federal department of education.

The extremist Republican vision calls for government to reward those at the top of the income scale with further relief from taxation so that they can pay directly for their own security, open space, convenient transport, and multiple houses. Simultaneously, GOP extremists want to end government investments in public transport, public open spaces, public security, and housing assistance. Extremist Republicans have set out to destroy America's Public Square and with it the sense of shared obligation and investment in our future. They even propose to end the thirty-year pledge of the federal government to assist any deserving student with the opportunity for higher education—the essential link to the American dream.

The extremist leaders of the Republican party have a narrow, intolerant view of how Americans should live their lives. They oppose equality for women in personal matters such as the marriage contract and in sexual politics. Simultaneously, they seek to end federal support for contraceptive health services for poor women and the right of all women to decide when or if to bear a child. They applaud technological breakthroughs like the "computer superhighway," but do not trust citizens enough to allow its uncensored use. They attack a popular culture that features excessive violence and easy sex, then hail the marketplace that feeds the popular appetite for both. They hail the American spirit, but exploit economic insecurity with attacks on aliens, legal and not. They impugn the patriotism of those who fear talk of "a Christian nation," and who reject official prayer in public schools.

These Republicans are hypocritical. They scold the poor for not working and accepting responsibility for their children, while they saw the rungs on the opportunity ladder that the striving poor need to grab to escape poverty. They say they are against racial discrimination, but then encourage Republicans like David Duke, whose appeal is based on racial hatred. They play tough on crime and then endorse a convicted Oliver North to represent Virginia in the U.S. Senate.

The GOP "Contract with America" is very much in line with the big talk–no pain approach. When asked to specify the cuts required to reach the contract's goal of balancing the budget in seven years, the House Majority Leader Dick Armey of Texas refused, on the grounds that to do so would cause his supporters' "knees to buckle." The new extremists, in short, are phonies; they dishonor the conservative tradition.

A PROGRESSIVE RESPONSE

Progressives understand that the postwar American prosperity was spurred on by much higher rates of personal savings and by high levels of government investment in a national highway system, new airports and infrastructure, and a huge expansion in public higher education. (Forty-four percent of today's colleges and universities were established after 1960—almost all of them public). The federal government financed basic and applied research on an unprecedented scale, in aerospace and military applications, and biomedical research and basic science. It subsidized and expanded the home-mortgage market and financed housing for poor families. And during the much-maligned Great Society, the nation finally guaranteed a dignified retirement for working Americans by establishing Medicare to end the near-automatic impoverishment of the elderly.

Today, progressives are confused about what to do to restore a broad-based prosperity. Bill Clinton has tried to get by with a conflicting economic policy that on the one hand relies on the Reaganist prescription to reduce federal deficits by gutting federal spending, and, on the other, recognizes the need for increased federal spending for research, development, infrastructure investment, higher education, and housing. Thirty-six percent of the Democratic representatives voted for a balanced budget amendment in 1995, an invention of the Right to accomplish by way of constitutional amendment what they are unwilling to support through the legislative process. In short, Democrats are acting more like crypto-Republicans than like representatives of a political philosophy that offers concrete opportunity to middle-class aspirations.

A progressive majority coalition cannot be rebuilt on campaign cleverness or by exploiting the fears of what the right-wing takeover of the

GOP portends. Not alone, anyway. Nor is the test whether Clinton wins a second term: assuming no economic crash or Whitewater disaster, a right-wing opponent or a rightist third party in the field, Clinton could win without disturbing the underlying preference of American voters for Republican presidents. No, for progressives to come back, they need to be firm and consistent about some general principles, some of which are tactical and political, some philosophical fundamental. All should have a familiar feel after reading the preceding eight chapters.

Principle One: Progressives support both higher levels of public investment and strengthening marketplace forces. The United States has reached a point where its air traffic control system shuts down periodically, where bridges on interstate highways collapse, where its greatest public research university (the University of California) is slowly deteriorating, and where no viable solution to the disposal of radioactive wastes has yet been implemented. Restoring a broad-based prosperity requires not only a market system that stimulates entrepreneurial activity, but a level of public investment that ensures an efficient transportation system, maintenance of our competitive edge in research and development, and management and preservation of our environment.

Principle Two: Progressives believe in the place of private behavior and personal values in shaping the public interest and achieving economic prosperity. Progressives should be consistent in advancing policies that strengthen two-parent families, the work ethic, and taking financial responsibility for one's children. The evidence is overwhelming that parental nurturing is essential to educational achievement, which is in turn a big determinant of lifetime earnings potential. The nation cannot afford to witness the further weakening of families.

Principle Three: Progressives represent the interests of the working and middle classes and reject the idea that incentives for investors and entrepreneurs are sufficient to bring about broad-based prosperity. Republicans have waged successful class warfare against wage-earners and the poor for fifteen years, by decreasing taxes on the very rich, increasing them on the middle-class, and exploiting the poor. The result has been intentional deficits, a persistent budget crisis, and a massive transfer of wealth and income from those who work to those who invest—just 1 percent of Americans own almost half of all financial assets![17] Progressives not only must advance principles of fair taxation that reflect ability to pay, but also must renew the belief that the United States can afford to provide universal health care, educational opportunities, and lifelong training. "Trickle-down" has not trickled—it is time to try something else.

Principal Four: Progressives believe American self-government is endangered by a failure of citizenship. Government and the political system do not fail by themselves. Citizens, individually and collectively, contribute to the failure. Progressives should help set the standards of citizenship required to preserve American democracy. One standard should be that citizens will not accept public services they are unwilling to pay for. Progressives should be consistent in calling for a restoration of standards of civility in public discourse, as well as in society at large. We know that litter laws do not clean our highways, that "motor voter" laws do not register every potential voter, or that job training programs do not inculcate the work ethic in every trainee. Only citizens, acting individually, with a sense of civic virtue can make our system work.

Principle Five: Progressives support ending ineffective and unnecessary programs and are enthusiastic about making government more efficient, decisive, and effective. Bill Clinton will not receive the credit he and Vice President Al Gore have earned for acting on their "reinvent government" pledge. Reducing the federal work force by 102,000 employees by 1994 and saving an estimated $26 billion is a noticeable achievement, even in a $1.5 trillion budget. But most Americans come into contact with their government in a post office line, or through an indecipherable IRS instruction, or through a rude clerk at a motor vehicle agency. Progressives need either to make civil service work for its customers, or take on the nasty fight to reform it.

Principle Six: Progressives operate with a long-term perspective and a prudent fiscal philosophy that emphasizes "cash payment" for current needs and incurring debt only for investments with long-term benefits. Progressives are associated with Keynesian economics, which anticipates cyclical budget deficits to "jump start" lagging economies by providing unemployment payments and accelerating public works projects. That is very different from the policy of Republican extremists to use debt to finance tax cuts. Debt is an appropriate way to finance investments that produce long-term benefits where future beneficiaries can pay their share. With living standards for most Americans steadily deteriorating, it would be sensible to invest in badly needed infrastructure improvements and higher education to increase economic growth, enhance the skill base of the American labor force, and increase returns on private investment.

Principle Seven: Progressives believe that the American dream relies on higher education being available for all who seek and qualify for it. Only 22 percent of college students attend private institutions, a figure unchanged for two decades. For this principle to be honored means, then, that *public* higher education must be accessible, efficient, and affordable. The great American promise of higher education is endangered as public institutions struggle to minimize tuition increases, maintain course offerings so students can graduate in a reasonable time, and still support research and graduate programs. Family incomes have increased hardly at all since 1975, but college costs have risen at twice the rate of inflation. Progressives must reverse these discouraging trends even as extremists seek to shrink the public commitment to higher educational opportunity.

Principle Eight: Progressives support the historic struggle for racial justice and an inclusive American society. This is where we end, back on the subject of race in America.

"[W]hite America has been historically weakwilled in ensuring racial justice," Cornel West writes, "and has continued to resist fully accepting the humanity of blacks."[18] The goal of a racially harmonious society is not a black concern or a white concern, but an American concern. Because white Americans dominate its institutions, they set the tone in determining if equal opportunity and racial goodwill will prevail.

A progressive coalition needs strong political and moral leadership. Lyndon Johnson, Robert Kennedy, and Martin Luther King, Jr., in their very different ways, helped black and white Americans consider new possibilities for racial harmony. Kennedy was almost alone among progressive Democrats in appealing directly to working-class whites and blacks, criticizing black nationalism, and initiating programs to fight ghetto poverty.

Americans need a president to remind them, as Bill Clinton has, that "*Them* is the dread word in American politics. The Republicans blame all the problems on *them*. Sometimes, the Democrats say, 'We're going to help *them*.' People don't need help as *them*; they need help to be part of *us*, of defining their own future." America need leaders to emphasize common interests and to demonstrate personally that black and white Americans are bound together. But, ultimately, the problems are much larger than anything that can be resolved by hearing the right words or seeing the right examples.

Senator Bill Bradley sets an example, personally and politically:

> I ask every American to become a part of the dialogue that lifts this discussion to the higher ground. Beginning with ourselves, each of us must address our own personal understanding or misunderstanding of race. Ask yourself, when was the last time you had a conversation about race with someone of a different race? Ask yourself what values are shared by all races? And begin to ask our leaders how they have confronted their own understanding or misunderstanding about race in their own real lives—not just their political careers.[19]

There is no other way, is there? Individual Americans must demonstrate the respect for those of other races and backgrounds by speaking directly and openly about their shared problems and their different experiences.

Race can be discussed in a way that encourages people to think optimistically of America's promise of equal opportunity. The answer resides between the icy indifference of most conservatives to the plight of black Americans and the group-think of racial nationalists.

Race can be discussed in a way that acknowledges that most Americans, most of the time, treat others with civility, if not respect. This discussion need not ignore or revise our horrific racial history or diminish the influence of our very different racial, ethnic, and religious backgrounds. But racial harmony will not be achieved if we insist that the nature and quality of our participation in American society is determined by skin color.

At bottom, no law can tell any parent to love their child, and no court can tell Americans of different races, tongues, and religions to treat one another with civility, respect, and curiosity. Only we—you and I—can do that.

NOTES

CHAPTER 1

1. David Broder, "Flynn, Jackson Seek Clinton's Urban Commitment," *Washington Post,* June, 13, 1992, p. A12.

2. Thomas B. Edsall and David Broder, "Weekend of Meetings on Strategy Bringing Clinto n to Washington," *Washington Post,* June 12, 1992, p. A16.

3. "Remarks of Governor Bill Clinton to the Rainbow Coalition National Convention," Washington, D.C. (June 13, 1992), from text provided by Clinton-Gore for President.

4. Thomas B. Edsall, "Clinton Stuns Rainbow Coalition," *Washington Post,* June 14, 1992, p. A8.

5. Poll data summarized and reported in *American Enterprise,* September/October, 1992, p. 82.

6. "Stunned" is the right word; see Edsall, "Clinton Stuns Rainbow Coalition."

7. The "exclusion" cite is found in Gwen Ifill, "Democratic Group Argues over Goals," *New York Times,* May 7, 1991, p. A21; others in Dan Balz and David S. Broder, "Democrats Argue over Quota Clause," *Washington Post,* May 7, 1991, p. A9.

8. Clinton denied the premise of the June 12 Edsall-Broder story that his campaign was split over the Souljah speech, with some advisers pushing an accommodating approach to Jackson and others a confrontational one. See Thomas B. Edsall, "Clinton Hits Bush Role at Rio Meet," *Washington Post,* June 13, 1992, p. A12.

9. David S. Broder and Thomas B. Edsall, "Clinton Finds Biracial Support for Criticism of Rap Singer," *Washington Post,* June 16, 1992, p. A7

10. R. W. Apple, Jr. "Jackson Sees a 'Character Flaw' in Clinton's Remarks on Racism," *New York Times,* June 19, 1992, pp. A1, A24.

11. Ronald Walters, " . . . Clinton's Gall," *Washington Post,* June 16, 1992, p. A21.

12. Michael K. Frisby, "Clinton Debate with Rapper Rages," *Boston Globe,* June 18, 1992, p. 22.

13. Derrick Z. Jackson, "Where Dissatisfaction with Clinton Is Running High . . . ," *Boston Sunday Globe,* July 26, 1992, p. 63.

14. "Clinton's Cheap Shot . . . ," *Boston Globe,* June 19, 1992, p. 14.

15. Anna Quindlen, "All of These You Are," *New York Times,* June, 28, 1992, section IV, p. 17.

16. Andrew Kopkind and Alexander Cockburn, "The Democrats, Perot, and the Left," *Nation,* July 20/27, 1992, p. 82.

17. Clarence Page, "Bill Clinton's Notsaposta Say That, Is He?" reprinted in *Liberal Opinion Week,* June 28, 1992, p. 28.

18. Carl Rowan, "Bill Clinton, Jesse Jackson and Sister Souljah," reprinted in *Liberal Opinion Week,* June 28, 1992, p. 6.

19. Gwen Ifill, "Clinton Stands by Remark on Rapper," *New York Times,* June 15, 1992, p. A16.

20. Gwen Ifill, "Clinton, in Need of Lift, Deftly Plays Racial Card," *New York Times,* June 17, 1992, p. A22.

21. Ibid.

Chapter 2

1. Polite versions use the word "out-segged." I rely on the more likely version, quoted by Theodore H. White, *The Making of the President, 1968* (New York: Atheneum, 1969), p. 344.

2. C. Vann Woodward, *The Strange Career of Jim Crow* (New York: Oxford University Press, 1974), p. 170.

3. A good summary of discriminatory federal policies and practices can be found in Douglas Massey and Nancy A. Denton, *American Apartheid: Segregation and the Making of the Underclass* (Cambridge, Mass.: Harvard University Press, 1993), pp. 51–57.

4. *Public Papers of the Presidents: Lyndon B. Johnson, 1963–1964* (Washington, D.C.: U. S. Government Printing Office, 1966), p. 474.

5. William Brink and Louis Harris, *Black and White: A Study of U.S. Racial Attitudes Today* (New York: Simon and Schuster, 1966), p. 109.

6. Nicholas Lemann, *The Promised Land: The Great Black Migration and How It Changed America* (New York: Alfred A. Knopf, 1991), p. 117

7. Theodore H. White, *The Making of the President, 1960* (New York: Atheneum, 1961), p. 234.

8. Charles R. Morris, *A Time of Passion: America 1960–1980* (New York: Harper and Row, 1984), pp. 91–92.

9. Lemann, *The Promised Land,* pp. 148–49

10. Daniel P. Moynihan, *Maximum Feasible Misunderstanding: Community Action in the War on Poverty* (New York: The Free Press, 1969), p. 170 (Moynihan's emphasis).

<mark>NOTES</mark>

11. The full text is published in Lee Rainwater and William L. Yancey, *The Moynihan Report and the Politics of Controversy* (Cambridge, Mass.: MIT Press, 1967), pp. 39–124.

12. Ibid., p. 43.

13. Ibid., p. 93.

14. Johnson's speech is reprinted in full in Rainwater and Yancey, *The Moynihan Report*, pp. 125–32.

15. Ibid., p. 126.

16. Ibid., p. 128.

17. Ibid., p. 130.

18. Brink and Harris, *Black and White*, pp. 278, 220.

19. Ibid., p. 130.

20. Daniel P. Moynihan, "The President and the Negro: The Moment Lost," *Commentary*, February 1967, p. 33.

21. Adolph Reed, Jr., and Julian Bond, "Equality: Why We Can't Wait," *Nation*, December 9, 1991, p. 733.

22. Jewell Handy Gresham, "The Politics of Family in America," *Nation*, July 24/31, 1989, p. 118 (emphasis added).

23. William Ryan, "Savage Discovery," *Nation*, November 22, 1965, pp. 380–84; reprinted in Rainwater and Yancey, *The Moynihan Report*, pp. 457–66.

24. William Ryan, *Blaming the Victim* (New York: Vintage Books, 1976), pp. 6–7 (Ryan's emphasis).

25. Ryan, "Savage Discovery," p. 464.

26. Cecil Williams, "Crack is Genocide, 1990's Style," *New York Times*, February 15, 1990, p. A29.

27. Ibid.

28. Ryan, "Savage Discovery," p. 464 (Ryan's emphasis).

29. Ibid.

30. James Farmer, "The Controversial Moynihan Report," syndicated column of December 18, 1965. Reprinted in Rainwater and Yancey, *The Moynihan Report*, p. 410.

31. Ibid., pp. 410–11 (author's emphasis).

32. Kenneth S. Tollett, "Racism and Race-Conscious Remedies," *American Prospect*, Spring 1991, p. 93.

CHAPTER 3

1. Aaron Wildavsky, "The Empty-Head Blues: Black Rebellion and White Reaction," *Public Interest*, Spring 1968, p. 3.

2. William Brink and Louis Harris, *Black and White: A Study of U.S. Racial Attitudes Today* (New York: Simon and Schuster, 1966), p. 127.

3. Ibid., p. 109.

4. Howard Schuman, Charlotte Steeh, and Lawrence Bobo, *Racial Attitudes in America: Trends and Interpretations* (Cambridge, Mass.: Harvard University Press, 1985), pp. 88–91.

5. Kenneth B. Clark, *Dark Ghetto: Dilemmas of Social Power* (Middletown, Conn.: Wesleyan University Press, 1965), pp. 237–38.

6. James Baldwin, Nathan Glazer, Sidney Hook, and Gunnar Myrdal, "Liberalism and the Negro: A Round-Table Discussion," *Commentary*, March 1964, p. 39.

7. Clayborne Carson, *In Struggle: SNCC and the Black Awakening of the 1960s* (Cambridge, Mass.: Harvard University Press, 1981), pp. 191–211 in particular.

8. Stokely Carmichael and Charles V. Hamilton, *Black Power: The Politics of Liberation in America* (New York: Vintage Books, 1967), p. 53.

9. Theodore H. White, *The Making of the President, 1968* (New York: Atheneum, 1969), pp. 233–35.

10. Thomas Byrne Edsall and Mary D. Edsall, *Chain Reaction: The Impact of Race, Rights and Taxes on American Politics* (New York: W. W. Norton and Company, 1991), pp. 88–89.

11. The thesis that 1964 marked such a watershed for both parties is best developed by Edsall and Edsall, *Chain Reaction*, pp. 32–46 in particular.

12. Lee Rainwater and William L. Yancey, *The Moynihan Report and the Politics of Controversy* (Cambridge, Mass.: MIT Press, 1967), p. 248.

13. Lyndon Baines Johnson, *The Vantage Point: Perspectives of the Presidency, 1963–1969* (New York: Holt, Reinhart, and Winston, 1971), p. 330.

14. Joseph A. Califano, Jr., *The Triumph and Tragedy of Lyndon Johnson: The White House Years* (New York: Simon and Schuster, 1991), p. 131.

15. Michael Harrington, *The Other America: Poverty in the United States* (New York: Macmillan, 1962), p. 62.

16. Clark, *Dark Ghetto*, p. 21.

17. Benjamin DeMott, *The Imperial Middle: Why Americans Can't Think Straight about Class* (New York: William Morrow and Company, 1990), p. 43.

18. Laura Carper, "The Negro Family and the Moynihan Report," *Dissent* March/April 1966, reprinted in Rainwater and Yancey, *The Moynihan Report*, p. 474.

19. Edward C. Banfield, *The Unheavenly City: The Nature and Future of Our Urban Centers* (Boston: Little, Brown and Co., 1970).

20. Nicholas Lemann, *The Promised Land: The Great Black Migration and How It Changed America* (New York: Alfred A. Knopf, 1991), pp. 178–79.

21. Michael K. Brown and Seven P. Erie, "Blacks and the Legacy of the Great Society: The Economic and Political Impact of Federal Social Policy," *Public Policy* 29, no. 3 (Summer 1981): 299–330.

22. U.S. Bureau of the Census, *U.S. Census of Population: 1960, Final Report PC(2)-7A, Occupational Characteristics* (Washington, D.C.: U.S. Government Printing Office, 1962), pp. 21–22; *1980 Census of Population, Occupation by*

Industry, PC80-2-7C (Washington, D.C.: U.S. Government Printing Office, 1984), pp. 1, 2, and 157.

23. Califano, *The Triumph and Tragedy,* p. 113.

24. Unpublished report of the White House Task Force on Cities, Paul N. Ylvisaker, chairman, Washington, D.C., July 7, 1967, p. i, author's files (emphasis in original).

25. Ibid., p. ii.

26. Cover letter from Paul N. Ylvisaker to President Lyndon Johnson, accompanying unpublished report by the Task Force on Cities, unnumbered.

27. In fact, a Gallup Poll conducted February 1–6, 1968, found that 63 percent of its sample agreed that judges were not treating criminals harshly enough, while only 2 percent thought they were too tough. On questions about what to do about rising crime, only 18 percent favored correcting underlying conditions, while 18 percent favored more parental discipline, 14 percent more police, 17 percent harsher sentencing, and 13 percent increased penalties.

28. Robert F. Kennedy, "Excerpts from Kennedy Speech on Coast," *New York Times,* October 24, 1966, p. 16.

29. "Kennedy Clashes with CORE Chief," *New York Times,* December 9, 1966, pp. 1, 27.

30. Ramsey Clark, *Crime in America: Observations on Its Nature, Causes, Prevention and Control* (New York: Simon and Schuster, 1970), p. 51.

31. President's Commission on Law Enforcement and Administration of Justice, *The Challenge of Crime in a Free Society* (Washington, D.C.: U.S. Government Printing Office, 1967), p. 15.

32. William Ryan, *Blaming the Victim* (New York: Vintage Books, 1971), p. 204.

33. Ibid., particularly pp. 215–18.

34. William H. Grier and Price M. Cobbs, *Black Rage* (New York: Basic Books, 1968), p. 71.

35. "Poll Finds Crime Top Fear at Home," *New York Times,* February 28, 1968, p. 29.

36. See Associated Press, "Humphrey Warns of Slum Revolts," *New York Times,* July 19, 1966, p. 19.

37. Banfield, *The Unheavenly City,* cite is title of chapter title beginning p. 185.

38. *Report of the National Advisory Commission on Civil Disorders* (New York: E. P. Dutton & Co., 1968), pp. 1, 2.

39. Ibid., p. 203 (emphasis added).

40. Ibid.; the broad policy choices are outlined on pp. 395–407, the specific national policies on pp. 410–82.

41. Ibid., pp. 201–2; the commission devotes 2 of 668 pages to the conspiracy theory.

42. Wildavsky, "The Empty-Head Blues," p. 5.

43. Interview with Victor Palmieri, Newark, New Jersey, 1991.

44. Califano, *The Triumph and Tragedy*, pp. 260–62.

45. Henry Raymont, "Riot Report Book Big Best Seller," *New York Times*, March 14, 1968, p. 49.

46. "The Choice for Americans," *New York Times*, March 3, 1968, section IV, p. 12.

47. "Challenge/Response," *New Republic*, March 16, 1968, p. 5.

CHAPTER 4

1. Angelo Baglivo, *Newark News* (paper has ceased publication).

2. Vicki Granet Semel, *At the Grass Roots in the Garden State: Reform and Regular Democrats in New Jersey* (Rutherford, N.J.: Fairleigh Dickinson University Press, 1978), Table 2, p. 102.

3. Ibid., Table 1, p. 99.

4. Ronald Sullivan, "Hughes Backs Jersey Party Reform as Liberal Democrats Unite," *New York Times*, November 15, 1968, p. 30.

5. Byrne's record was as important as his two most important predecessors, Woodrow Wilson and Richard Hughes. Under Byrne, New Jersey became the first state to finance gubernatorial elections with public funds and to represent consumers in utility rate cases. He enacted an income tax to reduce and stabilize property taxes and preserved a wide swath of the New Jersey Pinelands.

6. Survey # 761-K, Gallup Poll (May 15, 1968), reported in *The Gallup Poll: Public Opinion 1935–1971* (New York: Random House, 1972), p. 2127.

7. For a discussion of the influence of the Special Equal Rights Committee, see William J. Crotty, *Decision for the Democrats: Reforming the Party Structure* (Baltimore: Johns Hopkins University Press, 1978), pp. 10, 12, 16, 72–73, and 276–77.

8. Theodore H. White, *The Making of the President, 1968* (New York: Atheneum, 1969), pp. 273–74.

9. Crotty, *Decision for the Democrats*, p. 31.

10. Compiled by Nelson W. Polsby, *Consequences of Party Reform* (Oxford: Oxford University Press, 1983), Table 3.5, p. 114.

11. White, *The Making of the President, 1968*, pp. 175–77.

12. Polsby, *Consequences of Party Reform*, Table 2.5, p. 64.

13. Thomas Byrne Edsall and Mary D. Edsall, *Chain Reaction: The Impact of Race, Rights and Taxes on American Politics* (New York: W. W. Norton and Company, 1991), pp. 94–95.

14. Gary Warren Hart, *Right from the Start: A Chronicle of the McGovern Campaign* (New York: Quadrangle, 1973), p. 208.

15. George McGovern, *Grassroots: The Autobiography of George McGovern* (New York: Random House, 1977); see his discussion of the nomination on pp. 182–87.

16. Ibid., p. 186.

17. Richard M. Nixon, *RN: The Memoirs of Richard Nixon* (New York: Touchstone, 1990), pp. 30–45.

18. Robert B. Semple, Jr., "Nixon Scores Panel for 'Undue' Stress on White Racism," *New York Times*, March 7, 1968, p. 1.

19. John Ehrlichman, *Witness to Power: The Nixon Years* (New York: Simon and Schuster, 1982), pp. 228–29.

20. See House of Representatives vote on HR 15209 in *Congressional Quarterly Almanac 1969* (Washington, D.C.: Congressional Quarterly Press, 1970), pp. 80–81H.

21. For a more complete discussion of the Philadelphia Plan, see Hugh Davis Graham, *The Civil Rights Era: Origins and Development of National Policy* (Oxford: Oxford University Press, 1990), pp. 322–45.

22. Ibid., p. 344.

23. The study, by John F. Kain and Robert Schafer, "Regional Impacts of the Family Assistance Plan" (mimeograph, Harvard University, Cambridge, Mass., June 1971) is cited in Daniel P. Moynihan, *The Politics of a Guaranteed Income: The Nixon Administration and the Family Assistance Plan* (New York: Random House, 1973), pp. 385–86.

24. U. S. Senate Committee on Finance, "Family Assistance Act of 1970, Hearings on H.R. 16311" (Washington, D.C.: U.S. Government Printing Office, 1970), Part I, pp. 112–19; examples were prepared by the committee staff.

25. Ibid., p. 451.

26. Ibid.; see pp. 327–44 for Moynihan's analysis of NWRO and its proposal.

27. Deirdre Carmody, "McGovern Offers Plan on Poverty," *New York Times*, January 21, 1970, pp. 1, 38.

28. "Statement of Senator George McGovern" in U.S. Senate Finance Committee, "Family Assistance Act of 1970, Hearings on H.R. 16311," Part 3, pp. 143–55.

29. Theodore H. White, *The Making of the President, 1972* (New York: Atheneum, 1973), p. 128.

30. McGovern, *Grassroots*, p. 226.

31. James M. Naughton, "M'Govern Offers New Tax Program in Wall St. Talk," *New York Times*, August 30, 1972, pp. 1, 22.

CHAPTER 5

1. William Brink and Louis Harris, *Black and White: A Study of U.S. Racial Attitudes Today* (New York: Simon and Schuster, 1967), p. 246.

2. *The Gallup Poll: Public Opinion Volume III, 1959–71* (New York: Random House, 1972); Gallup Poll for December 11–16, 1964, p. 1912; Gallup Poll for December 11–16, 1965, p. 1981.

3. Jared Taylor, *Paved with Good Intentions: The Failure of Race Relations in Contemporary America* (New York: Carroll and Graf Publishers, Inc., 1992), p. 243.

4. Glenn C. Loury, "A Call to Arms for Black Conservatives," in Joseph Perkins, ed., *A Conservative Agenda for Black Americans*, 2d ed. (Washington, D.C.: The Heritage Foundation, 1990), p. 19.

5. Martin Luther King, Jr., "Next Stop: The North," *Saturday Review*, November 13, 1965, pp. 33–35.

6. Martin Luther King, Jr., "A Testament of Hope," *Playboy*, January 1965, reprinted in James M. Washington, ed., *A Testament of Hope: The Essential Writings and Speeches of Martin Luther King, Jr.*, (San Francisco: Harper and Row, 1986), p. 316.

7. Martin Luther King, Jr., "Black Power Defined," *New York Times Magazine*, June 11, 1967.

8. Cited in Washington, *Testament of Hope*, pp. 367–68.

9. Stokely Carmichael and Charles V. Hamilton, *Black Power: The Politics of Liberation in America* (New York: Vintage Books, 1967), p. vi.

10. Ibid., pp. 34–35.

11. Ibid., p. 53.

12. Ibid., pp. 54–55.

13. Ibid., p. 54.

14. Ibid., p. 40.

15. Tom Wolfe, *Radical Chic and Mau-Mauing the Flak Catchers* (New York: Farrar, Strauss, and Giroux, 1970).

16. See Gary Orfield, *Must We Bus? Segregated Schools and National Policy* (Washington, D.C.: The Brookings Institution, 1978), pp. 56–69 in particular.

17. See Abigail M. Thernstrom, *Whose Votes Count? Affirmative Action and Minority Voting Rights* (Cambridge, Mass.: Harvard University Press, 1987), p. 18.

18. James Baldwin, Nathan Glazer, Sidney Hook, and Gunnar Myrdal, "Liberalism and the Negro: A Round-Table Discussion," *Commentary*, March 1964, p. 38.

19. Martin Luther King, Jr., "Letter from Birmingham City Jail," reprinted in Washington, *Testament of Hope*, p. 292.

20. United Press International, "Kennedy Clashes with CORE Chief," *New York Times*, December 9, 1966, p. 1.

21. John Herbers, "Democrats Vote Pro-Busing Plank," *New York Times*, June 27, 1968, p. 1.

22. Cornel West, *Race Matters* (Boston: Beacon Press, 1993), pp. 24–25.

23. William Julius Wilson, *The Declining Significance of Race: Blacks and Changing American Institutions*, 2d ed. (Chicago: University of Chicago Press, 1980), p. 157.

24. Author's notes of remarks by Adelaide Sanford at a panel on "Model Programs and Innovative Strategies," Sixth National Policy Institute, Joint Center for Political and Economic Studies, Washington, D.C., January 24, 1992.

25. Derrick Bell, *Faces at the Bottom of the Well: The Permanence of Racism* (New York: Basic Books, 1992), p. 104.

26. Survey of 15,490 voters by Voter Research and Surveys, "Portrait of the Electorate," *New York Times*, November 5, 1992, table on p. B9.

27. Adolph Reed, Jr., "All for One and None for All," *Nation*, January 28, 1991, p. 87.

28. Joint Center for Political and Economic Studies, "Voices of the Electorate among the African American Population," Washington, D.C., July, 1992, p. 2.

29. Adam Clymer, "The 1984 National Primary," *Public Opinion*, August/September 1984, pp. 52–53.

30. E. J. Dionne, Jr., "Jackson Share of Votes by Whites Triples in '88," *New York Times*, June 13, 1988, p. B7.

31. Lerone Bennett, Jr., interview with Jesse L. Jackson, "I Could Have Won," *Ebony*, August 1984, p. 168.

32. Evan Thomas, "Pride and Prejudice," *Time*, May 7, 1984, p. 30.

33. Mark Rosenthal, "Jesse's Business," *New Republic*, May 9, 1988, p. 10.

34. William R. Doermer, "A Long-Awaited Embrace," *Time*, September 10, 1984, pp. 12–13.

35. David E. Rosenbaum, "Black Democrats in a Poll Prefer Mondale to Jackson as Nominee," *New York Times*, July 10, 1984, p. A1.

36. Christine M. Black and Thomas Oliphant, *All by Myself: The Unmaking of a Presidential Campaign* (Chester, Conn.: Globe Pequot Press, 1989), particularly pp. 165–70.

37. Joint Center for Political and Economic Studies, "Voices of the Electorate among the African-American Population," p. 2.

38. The Gallup Organization, "The Gallup Poll Party ID Trend to 1937," unpublished, reprinted in Harold W. Stanley and Richard G. Niemi, *Vital Statistics of American Politics* (Washington, D.C.: Congressional Quarterly Press, 1992), p. 161.

39. Voter Research and Surveys, (November 3, 1992), reported in *American Enterprise*, January/February 1993, p. 93.

40. Survey of 15,490 voters by Voter Research and Surveys, reported in *New York Times*, November 5, 1992, p. B9.

41. Jason DeParle, "Talk Grows of Government Being Out to Get Blacks," *New York Times*, October 29, 1990, p. B6.

CHAPTER 6

1. Harold W. Stanley and Richard G. Niemi, eds., *Vital Statistics on American Politics* (Washington, D.C.: Congressional Quarterly Press, 1992); calculation by editors from data from *National Election Studies* (Ann Arbor, Mich.: Center for Political Studies, University of Michigan), p. 158.

2. James Reston, "What Goldwater Lost," *New York Times*, November 4, 1964, p. 23.

3. Thomas B. Edsall and Mary D. Edsall, *Chain Reaction: The Impact of Race, Rights and Taxes on American Politics* (New York: W. W. Norton and Company, 1991), p. 41.

4. Kevin P. Phillips, *Emerging Republican Majority* (New Rochelle, N.Y.: Arlington House, 1969), p. 286 (emphasis in original).

5. Ibid., p. 287.

6. "Republicans Score Net Gain of 47 Seats," *1966 CQ Almanac* (Washington, D.C: Congressional Quarterly Press, 1967), p. 1398.

7. Daniel P. Moynihan, "The President and the Negro: The Moment Lost," *Commentary,* February 1967, p. 31.

8. It is somewhat surprising that the Great Society, as it was set up by LBJ, has proved to be very durable, even in the face of the Reagan Revolution. Medicare has helped prevent the automatic pauperization of retired Americans, and Great Society programs guarantee access to a college education for millions of Americans. General aid for public education, mass transit, family planning, libraries, even the arts, survived the determined opposition of Reagan and Bush. But the prolonged intellectual and political attacks by conservatives have been effective: "Great Society" remains the code for failed federal programs that were supposed to liberate the poor, especially the black poor.

9. Charles R. Morris, *A Time of Passion: America 1960–1980* (New York: Harper and Row, 1984), p. 128.

10. Joseph A. Loftus, "Moynihan Calls on A.D.A. to Seek Ties with Conservatives," *New York Times,* September 24, 1967, pp. 1 and 44.

11. Richard M. Scammon and Ben J. Wattenberg, *The Real Majority: An Extraordinary Examination of the American Electorate* (New York: Coward-McCann, Inc., 1970), pp. 57–58.

12. James Q. Wilson, "The Rediscovery of Character: Private Virtue and Public Policy," *Public Interest,* Fall 1985, p. 3.

13. Irving Kristol, in *Reflections of a Neo-Conservative: Looking Back, Looking Ahead* (New York: Basic Books, 1983), p. 89.

14. For a quick history of AEI, see James Allen Smith, *The Idea Brokers: Think Tanks and the Rise of the New Policy Elite* (New York: The Free Press, 1991), pp. 174–84.

15. Here I rely on E. J. Dionne, Jr.'s useful perspective on the New Right in his book *Why Americans Hate Politics* (New York: Simon and Schuster, 1991), pp. 227–36.

16. See for example, Walter W. Heller, "The Kemp-Roth-Laffer Free Lunch," *Wall Street Journal,* July 12, 1978, p. A20.

17. Edsall and Edsall, *Chain Reaction,* p. 208.

18. Text of speech by Daniel Patrick Moynihan to the Business Council of New York State, September 13, 1981, printed in Daniel Patrick Moynihan, *Came the Revolution: Argument in the Reagan Era* (San Diego: Harcourt Brace Jovanovich, 1988), p. 31.

19. Ibid., p. 34 (Moynihan's emphasis).

20. William Greider, *The Education of David Stockman and Other Americans* (New York: E. P. Dutton and Co., 1981), p. 46.

21. Ibid., p. 33.

22. David A. Stockman, *The Triumph of Politics: The Inside Story of the Reagan Revolution* (New York: Avon, 1987), p. 429.

23. Paul Craig Roberts, *The Supply-side Revolution: An Insider's Account of Policymaking in Washington* (Cambridge, Mass.: Harvard University Press, 1984), p. 96.

24. Jack Kemp et al., "A Message for Houston," *Wall Street Journal,* August 11, 1992, p. A14.

25. Stockman, *The Triumph of Politics,* p. 409.

26. Alexis De Tocqueville, *Democracy in America,* vol. 2 (New York: Alfred A. Knopf, 1987), p. 105.

27. Ibid., p. 317.

28. John Kenneth Galbraith, *The Culture of Contentment* (Boston: Houghton Mifflin Company, 1992), pp. 96, 97.

29. Median family income is from the U.S. Department of Commerce, Bureau of the Census, *Current Population Reports* (Washington, D.C.: U.S. Government Printing Office, 1981); the higher education costs are found in the U. S. Department of Education, *Digest of Education Statistics 1992* (Washington, D.C.: U. S. Government Printing Office, 1992) p. 307.

30. U.S. Department of Education, *Digest 1992,* pp. 318, 319.

31. Karen DeWitt, "Battle Is Looming on U.S. College Aid to Poor Students," *New York Times,* May 27, 1991, pp. A1, 9.

32. Elaine El-Khawas, "Campus Trends, 1992," American Council on Education: Washington, D.C., July 1992, p. v.

33. Deborah J. Carter and Reginald Wilson, "Minorities in Higher Education, 1992," American Council on Education, Washington, D.C., 1993, Table 1, pp. 41–42.

34. Thomas Joseph Kane, *College Entry by Blacks since 1970: The Role of Tuition, Financial Aid, Local Economic Conditions and Family Background* (Cambridge, Mass.: Malcolm Wiener Center for Social Policy, John F. Kennedy School of Government, Harvard University, 1991), p. 176.

35. Ibid., p. 177.

36. Carter and Wilson, "Minorities in Higher Education," Table 2, pp. 44–55.

37. Ibid., Table 5, p. 59.

38. Federal National Mortgage Association, "Fannie Mae National Housing Survey," Washington, D.C., June 1992, p. 6.

39. Iver Peterson, "Home Ownership—a Receding Dream," *New York Times,* October 20, 1991, section X, pp. 1, 12.

40. William Kristol and Jay P. Lefkowitz, "Our Students, Still at Risk," *New York Times,* May 3, 1993, p. A15.

41. Theodore R. Sizer, "Recommendations for Improving Education in Metropolitan Areas: A Supplement to the Report of the Task Force on Cities," unpublished mimeograph, Washington, D.C., July 5, 1967, p. 8.

42. William J. Bennett, "A New Civil Rights Agenda," *Wall Street Journal,* April 1, 1991, p. A12.

43. Benno C. Schmidt, Jr., "Educational Innovation for Profit," *Wall Street Journal,* June 5, 1992, p. A10.

44. John E. Chubb and Terry M. Moe, *Politics, Markets, and America's Schools* (Washington, D.C., The Brookings Institution, 1990), pp. 218–19.

45. Ibid., p. 191.

46. Ibid., p. 188.

47. Ibid., p. 217.

48. Amy Stuart Wells, "School Choice Program is Upheld in Wisconsin," *New York Times,* August 8, 1990, p. B6.

49. Chubb and Moe, *Politics, Markets, and America's Schools,* p. 219.

50. Schmidt, "Educational Innovation for Profit."

51. See the discussion of student achievement in Chubb and Moe, *Politics, Markets, and America's Schools,* pp. 101–40.

52. Patrick M. Reilly, "Whittle Seeks Edison Funding of $750 Million," *Wall Street Journal,* May 5, 1993, p. B1.

53. Sara Mosle, "Dim Bulb," *New Republic,* January 18, 1993, pp. 16, 19–20. I have reworked her numbers to conform with Whittle's later estimates of scale.

54. National Center for Education Statistics, *Digest 1992,* Table 306, p. 312; Jason DeParle, "Report Cites Flaws in Regulation of Trade Schools," *New York Times,* September 12, 1990, p. B7; and Robert G. Bottoms, "Sure We Need Beauticians. . . ," *New York Times,* September 17, 1990, p. A23.

55. DeParle, "Report Cites Flaws."

56. Katherine Boo, "Beyond Beauty Schools," *Washington Monthly,* March 1991, p. 29.

57. Boo, "Beyond Beauty Schools," p. 30.

58. Julie Johnson, "Loan Enforcers Focus on Trade Schools," *New York Times,* June 11, 1989, section IV, p. 7.

59. DeParle, "Report Cites Flaws."

CHAPTER 7

1. See, for example, William Julius Wilson, *The Declining Significance of Race: Blacks and Changing American Institutions* (Chicago: University of Chicago Press, 1978); Gary Orfield, *Must We Bus? Segregated Schools and National Policy* (Washington, D.C.: The Brookings Institution, 1978); David T. Ellwood, *Poor Support: Poverty in the American Family* (New York: Basic Books, 1980). The descriptive statement for *Reconstruction* appears on its masthead, *Reconstruction* 1, no. 1 (Winter 1990): inside front cover.

2. Barney Frank, *Speaking Frankly: What's Wrong with the Democrats and How to Fix It* (New York: Times Books, 1992), p. 55.

3. Nicholas Lemann, *The Promised Land: The Great Black Migration and How It Changed America* (New York: Alfred A. Knopf, 1991); Thomas B. Edsall and Mary D. Edsall, *Chain Reaction: The Impact of Race, Rights and Taxes on American Politics* (New York: W. W. Norton and Company, 1991); Jim Sleeper, *The Closest of Strangers: Liberalism and the Politics of Race in New York* (New York: W. W. Norton and Company, 1990); and E. J. Dionne, Jr., *Why Americans Hate Politics* (New York: Simon and Schuster, 1991).

4. "The New Politics of Race," *Newsweek,* May 6, 1991, p. 30.

5. Star-Ledger/Eagleton Poll, "Discrimination—The Viewpoint of New Jerseyans," press release from the Eagleton Institute of Politics, Rutgers University, New Brunswick, N.J., March 14, 1993, p. 6.

6. Andrew Hacker, *Two Nations: Black and White, Separate, Hostile, Unequal* (New York: Charles Scribner's Sons, 1992).

7. Frank, *Speaking Frankly,* pp. 36–37.

8. "HBO/Joint Center Poll," Joint Center for Political and Economic Studies, Washington, D.C., July 8, 1992. See Table 2 for question on political philosophy; Table 3 for question on party preference.

9. Stanley Greenberg, telephone interview with author, March 24, 1993.

10. Kenneth S. Tollett, "Racism and Race-Conscious Remedies," *American Prospect,* Spring 1991, p. 91.

11. Stephen L. Carter, *Reflections of an Affirmative Action Baby* (New York: Basic Books, 1991), p. 14.

12. Michel Marriott, "Storm at Georgetown Law on Admissions," *New York Times,* April 17, 1991, p. A14; Timothy Maguire, "My Bout with Affirmative Action," *Commentary,* April 1992, p. 51.

13. Senator John Kerry, "Race, Politics, and the Urban Agenda," speech at Yale University, New Haven, March 30, 1992, p. 6.

14. Derrick Z. Jackson, "Kerry's Profiles in Crumble," *Boston Globe,* April 5, 1992, p. 7.

15. Jewell Handy Gresham, "The Politics of Family in America," *Nation,* July 24/31, 1989, p. 119 (emphasis added).

16. For evidence on the effects of single-parent families, see, for example, Barbara Dafoe Whitehead, "Dan Quayle Was Right," *Atlantic Monthly,* April 1993, p. 47.

17. Micaela Di Leonardo, "Boyz on the Hood," *Nation,* August 17/24, 1992, p. 186.

18. Senator Bill Bradley, "Race and the American City," Washington, D.C., March 26, 1992, p. 5 (provided by office of Senator Bradley).

19. Ibid., p. 6.

20. "A Call to End Racism," *Sunday Record* (Hackensack, N.J.), March 29, 1992, p. A30.

21. "No Place Seems Safe," *New York Times,* March 29, 1992, section IV, p. 16.

22. Herbert McClosky and John Zaller, *The American Ethos: Public Attitudes toward Capitalism and Democracy* (Cambridge, Mass.: Harvard University Press, 1984); on p. 65 the authors report: "This assumption of the equality of human

worth is so deeply ingrained in American political culture as to be axiomatic for most people."

23. Arthur M. Schlesinger, Jr., *The Disuniting of America: Reflections on a Multicultural Society* (New York: W. W. Norton and Company, 1992), p. 134.

24. Lee Sigelman and Susan Welch, *Black Americans' Views of Racial Inequality: The Dream Deferred* (Cambridge: Cambridge University Press, 1991), p. 129.

25. Author's transcription of interview with Derrick Bell, "Daily Edition," Monitor Radio, January 15, 1991.

26. Jesse Jackson, "Don't Fan the Flames," syndicated column reprinted in *Liberal Opinion Week*, May 13, 1991, p. 7.

27. Lani Guinier, "The Triumph of Tokenism: The Voting Rights Act and the Theory of Black Electoral Success," *Michigan Law Review* (March 1991): 1103.

28. Ibid., p. 1108.

29. Author's notes of speech by Leonard Jeffries at the New Jersey Black Issues Convention, Newark, New Jersey, September 21, 1991.

30. Author's transcription of speech by Adelaide Sanford at the Sixth National Policy Institute, Joint Center for Political and Economic Studies, Washington, D.C., January 23, 1992.

31. Louis Menand, "What Are Universities For?" *Harper's*, December 1991, pp. 47–56.

32. John H. Bunzel, "Alienation and the Black College Dropout," *Wall Street Journal*, April 3, 1991, p. A20.

33. Schlesinger, *The Disuniting of America*, p. 134.

34. Cornel West, *Race Matters* (Boston: Beacon Press, 1993), p. 4.

35. The first statistic is from a June 13–15, 1991, survey by the Gallup Organization; the results on preferences are from a survey by Princeton Survey Research Associations, Inc. for the Times-Mirror Center for the People and the Press, May 1990. Both results are reported in *American Enterprise*, September/October 1991, p. 82.

36. ABC News/Washington Post survey conducted in September–October 1989, reported in Sigelman and Welch, *Black Americans' Views of Racial Inequality*, p. 57.

37. Ibid.

38. See "Home Mortgage Disclosure Act: Expanded Data on Residential Lending," *Federal Reserve Bulletin*, Washington, D.C., November 1991, pp. 859–81; and Paulette Thomas, "Federal Data Detail Pervasive Racial Gap in Mortgage Lending," *Wall Street Journal*, March 31, 1992, pp. A1 and A10–11, which refines data in the Federal Reserve study.

39. In Margery Austin Turner, Raymond J. Struyk, and John Yinger, "Housing Discrimination Study: Synthesis," The Urban Institute, Washington, D.C., August 1991.

40. The House Wednesday Group, U.S. House of Representatives, "Moving Ahead: Initiatives for Expanding Opportunity in America," Washington, D.C., October 22, 1991.

41. Joseph Perkins, ed., *A Conservative Agenda for Black Americans,* 2d ed. (Washington, D.C.: The Heritage Foundation, 1990).

42. William J. Bennett, "A New Civil Rights Agenda," *Wall Street Journal,* April 11, 1991, p. A14.

43. Ronald Sullivan, "Rights Agency Accuses Times and Pressmen's Union of Job Discrimination," *New York Times,* September 3, 1991, p. A20.

44. Elizabeth Kadetsky, "Muscling In on Construction Jobs," *Nation,* July 13, 1992, p. 47.

45. Robert B. Reich, *The Work of Nations: Preparing Ourselves for 21st Century Capitalism* (New York: Vintage Books, 1991), p. 273.

46. James M. Markham, "Residents, Not City, Called Key to Cleaner Streets," *New York Times,* October 19, 1971, p. 39.

47. Ernest F. Hollings, "Some Advice to the New Kid in Town: Just Remember You're a 'New Democrat,'" *Los Angeles Times,* June 27, 1993, p. M6.

48. Citizens for Tax Justice, "Inequality and the Federal Budget Deficit," Washington, D.C., September, 1991, pp. 6, 8 (emphasis in original).

49. Martin L. Gross, *The Government Racket: Washington Waste from A to Z* (New York: Bantam Books, 1992), p. 260.

50. Ibid, pp. 262, 257.

51. Robert Eisner, *How Real Is the Federal Deficit?* (New York: The Free Press. 1986), pp. 26–32.

52. Charles R. Morris, "It's *Not* the Economy, Stupid," *Atlantic Monthly,* July 1992, p. 62.

53. Kevin P. Phillips, *The Politics of Rich and Poor: Wealth and the American Electorate in the Reagan Aftermath* (New York: Random House, 1990), pp. 89–90.

54. Alan Wolfe, "Proposal for a Study of a New American Social Contract," unpublished manuscript, October 1992, p. 2.

CHAPTER 8

1. Richard B. Freeman, "Employment and Earnings of Disadvantaged Young Men in a Labor Shortage Economy," in Christopher Jencks and Paul Peterson, *The Urban Underclass* (Washington, D.C.: The Brookings Institution, 1991), pp. 103–21.

2. U.S. Bureau of the Census, "Poverty in the United States: 1991," *Current Population Reports,* Series P-60, no. 181 (Washington, D.C.: U.S. Government Printing Office, 1992), Table H, p. xxi.

3. Terry K. Adams, Greg J. Duncan, and Willard L. Rodgers, "The Persistence of Urban Poverty," in Fred R. Harris and Roger W. Wilkins, eds., *Quiet Riots: Race and Poverty in the United States* (New York: Pantheon Books, 1988), pp. 94–95.

4. Edward C. Banfield, *The Unheavenly City: The Nature and the Future of Our Crisis* (Boston: Little, Brown and Company, 1970), p. 211.

5. Charles Murray, *Losing Ground: American Social Policy 1950–1980* (New York: Basic Books, 1984), p. 9 (emphasis supplied).

6. E. J. Dionne, *Why Americans Hate Politics* (New York: Simon and Schuster, 1991), p. 334.

7. Mickey Kaus, *The End of Equality* (New York: Basic Books, 1992,) p. 125.

8. Ibid., p. 135 (emphasis supplied).

9. David T. Ellwood, *Poor Support: Poverty in the American Family* (New York: Basic Books, 1988), p. 46.

10. Barbara Dafoe Whitehead, "Dan Quayle Was Right," *Atlantic Monthly*, April 1993, p. 48.

11. Daniel Patrick Moynihan, *Family and Nation* (San Diego: Harcourt Brace Jovanovich, 1987), p. 38.

12. James S. Coleman et al., *Equality of Educational Opportunity* (Washington, D.C.: U.S. Government Printing Office, 1966).

13. Diane Ravitch, *The Troubled Crusade: American Education 1945–1980* (New York: Basic Books, 1983), p. 158.

14. See David E. Pitt, "Bronx Principal Is Arrested as a Street Buyer of Crack," *New York Times*, November 10, 1988, p. B18; Neil A. Lewis, "Arrest of Principal Rekindles a Debate over School Tenure," *New York Times*, November 12, 1988, pp. A1, A31; Joseph Berger, "Inert System Let Shaky Principal Go," *New York Times*, December 27, 1988, pp. A1, B4; and "New Principal Rules Sought," *New York Times*, January 29, 1991, p. B3.

15. Suzanne Daley, "Why They're Pleading to Get into P.S. 87," *New York Times*, March 16, 1988, pp. B1, B5.

CHAPTER 9

1. Lester C. Thurow, "Companies Merge; Families Break Up," *New York Times*, September 3, 1995, section IV, p. 11.

2. The HBO/Joint Center Poll reported that black Americans were more likely to identify themselves as conservative or somewhat conservative (33.9 percent) than liberal or somewhat liberal (28.3 percent). "Voices of the Electorate among the African-American Population," July, 1992, Joint Center for Political and Economic Studies, Washington, D.C., July 1992, Table 2.

3. The abortion questions were asked by the National Opinion Research Center, 1987–1990 and combined; the religious and moral questions were asked by the Princeton Survey Research Associates, Inc., for the Times Mirror Center for the People and the Press, May 1–31, 1990, and were reported in *American Enterprise*, September/October 1991, pp. 84–85.

4. Although only 20 percent of black respondents (compared with 25 percent of white) characterized race relations in the United States as "generally good," 58 percent (and 79 percent of whites) said race relations in their own communities

were generally good; these findings came from a CBS/*New York Times* poll conducted May 6–8, 1992—immediately after the Los Angeles riots—and were reported in *American Enterprise,* July/August 1992, p. 95.

5. Hugh B. Price, "Keynote Address: National Urban League Convention," Indianapolis, July 24, 1994, p. 15.

6. See, for example, Marttila and Kiley, Inc., "Highlights from an Anti-Defamation League Survey on Racial Attitudes in America," Boston, June 11, 1993, pp. 64–67.

7. Charles R. Morris, "It's *Not* the Economy, Stupid," *Atlantic Monthly,* July 1993, p. 50.

8. Ruy Teixeira, " . . . What if We Held an Election and Everyone Came?" *American Enterprise,* July/August 1992, p. 57.

9. Kevin Phillips, *Boiling Point: Democrats, Republicans, and the Decline of Middle-Class Prosperity* (New York: Random House, 1993), p. 248.

10. Stanley B. Greenberg, Al From, and Will Marshall, *The Road to Realignment: The Democrats and the Perot Voters* (Washington, D.C.: Democratic Leadership Council, July 1993), pp. iii–14.

11. Ibid., pp. ii–2.

12. Ibid., pp. ii–26, and figures 4 and 5.

13. Ibid., p. ii–17.

14. Ibid., pp. iii–26, iii–28, iii–18.

15. Phillips, *Boiling Point,* p. 248.

16. Dan Weissman, "Whitman Opposes Tax Deduction Proposed by Republican Legislators," *Star-Ledger* (Newark), February 25, 1993, p. 17.

17. See Edward N. Wolff, *Top Heavy: A Study of the Increasing Inequality of Wealth in America* (New York: The Twentieth Century Fund Press, 1995), p. 7.

18. Cornel West, *Race Matters* (Boston: Beacon Press, 1993), p. 3

19. Bill Bradley, "Speech on Race and Civil Rights in America," Washington, D.C., July 16, 1991, p. 9.

INDEX

Abel, I. W., 81
Abortion, 2, 121, 124, 186, 195
Adams, Terry, 169
Adarand Constructors v. Pena, 188
Adubato, Steve, 177
Adult literacy, 31, 32
AFDC. *See* Aid for families with
    dependent children
Affirmative action, 106, 107, 109,
    131, 151, 154–55; in the mili-
    tary, 189–90
Affluent society, 43, 141–42
Afro-Americans. *See* Black Americans
Agnew, Spiro, 89–90
Aid for families with dependent
    children (AFDC), 43, 92–93
Alexander, Lamar, 198
Allen, Ivan, 60
American Council on Education,
    134
American Dream, 176, 185
American Enterprise Institute
    (AEI), 123–24
American Prospect (journal), 46,
    110, 147
American society, 91, 152, 156,
    160–61, 203; division in, 67,
    144, 157, 160; multiracial, 108,
    148–49, 165; myth of, 159–60;
    principles, 2–3, 104, 123, 154,
    157, 183–84

American values, 150, 175, 189;
    assimilation of, 57, 102; and
    lower class, 7, 57, 169–70;
    protection of, 3, 148; and
    Republican party, 3, 8–9, 121,
    158–59; restoration of, 170–71
Antidiscrimination laws, 26, 51,
    61, 158, 191
Antipoverty programs, 170, 171,
    187; administration, 184;
    criticism of, 130–34, 179–82,
    183; federal aid, 91–95; suc-
    cess, 178, 182, 183–84. *See
    also* War on Poverty; Welfare
Anti-Semitism, 104, 111
Antiwar movement, 75, 77, 79,
    84, 85
Armey, Dick, 199

Baby boomers, 121, 132
Baldwin, James, 103
Bane, Mary Jo, 147
Banfield, Edward, 56–57, 66,
    169–70
Baptists, 21, 109
Baroody, William, 123–24
Barry, Marion, 106
Bell, Derrick, 108, 155
Bennett, William J., 137, 150
Bernhard, Berl, 54
Berry, Edwin "Bill," 60

Biaggi, Mario, 93
Bipartisan coalition, 5, 23–25,
    117; restoration, 21, 159,
    182–83, 194–95; shattering, 4
Biracial coalition, 24, 186, 187,
    188–89, 202
Black activists, 20, 39, 42, 71, 147,
    150–51. See also Black nationalists
Black Americans, 35–37, 121;
    attitudes of, 109, 116, 150,
    186–87, 191; beliefs about, 44–45,
    169; constituents, 3, 18, 21, 27,
    113–14; economic conditions, 35,
    107, 131–32, 165; expectations of,
    25, 28, 35, 37; respect for, 8, 19, 47,
    98, 104,115, 175, 203; voting, 27,
    53, 193. See also Civil rights
    movement; Discrimination; See
    also subjects beginning with
    race or racial
Black children, 35, 107, 160
Black churches, 110, 113
Black civilization, 156
Black conservatives, 109–10, 221 n2
Black crime, 27, 30; excusing, 2,
    63, 64–65, 108–9
Black elite, 100, 105, 108
Black family, 106, 153; economic
    conditions, 91–95, 152; problems
    in, 30, 34–37, 39, 42, 43, 46, 99,
    151–52, 160
Black leadership, 30, 52, 152;
    attitudes, 186; criticism of, 46,
    116, 150; and Democratic party,
    14, 19, 20, 154, 187; and govern-
    ment, 38, 89; and liberals, 58,
    103, 105–8; and M. L. King, 98
Black nationalists, 56, 111, 148,
    154, 155, 203
Black Northerners, 21, 25–26, 100, 119
Black Panthers, 102
Black politicians, 155, 189; and
    Democratic party, 18, 75, 77, 78,
    114–15, 188

Black power, 52–53, 64, 100–103,
    105, 155
Black Power: The Politics of
    Liberation in America (Carmichael
    and Hamilton), 100–102
Black servicemen, 190
Black Southerners, 24–25, 29–30, 37;
    economic conditions, 92; suffrage,
    54, 78, 89, 103; voting, 113, 150
Blaming the Victim (Ryan), 43, 65
Blue collar. See Working class
Bond, Julian, 41
Boo, Katherine, 143
Boston (Mass.), 51
Boston Globe, 17, 151
Bradley, Bill, 147, 153, 203
Brink, William, 39
Brooke, Edward, 89
Brookings Institution, 137–38
Brown, H. Rap, 98
Brown, Michael, 58–59
Brown v. Board of Education, 24
Buckley, William F., 122
Budget, 162–64, 199, 200; as cam-
    paign issue, 9, 125; under Demo-
    cratic administrations, 2, 40–41,
    60, 162, 183, 201; under Repub-
    lican administrations, 10, 127,
    132; and welfare reform, 172,
    173. See also Government
    spending
Burns, Arthur F., 91
Bush, George, 9, 10, 56, 147; as
    presidential candidate, 13, 15,
    194–95
Bush administration, 132, 133,
    159, 198
Business leadership, 25, 26–27, 123
Busing, 8, 20, 51, 53, 86, 105
Byrne, Brendan, 76–77

Cahill, William, 89
Califano, Joseph, 54–55, 59–60
California, 14, 42, 102, 134

CAPs. *See* Community action
    programs
Carey, Denny, 74
Carmichael, Stokely, 52–53, 100–102
Carper, Laura, 56
Carter, Jimmy, 83, 125, 193
Carter, Stephen, 109, 110, 151
Carter administration, 124
Catholic Americans, 75; and blacks,
    27, 53; constitutents, 63; voting,
    5, 27
Census, 169; (1960), 29–30; (1990),
    115
Chicago (Ill.), 178
Children, 2, 107, 160, 171, 172,
    173–74
Chisholm, Shirley, 93, 110
Christianity and politics, 124, 193,
    198; and blacks, 25, 103–4, 110,
    113
Chubb, John, 137–39, 141
Citizenship (concept), 161–62, 201
Civil disorders, 121; excusing, 2,
    63–68, 70, 71; solutions for, 58,
    68–70. *See also* Riots; Violence
Civility, 161–62, 203
Civil rights, 6, 38, 130, 137; as
    campaign issue, 117; and
    Democratic party, 8, 37; and
    New Right, 124; and Republican
    party, 89, 91, 159. *See also* Voting
    rights
Civil Rights Act (1964), 5, 23, 25, 88
Civil rights laws, 24–25, 46, 108
Civil rights leadership, 40, 91
Civil rights movement, 26, 49, 52,
    159; and Black Power, 100–102;
    and L. B. Johnson, 21, 24, 38;
    moral force of, 5, 24–25, 26–27,
    37, 51; and War on Poverty,
    38, 40
Clark, Kenneth, 29, 52, 55
Clark, Ramsey, 64
Class. *See* Social classes

Clinton, Bill, 201, 202; credibility,
    1; criticism of, 16–18, 143–44,
    191–92; policies, 10, 144, 162,
    182–83, 199; as presidential
    candidate, 13–15, 16–21, 114, 139,
    191; support for, 18–19, 113
Clinton administration, 1–2, 3,
    144, 160, 171–73
Cloward, Richard, 103
Cobbs, Price, 65–66
Cockburn, Alexander, 17–18
Coleman report, 90, 179
Commission on Party Structure and
    Delegate Selection (Democrats), 81–82
Community action programs (CAPs),
    29, 32–33, 168, 177–78; adminis-
    tration, 40, 57–58; criticism of,
    33; premise, 31; success, 178
Community responsibility: denial
    of, 50, 66
Congress, 8, 10, 53, 165; and B.
    Clinton, 1, 162, 171, 172, 175,
    182–83, 192, 195; and L. B.
    Johnson, 23, 39, 40, 54, 58,
    62, 71; and R. Nixon, 91, 93–94;
    and R. Reagan, 129, 132, 133
Congressional elections, 188–89;
    (1964), 23; (1966), 5, 119;
    (1994), 2, 143–44, 146, 191–92
Conservatives, 123–24, 144; edu-
    cational policies, 138, 139–40;
    labeling, 47, 110, 122, 196;
    policies, 4, 130–31, 137, 160,
    171, 176, 177; principles, 9, 118,
    136, 138; and racial issues, 16,
    23, 40, 99, 107, 109–10, 159,
    203; support for, 71. *See also*
    Black conservatives; Republican
    party, effect of conservatives on
Conservative values, 3, 121, 123,
    124, 150, 152, 186
Constituents. *See* Voters
"Contract with America," 143–44,
    176–77, 199

Council on Urban Affairs, 90
Courts, 53, 71, 131, 180. *See also*
    Supreme Court
Credentials Committee (Democratic
    National Convention), 80, 87
Crime, 29, 44, 147, 150, 209 *n*27;
    as campaign issue, 5–6, 14, 15,
    27–28, 62, 63, 71, 120; causes,
    64–66; war on, 10, 28, 120.
    See also Black crime; Drugs,
    and blacks
Criminal justice system, 70; accused of
    racism, 63, 64, 65, 66, 108, 169
Criminals, 6, 15, 63, 66
Cultural revolution, 121–22, 146,
    186, 194

Daley, Richard, 81
Dark Ghetto (Clark), 29, 51
*Declining Significance of Race,
    The* (Wilson), 106–7, 147
Deficit, 126, 164, 183, 220, 201;
    reduction, 2, 163; spending,
    125, 126–28, 196–97
Democratic leadership, 62, 74, 77, 85
Democratic Leadership Council, 16
Democratic National Convention,
    77; (1968), 73, 78–79, 80; (1972),
    85, 87, 112; (1988), 113
Democratic party, 77–78, 125;
    campaign issues, 5–6, 15, 71, 79,
    83–84, 85–88, 94–95, 104, 139,
    191; constituents, 1, 3, 15, 27–28,
    91, 112, 113–14, 115, 192, 193;
    effect of liberals on, 6–8, 75–77,
    79, 80–84, 118, 147, 149–50; lib-
    erals in, 14, 74–75; in New Jersey,
    74–77; principles, 2–3, 7–8, 21, 66,
    148, 193; and racial issues, 6–8,
    16, 17, 21, 40, 78, 112, 154;
    reforms, 76–77, 80–85
Democratic politicians, 7–8, 60, 7
    4–77, 95, 188. *See also* Black
    politicians, and Democratic

party; also specific politicians,
    e.g. Jackson, J.
DeMott, Benjamin, 56
Desegregation. *See* Integration
Detroit (Mich.), 66, 180
Di Leonardo, Micaela, 152
Dionne, E. J., 147–48, 170–71
Discrimination, 29, 35, 104, 154;
    beliefs about, 8, 26–27, 43,
    157–59, 169, 171; and Demo-
    cratic party, 16; and Republican
    party, 149, 199. *See also* Anti-
    discrimination laws; Housing dis-
    crimination; Job discrimination;
    Segregation
Diversity in the workplace, 191
Downs, Anthony, 60
Drugs: and blacks, 43–44, 108–9;
    war on, 10, 120
DuBois, W. E. B., 107
Dukakis, Michael, 10, 81, 110, 193;
    and J. Jackson, 18, 20, 112, 113
Duke, David, 15, 199
Dunlop, John, 60

Eagleton, Thomas, 87, 95
Earned income credit, 2, 171, 173,
    175, 182–83
Economic growth, 60, 65, 127, 131,
    168; and government, 9, 187,
    192, 196, 199, 200–201, 202
Economic interests, 8, 115, 121, 148
Economic policy, 164–65, 192, 199,
    201–2; under Democratic ad-
    ministrations, 40, 162–63, 192;
    under Republican administrations,
    9–10, 124, 125, 128–29, 132,
    163–64, 196–98
Economy, 3–4, 168–69, 195; as
    campaign issue, 2, 118, 124, 125, 134,
    162; effect on blacks, 35, 107, 175
Edison Project, 137, 141
Edsall, Mary D., 5, 86, 118–19, 147,
    176

Edsall, Thomas B., 5, 86, 118–19, 125, 147, 176
Education, 130; and blacks, 108, 134, 135, 180; compensatory, 176, 179–80; as campaign issue, 114; federal aid, 23, 54, 68, 160, 180; opportunities, 131, 187, 201; reforms, 181–82, 198. *See also* Higher education; Race differences, in educational performance; Schools; School integration
Educational achievement, 109, 136, 141, 179, 181, 182, 198
Educational vouchers, 68, 136–37, 139–42, 198
Eisner, Robert, 163
Elderly, 5, 199
Elementary and Secondary Education Act, 179–80
Elite, 102, 105, 118, 123–24, 136, 139. *See also* Black elite
Ellwood, David, 147, 173
Employment, 2–3, 197; and blacks, 58–59, 62, 68, 114, 131; opportunities, 99, 103, 131, 188, 190–91. *See also* Job discrimination; Job integration; Unemployment
Empowerment: of blacks, 50, 56, 58, 159; of poor, 177
Equality, 24, 45, 147, 160, 173, 194; and liberty, 98–99, 129–30
Equal opportunity, 25, 51, 71, 129–30, 131, 154–55, 156, 203; and Democratic party, 5, 16, 38, 108; and Republican party, 130–32, 160, 194, 199; structure, 175–76. *See also* Education, opportunities; Employment, opportunities; Higher education, opportunities
Erie, Steven, 58–59
Espy, Mike, 18
Ethnic minorities: attitudes, 27; economic conditions, 28, 190; and politics, 84, 85, 89;

preferences for, 7. *See also* Black Americans; Hispanic Americans

Falwell, Jerry, 124
Family, 147, 150, 160, 173–74; dissolution, 30, 116, 174; economic conditions, 9, 121, 133–34, 135, 185–86, 197, 202; role of, 2, 34. *See also* Black family; Lower-class family
Family assistance plan (FAP), 91–94, 103
Family-leave act, 2, 195
Family responsibility, 35, 150; denial of, 41, 42, 43, 45, 46, 50; by fathers, 171, 174
Family values, 170, 171, 173, 186, 194
FAP. *See* Family assistance plan
Farmer, James, 45, 47
Farrakhan, Louis, 104, 111–12
Feminists, 84, 85, 112, 121
Feulner, Edwin, 124
Finch, Robert, 90, 91
Florio, Jim, 128
Food stamps, 173
Ford, Gerald, 123
Ford Foundation, 29, 30, 60
Frank, Barney, 147, 149–50
Fraser, Donald, 81

Galbraith, John Kenneth, 130
Gay, Dan, 76
Gays, 121; and politics, 1, 84, 85, 192
Ghetto. *See* Urban poor
Gingrich, Newt, 195
Ginsberg, David, 70
Goldmark, Peter, 70
Goldwater, Barry, 53, 117–19
Goodwin, Richard, 37
Gore, Al, 202
Government, 54, 147, 165; attitudes toward, 4, 146; intervention by, 9, 27, 51, 89, 124, 128, 130, 170; and

Reaganites, 123–24, 128–29, 130–32, 136; role, 1, 38–39, 78, 126, 128–29, 136, 144, 162. *See also* Intergovernmental relations; State governments

Government programs, 59–60, 68–69; and conservatives, 129, 130–32, 138, 160, 177; cutting, 62, 126, 129; effectiveness, 57, 167, 176; universality, 175, 184. *See also* specific programs, e.g. Antipoverty programs

Government spending, 9, 54, 127, 160, 171, 173; by Republican administrations, 10, 126–27, 129, 132, 163–64, 170, 172. *See also* federal aid under subjects, e.g. Higher education, federal aid

Gramm, Phill, 192

"Gray Areas" project, 29

Great Society, 49–50, 60, 123; criticism of, 68, 120; goals, 58; impact, 59, 132; opposition to, 119–20; programs, 23, 57, 136, 199; support for, 5, 53. *See also* War on Poverty

Greenberg, Stanley, 193–94

Gresham, Jewell Handy, 41

Grieder, William, 126

Grier, William H., 65–66

Gross, Martin, 163

Group rights, 101–2, 154, 157, 203

Guaranteed income. *See* Income guarantees

Guinier, Lani, 2, 155

Hacker, Andrew, 148

Hackett, David, 30

Hamilton, Charles, 52–53, 100–102

Harrington, Michael, 55

Harris, Fred, 81, 92

Harris, Louis, 27, 39

Hart, Gary, 86, 112

Hayakawa, S. I., 121

Head Start (program), 32

Health care, 109, 114, 131, 132, 148, 198, 201; reform, 2, 173, 192, 194

Heller, Walter, 30, 125

Helstoski, Henry, 76

Heritage Foundation, 124, 137, 158–59

Higher education, 46, 121, 151, 156; federal aid, 5, 10, 131, 32, 133–35, 142–43, 175; opportunities, 5, 54, 103, 132–36, 165, 169, 198, 202; state aid, 133–34

Hill, Herbert, 91

Hispanic Americans: discrimination against, 158, 191; education, 134, 135; and politics, 85, 107, 192, 193

Hollings, Ernest, 162

Home ownership, 135–36

Homosexuals. *See* Gays

Hooks, Benjamin, 109

House of Representatives, 93, 129, 195; and racial issues, 53, 112, 158

Housing discrimination, 8, 26, 27, 158–59, 191

Housing integration, 8, 51, 61, 68, 99

Housing subsidies, 68, 131

Hughes, Richard J., 76, 80, 168, 179

Humphrey, Hubert, 66–67, 81; as presidential candidate, 74, 78–79, 80–81, 94–95

Illegitimacy. *See* Unwed motherhood

Income, 28, 134, 146, 185; and inflation, 9, 133, 135, 202

Income guarantees, 92–94, 103; as campaign issue, 86, 94–95

Income tax: cutting, 10, 127, 128, 196–97; and Democratic party, 148, 162–63. *See also* Earned income tax credit

Income transfers, 142, 177, 200

Individual responsibility, 131, 173, 183; denial of, 41, 43 45–47, 50, 70, 104

Individual rights, 101, 154, 157
Isolation, Political, 100, 116
Integration, 8, 51, 52, 53–55;
    accomplishing, 103, 148, 156;
    black expectations from, 25, 28, 35;
    and B. Clinton, 20; Democrat
    position on, 2, 47, 50, 60–62, 105;
    government funds supporting,
    60–61, 68, 119; and L. B.
    Johnson, 5; opposition to, 52–53,
    101, 102, 155; and progressives,
    154–55, 187, 202. See also School
    integration; Segregation;
    Separatism
Intellectuals, 130, 170; conservative,
    123–24; in Democratic party, 60,
    95, 118, 122–23; and racial issues,
    47, 71, 100
Interest groups. See Special interests
Intergovernmental relations, 54,
    61–62, 121, 132, 133–34, 183

Jackson, Derrick, 17, 151
Jackson, Jesse L., 155; and B.
    Clinton, 15–16, 19; and
    Democratic party, 13–14, 18,
    19–20, 115, 193; and Jewish
    Americans, 104, 111–12; as
    presidential candidate, 110–13
Javits, Jacob, 89
Jeffries, Leonard, 106, 156
Jencks, Christopher, 147
Jewish Americans: and blacks, 25,
    104, 106, 111–12; and politics,
    3, 99, 192
Job Corps, 31, 132
Job creation, 167, 172
Job discrimination, 8, 26, 158, 159
Job integration, 28, 51, 62, 90–91,
    189–90
Job opportunities. See Employment,
    opportunities
Johnson, Lyndon Baines, 62, 67,
    122, 168; criticism of, 50, 120;

Howard University speech, 37–40,
    50, 53; as presidential candidate,
    27, 117; and racial issues, 5, 21,
    23–24, 49, 70, 89, 202; State of
    the Union message (1965), 28;
    support for, 113, 114
Johnson administration, 7, 29, 30–33
Judiciary, 8, 53, 71, 131. See also
    Supreme Court

Kane, Thomas, 134–35
Kaus, Mickey, 172–73
Kean, Tom, 194
Kemp, Jack, 125, 127–28, 159, 177
Kennedy, John F., 23, 29, 63, 70
Kennedy, Randall, 110, 116, 147
Kennedy, Robert F., 53, 63–64, 105,
    202; as presidential candidate,
    67, 73–74, 75, 79
Kennedy administration, 7, 29, 30
Kerner, Otto, 67
Kerner Commission, 58, 61, 66–70,
    89
Kerry, John, 151
King, Martin Luther, Jr., 6, 51, 75,
    103–4, 161; assassination, 67, 89,
    105, 111; influence of, 5, 25,
    98–100, 101, 107, 202; and J. F.
    Kennedy, 29; opinion of, 97–98
Kopkind, Andrew, 17–18
Kriegel, Jay, 70
Kristol, Irving, 47, 123, 136

Labor market, 168–69, 171, 202.
    See also Employment
Labor unions, 25; and blacks, 90–91,
    120, 159; and Democratic
    party, 14, 75, 112, 148, 192
Laffer, Arthur, 125
Laffer Curve, 125
Laird, Melvin, 123
Latinos. See Hispanic Americans
Law enforcement, 66, 70, 71, 120
Leadership, 33, 62, 115, 183;

need for, 61, 177, 202; *See also*
    Black leadership; Business
    leadership; Civil rights leader-
    ship; Democratic leadership;
    Republican leadership
Left (politics), 14, 42, 193; and B.
    Clinton, 16–18; and Black Power,
    105; and class issues, 56–57;
    and J. Jackson, 111–12; and L.
    B. Johnson, 21; marginalization
    of, 50; and race issues, 6, 13,
    45, 56
Legislation, 46, 53, 59, 121, 124;
    See also Antidiscrimination laws;
    Civil rights laws; specific acts,
    e.g. Civil Rights Act (1964)
Legislative districts, 187, 188–189
Lemann, Nicholas, 29, 31, 147
"Letter from the Birmingham City
    Jail" (King), 103–4
Levenson, Larry, 60
Lewis, John, 52, 187
Liberal elite, 124, 139
Liberalism, 8, 176; history, 4
Liberals, 60, 171; and B. Clinton, 16,
    17; and black separatists, 102; and
    class issues, 55–57; and crime
    issues, 63–6, 70; credibility, 11, 20,
    21, 120; criticism of, 20, 46, 47,
    52, 55–57, 121–22, 147–48, 149–53;
    and integration, 50, 51–55, 62,
    120; labeling, 4, 5, 10–11; and
    M. L. King, 99, 103–4; and R.
    Nixon, 93–95; and racial issues,
    6–8, 15, 20, 42, 44–45, 104–5,
    107–8; and social services, 30–31,
    57–59; *See also* Democratic
    party, effect of liberals on;
    Democratic party, liberals in;
    Republican party, liberals in
Liberty, 98, 129
Lindsay, John V., 69–70, 88
Living standards. *See* Quality of
    life; Standard of living

Local liberalism, 176
Long-term strategy, 9, 176–77,
    201–2
Los Angeles (Calif.), 13–14, 42, 147
Losing Ground (Murray), 170
Loury, Glenn, 98, 109
Lowenstein, Allard K. 76
Lower class, 55, 95, 165; behav-
    ior, 66, 68, 70, 153; concen-
    tration of, 7, 56; education, 134,
    140–41, 179. *See also* Poor;
    Working class
Lower-class family, 7, 91–95,
    140–41, 152, 173, 174
Low-income housing, 8, 70, 132,
    152, 176; ownership, 159

MacInnes, Gordon, 73; beliefs of,
    3, 196; in community action
    programs, 32–33, 168, 177–78;
    as state senator, 128, 176, 180–82,
    187, 190, 195, 196
Malcolm X, 98
Marburger, Carl, 180
McCarthy, Eugene, 53, 67, 74,
    75, 78, 79, 93–94
McGovern, George, 76, 81, 147;
    as presidential candidate, 4,
    79, 83, 85–87, 88, 94–95, 192,
    193
McGovern–Fraser Commission.
    See Commission on Party
    Structure and Delegate
    Selection (Democrats)
McKissick, Floyd, 105
Meaner, Robert B., 76
Media, 4, 29, 40, 42, 70, 147; in
    election campaigns, 17, 79, 25;
    and J. Jackson, 111; and M. L.
    King, 100; on racial issues, 25, 27,
    29, 40, 42, 102, 151, 153
Medicare, 5, 10, 23, 54, 199
Medicaid, 23, 54, 92, 131, 178
Menand, Louis, 156

Middle class, 55–56, 75, 125, 134, 194;
  becoming, 8, 58, 68, 170, 187;
  and blacks, 52–53, 58, 68, 151;
  constituents, 6, 15, 86, 124, 187,
  192, 193; criticism of their values,
  102; economic conditions, 133, 196,
  200; as a goal, 52–53, 56, 57, 68, 177
Middle class blacks, 8, 55, 58, 107,
  131, 187
Military, 147, 189–90; government
  spending on, 126, 132
Miller v. Johnson, 188
Mills, Wilber, 93
Mississippi, 103
Model Cities Act (1966), 54–55, 58
Moe, Terry, 137–39, 141
Mondale, Walter, 81, 110, 193; and
  J. Jackson, 18, 20, 112
Moral Majority, 124
Morris, Charles, 31, 121–22, 163, 192
Morris County (N.J.), 176, 195
Mosle, Sara, 141
Moynihan, Daniel Patrick, 33–34,
  55, 119, 146, 174; criticism of,
  54, 95, 105, 122; and Johnson
  administration, 34, 40–41, 42, 50;
  and Nixon administration, 90,
  91; and Reagan administration,
  126
Moynihan Report, 34–38, 41–42, 50,
  60, 177; criticism of, 37, 41, 2–47,
  56; and L. B. Johnson, 37–38, 39;
  and the media, 41
Multiculturalism, 108, 109, 136,
  155–57, 180
Murray, Charles, 130, 170
Muskee, Edmund, 83

NAACP. See National Association
  for the Advancement of Colored
  People
National Advisory Commission on
  Civil Disorders. See Kerner
  Commission

National Association for the Ad-
  vancement of Colored People
  (NAACP), 113
National Black Leadership Council,
  152
National Review (journal), 122
National Welfare Rights Organization
  (NWRO), 93–94, 103–4
Nation at Risk, A, 136
Nation of Islam, 104, 111–12
NDC. See National Democratic
  Coalition
Negroes. See Black Americans
"Negro Family: The Case for National
  Action." See Moynihan Report
Neighborhoods, 51, 56, 69, 183;
  growing, 27, 29, 53; and integra-
  tion, 8, 51; rebuilding, 55
Neighborhood Youth Corps, 31, 32
Neoconservatives, 47, 66, 122, 123
Neoliberals, 147, 161
New Democratic Coalition (NDC),
  74–77
Newark (N.J.), 60, 69, 179, 180, 181
New Jersey, 176, 177–78; blacks in,
  158; Democratic party, 74–77, 183,
  187, 189; economic policy, 76–77,
  128, 196–98; schools, 180–82
New Right, 124
New York (N.Y.), 152, 161; edu-
  cation, 182; politics, 147; race-
  relations, 69–70, 104, 159
New York (State), 108
New York Times, 17, 42, 44, 70,
  117, 153, 182
Nixon, Richard, 90, 91; as presi-
  dential candidate, 5–6, 29, 88–90,
  95, 122, 193
Nixon administration, 90–95, 120, 195
Nonviolence, 52, 103; Black Power
  criticisms, 101; and M. L.
  King, 98, 99, 103–4
North, Oliver, 199
North, 26–27, 37, 106–7

Northerners, 9, 21, 25–28, 100;
    attitudes, 26, 27, 119
NWRO. *See* National Welfare
    Rights Organization

Office of Economic Opportunity
    (OEO), 31, 33
Orfield, Gary, 147
Orphanages, 172
Other America, The (Harrington), 55

Page, Clarence, 18–19
Payne, Donald, 112
Percy, Charles, 89
Perot, Ross, 10, 13, 15, 16, 193–94
Personal responsiblity. *See* Individual
    responsibility
Peters, Charles, 147
Philadelphia Plan, 90–91
Phillips, Kevin, 124, 163–64, 195
Piven, Frances Fox, 102–3
Political advantage, 114–15
Political affiliation, 19, 109, 113, 117,
    148, 187, 193, 221 *n*2; switching,
    8–9, 85, 88, 89, 121, 186, 188, 193
Political coalitions, 99, 100, 107, 122,
    150–51; obstacles to, 101, 106, 151.
    See also Bipartisan coalitions;
    Progressive coalitions
Political culture, 4, 25, 57, 73, 84–85,
    86, 144
Political platforms, 87–88, 147–48. *See
    also* Democratic party, campaign
    issues; Republican party, cam-
    paign issues; *also* campaign issues
    under subjects, e.g. Vietnam War,
    as a campaign issue
Politicians. *See* Black politicians;
    Democratic politicans
Poor, 99–100, 173, 199; attitudes
    toward, 56–57; constituents, 193;
    education, 136–37; preferences
    for, 99; programs for, 39, 54, 164,
    169; and Republican party, 129,
    130–32, 200; statistics, 131. *See*

also Antipoverty programs; Urban
    poor; Welfare recipients
Popular culture, 148–49, 198
Poverty: as a campaign issue, 86, 194;
    causes of, 7, 35–38, 177; racializ-
    ing, 36–37, 39–40, 45–47. *See
    also* War on Poverty
Powell, Colin, 176
Preferences for blacks, 106, 153; con-
    sequences of, 151, 189; M. L.
    King position on, 6, 99; opposition
    to, 16, 38–39, 40, 158, 194;
    support for, 6–7, 155. *See also*
    Affirmative action; Quotas
Presidency, 62; tests of, 3–4. *See also*
    Bush administration; Clinton ad-
    ministration; Johnson administra-
    tion; Kennedy administration;
    Nixon administration; Reagan
    administration
Presidential elections, 6, 8, 115, 120,
    193; (1960), 29; (1964), 5, 21,
    27–28, 53, 117, 118–19; (1968),
    5–6, 73–74, 75, 77–79, 88–90, 122;
    (1972), 85–87, 88, 94–95, 105;
    (1980), 9, 125; (1984), 110, 112;
    (1988), 10, 110, 193; (1992), 10,
    13–15, 16–21, 114, 146, 191, 194–95
President's Commission on Law
    Enforcement and Administration
    of Justice, 64–65
President's Committee on Juvenile
    Delinquency, 30
Price, Hugh B., 187
Private schools: subsidizing, 136, 137,
    139–40, 141–42
Privatization: of government services,
    176; of public schools, 136–42, 160
Professional blacks, 187; and B.
    Clinton, 16–17; on racisim, 8, 42,
    45, 56–57, 151; reaction to, 107–8
Progressive coalition, 1, 6, 71; restor-
    ation, 3, 4, 144, 185–86, 187,
    188–91, 192–93, 199–203;
    shattering, 4, 5–7, 107–8

Progressives, 58, 194, 199–200; credibility, 175; goals, 3, 11, 146, 149, 154–55, 162; labeling, 4–5, 145; principles, 200–203; and racial issues, 150, 159

Progressivism: history, 4

Promised Land, The (Lemann), 29

Public housing. *See* Low-income housing

Public interest, 123, 129–30, 165, 171, 190, 200

Public Interest, The (journal), 47, 122–23

Public investment, 131–32, 184; benefits from, 164–65, 175–76; in education, 143; opposition to, 9–10, 144, 198; support for, 5, 14, 187, 200, 201–2. *See also* Government spending

Public opinion, 146; on crime, 66, 209 *n*27; on leadership, 97–98; on political affiliation, 109, 113, 221 *n*2; on presidential candidates, 79, 112; on race relations, 26–27, 39, 117, 148, 154–55, 221 *n*4; on racism, 26, 109, 158; on welfare, 150

Public schools, 136–42, 160, 181, 186, 198. *See also* School integration

Public service jobs, 68, 172–73, 198, 201

Public services, 57–58, 138, 201; government spending on, 9–10, 57. *See also* Community action programs

Quality of life, 167, 170

Quindlen, Anna, 17

Quotas, 8, 80, 159, 189, 190; support for, 16, 90–91

Race differences, 35–36, 44, 161; in educational performance, 109, 151, 156; explaining, 6–7, 55, 68, 70; in poverty, 37–40

Race-neutral policies, 107, 150–51, 171, 175, 187

Race relations, 18–19, 40, 148–49, 186–87, 203; and liberals, 157, 160–61; in politics, 77, 78, 80, 188–89. *See also* Discrimination; Integration; Segregation

Racial integration. *See* Integration

Racial issues, 104, 118–19, 150, 189. *See also* Discrimination; Integration; Segregation; Separatism; *See also* racial issues under subjects, e.g. Conservatives, and racial issues

Racial justice, 89, 98, 108, 202–3

Racism, 7, 41, 89, 108; and B. Clinton, 14–15, 16–18; as cause of black problems, 35, 42, 45–47, 57, 68, 105–9, 156; and civil disorders, 67–68; and crime, 63, 64–66, 108, 169; and R. F. Kennedy, 63

Radical Chic (Wolfe), 102

Rainbow Coalition, 13–14

Ravitch, Diane, 180

Reagan, Ronald, 9–10; as presidential candidate, 125

Reagan administration, 128–29, 136, 149, 195; economic policy, 125, 126–27, 132, 133–34

Reaganomics, 9–10, 125, 126–28, 146, 163–64

Reconstruction (journal), 110, 147

Redistricting, 187, 188–89

Reed, Adolph, Jr., 41, 109

Reich, Robert, 160

Religious schools, 136, 140

Republican leadership, 88–89, 196, 198

Republican National Committee, 189

Republican party, 77–78, 85, 175, 191, 193–95; and blacks, 89, 113, 114; campaign issues, 9, 71, 114, 143–44, 180, 196; constituents, 113, 186, 193–94; and crime issues, 28, 66, 71; effect of conservatives on, 117–20, 124, 126, 143–44, 196–99; liberals in, 88–89, 90, 117, 194; policies, 47, 183, 186; principles, 88, 148, 202; and racial issues, 88–89,

117–20, 154, 158–59; role, 3;
  support for, 8–9, 19, 188–89
Republican Right, 9; effect of, 186,
  194–95, 199–200; policies, 10,
  198–99, 201
Reston, James, 117–18
Richardson, Elliott, 89
Right and left (politics), 47, 146, 193.
  See also Left (politics); New Right;
  Republican Right
Riots, 60, 147; causes, 67; criticism
  of, 63, 89, 98; results from, 42,
  58, 68
Roberts, Paul Craig, 127
Rockerfeller, Nelson, 89–90
Rodino, Peter, 112
Romney, George, 89
Rowan, Carl, 19
Rules Committee (Democrats), 80
Ryan, William, 42–43, 45, 47, 65

Sanford, Adelaide, 108, 156
"Savage Discovery" (Ryan), 42
Scalia, Antonin, 188
Schlesinger, Arthur, Jr., 154, 156–57
School integration, 62, 89, 103, 179,
  181; opposition to, 8, 24; support
  for, 51, 70, 147, 180
School principals, 181–82
Schools: choice of, 136–42, 143. *See
  also* Private schools; Public schools;
  Trade schools
School vouchers. *See* Educational
  vouchers
Scott, Hugh, 89
Segregation, 6, 25, 61, 104, 160; and
  Democratic party, 19, 21, 24, 37;
  in Democratic party, 77, 78, 80;
  legal end of, 5, 89, 180; and
  Republican party, 24, 118–20, 194.
See also Discrimination; Integration
Self-government, 123
Self-help, 98–99, 106, 109

Senate, 129, 149; and B. Clinton, 1,
  162, 195; and R. Nixon, 93–94;
  and racial issues, 24, 71; and R.
  Reagan, 9, 129
Separatism, 3, 42, 108, 154, 155; in
  Black Power movement, 52–53,
  101; and M. L. King, 99; and
  National Welfare Rights Organ-
  ization, 102–3. *See also* Integration;
  Segregation
Set-asides, 187, 188, 189
Short-term strategy, 176–77
Shriver, Sargent, 30–31, 32
Shultz, George, 90, 91, 120
Single-parent family, 2, 30, 152, 173;
  criticism of, 46, 160, 174
Sizer, Theodore, 60, 136–37
Sleeper, Jim, 147
Social classes, 123, 159–60, 200;
  behavior, 169–70; differences
  between, 52, 55–57, 160; and
  inequality, 107, 147. *See also*
  Upper class; Lower class; Middle
  class; Working class
Social issues, 186, 187, 195. *See also*
  Abortiion; Poverty; Racial issues;
  Urban issues
Social policy, 120, 128–29, 171. *See
  also* Antipoverty programs; Urban
  policy
Social Security, 9, 10, 126, 141–42
Social services, 30–31, 54; opposition
  to, 170; results from, 58–59;
  government spending on, 50,
  57–58
Social statistics, 37, 44, 65, 131, 169
Social workers, 50, 59
Societal values, 1, 57; transmittal of,
  2, 35. *See also* American values
Souljah, Sister, 14–15, 16–19
South, 91–92; politics, 47, 53, 189;
  schools, 5, 103; segregation, 21,
  24, 118–19

Southerners, 80, 89; and politics, 9,
    78, 114, 118–19, 193. *See also*
    Black Southerners
Special Equal Opportunity Committee
    (Democrats), 78, 80
Special interests, 23, 84, 112, 114, 129
Standard of living, 9, 121, 185, 186,
    196, 201
Starr, Paul, 147
State governments, 133, 138, 196–98.
    See also Intergovernmental relations
Steele, Shelby, 109
Stockman, David, 126–27, 129
Striving poor, 173; programs for,
    164, 169, 199
Student Nonviolent Coordinating
    Committee (SNCC), 52
Student protests, 52, 121
Suburbanization, 29–30, 107, 131
Suburbs: discrimination in, 61–62, 68
Suburban voters, 19, 159, 160
Sunstein, Cass R., 46
Supreme Court, 24, 46, 106, 140,
    149, 188, 190
Surveys. *See* Public opinion

Taxation, 9, 198, 200–201; under
    Democratic administrations, 2, 125,
    162–63; under Republican admin-
    istrations, 10, 125, 126, 127; state,
    128, 133, 196–97. *See also* Income tax
Taylor, Jared, 98
Teixeira, Ruy, 193
Thomas, Clarence, 106, 109, 149
Thompson, Frank, 76
Thurmond, Strom, 88, 89
Thurow, Lester C., 185
Tocqueville, Alexis de, 129–30, 161
Tollett, Kenneth, 46, 150–51
Trade schools: criticism of, 142–43, 176
Traditional values. *See* American
    values; Family values
Trenton (N.J.), 168

Underclass, 121, 130, 172, 173, 174
Unemployment, 2, 65, 168, 197; and
    blacks, 35, 37, 65, 92, 93; insurance,
    148
Unheavenly City, The (Banfield),
    169–70
Unions. *See* Labor unions
Unwed motherhood, 2, 37, 44; and
    blacks, 30, 35, 43, 46; as campaign
    issue, 124; causes, 9
Upper class, 56, 75, 146, 193;
    economic conditions, 162, 185,
    200; voting, 198
Urban issues, 27, 29, 61, 68, 131,
    187
Urban policy, 49, 54–55, 61–62, 168,
    177
Urban poor, 28, 49; escape from, 169;
    and M. L. King, 100; policies for,
    36, 54–55, 61–62, 175–76, 177–78;
    policy problems, 7, 28–29, 30–31,
    62, 183; problems of, 35, 40, 50,
    51, 67, 106–7, 160, 167; and
    welfare, 91–92, 103
Urban renewal, 33, 55

Values. *See* American values;
    Conservative values; Family values;
    Societal values
"Vanishing Black Family, The," (CBS
    program), 152
Victim blaming, 42–43, 44–46, 63,
    65, 106, 109
Vietnam War, 5, 7, 33, 40, 58, 60,
    114, 125; as campaign issue, 5,
    75, 76, 77, 78, 79, 85; effect on
    domestic issues, 32, 62
Viguerie, Richard, 124
Violence, 30, 58, 105; causes, 63, 66,
    153; fear of, 27, 102, 153; by
    local government, 25. *See also*
    Civil disturbances; Crime; Riots
Voodoo economics, 9, 125

Voters, 5, 8, 13, 19, 86, 122, 126, 160,
    193; attitudes, 10, 15,   125, 129,
    149, 177, 193–94; goals, 3. *See
    also* Black Americans, constituents;
    Democratic party, constituents;
    Middle class, constituents;
    Political affiliation; Republican
    party, constituents; Suburban voters;
    White Americans, voting; Working
    class, constituents
Voting rights, 24, 51, 89, 97
Voting Rights Act (1965), 5, 54, 78, 97
Voting Rights Act (1982), 188
Vouchers for schools. *See* Educational
    vouchers

Wallace, George, 24, 27, 53, 79, 86,
    193
Wall Street Journal, 9, 125, 127
Walters, Ronald, 16–17
Wanniski, Jude, 125
War on Poverty, 32–33, 38, 39–40, 57;
    creating, 23, 28–29, 30–32; oppo-
    sition to, 119–20; and R. Nixon, 90–95
Washington Monthly, 147, 160–61
Wattenberg, Ben, 66, 122
Welfare, 37, 119, 147, 171; as cam-
    paign issue, 86, 87, 119; as an
    entitlement, 103; opposition to,
    92, 194; and Republican adminis-
    trations, 9, 91–95; as race neutral,
    150–51; reform, 10, 150, 170–73.
    See also Antipoverty programs
Welfare recipients, 70, 114, 172; atti-
    tudes toward, 43; services for,
    57–59, 171; work requirements
    for, 3, 92, 95, 132, 171, 172–73
Welfare Reform Act (1988), 171
West, Cornel, 106, 110, 116, 157, 202
Weyrich, Paul, 124
White, Theodore H., 29–30, 80, 82
White Americans, 29, 186; attitudes
    toward blacks, 69, 105, 120, 151,
    153, 154–55; attitudes toward

integration, 5, 8, 51; black attitudes
    toward, 187; blaming, 38, 39, 42,
    43, 44–45, 68; effect of Black Power
    on, 100–101, 102; resistance to
    integration, 5, 24, 41, 51. *See also*
    Northerners; Southerners
White backlash, 53, 63
Whitehead, Barbara Dafoe, 174
White House Task Force on Cities
    (Ylvisaker Task Force), 60–62, 136
White liberals: labeling, 103, 149. *See
    also* Liberals
White power, 18
White racism. *See* Racisim
White-rights organizations, 98
Whitman, Christine Todd, 128, 196–98
Whittle Communications, 137, 141
Wildavsky, Aaron, 49, 68
Wilder, Douglas, 18
Wiley, George, 103–4
Wilkins, Roger, 17
Wilkins, Roy, 58
Williams, Cecil, 44
Wilson, James Q., 123, 171
Wilson, William Julius, 42, 106–7,
    110, 116, 147, 150–51
Wisconsin, 139
Wolfe, Alan, 165
Wolfe, Tom, 102
Women, 9, 121, 173, 198; and
    politics, 3, 60, 84, 85, 86, 112, 192
Work. *See* Employment
Working class: constituents, 18, 86,
    88, 124, 187; and Democratic
    party, 6, 8, 15; economic condi-
    tions, 2, 127, 133; and racial
    issues, 51, 119–20; and Repub-
    lican party, 9, 91, 193; reuniting, 3
Working poor. *See* Striving poor

Ylvisaker, Paul, 29, 30, 60
Ylvisaker Task Force. *See* White
    House Task Force on Cities